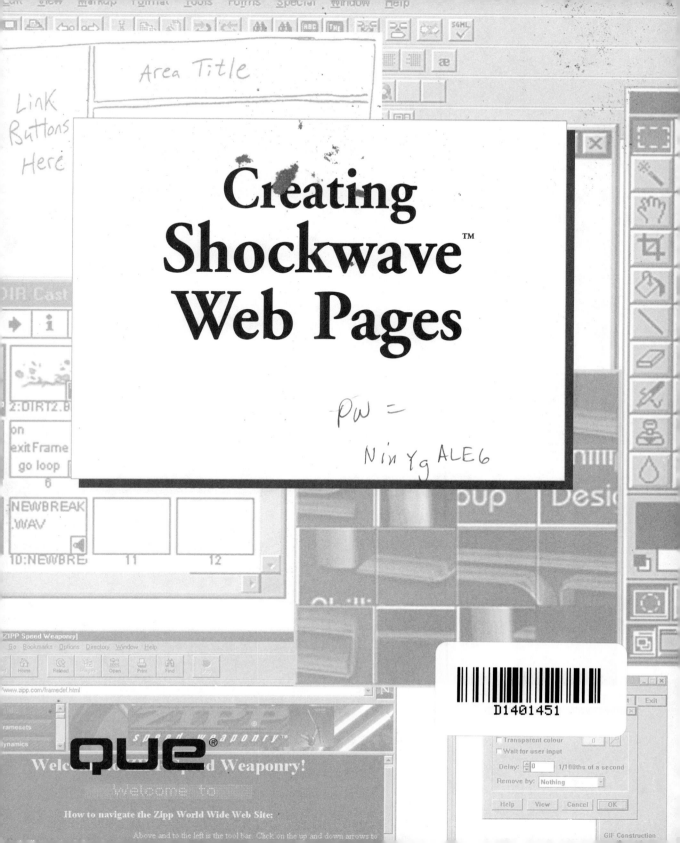

Creating Shockwave™ Web Pages

Written by

Perry Board
Rick Luna
Derek O'Dell

que

Creating Shockwave Web Pages

Copyright© 1996 by Que® Corporation.

Library of Congress Catalog No.: 96-69966

ISBN: 0-7897-0903-1

98 97 96   6 5 4 3 2 1

Interpretation of the printing code: the rightmost double-digit number is the year of the book's printing; the rightmost single-digit number, the number of the book's printing. For example, a printing code of 96-1 shows that the first printing of the book occurred in 1996.

All terms mentioned in this book that are known to be trademarks or service marks have been appropriately capitalized. Que cannot attest to the accuracy of this information. Use of a term in this book should not be regarded as affecting the validity of any trademark or service mark.

Screen reproductions in this book were created using Collage Complete from Inner Media, Inc., Hollis, NH.

Composed in *Stone Serif* and *MCPdigital* by Que Corporation

Credits

President
Roland Elgey

Publisher
Joseph B. Wikert

Publishing Manager
Jim Minatel

Title Manager
Steven M. Schafer

Editorial Services Director
Elizabeth Keaffaber

Managing Editor
Sandy Doell

Director of Marketing
Lynn E. Zingraf

Acquisitions Manager
Cheryl D. Willoughby

Acquisitions Editor
Stephanie McComb

Product Director
Benjamin Milstead

Production Editor
Sherri Fugit

Editors
Patricia Kinyon
Susan Ross Moore
Anne Owen
Caroline Roop

Product Marketing Manager
Kim Margolius

Assistant Product Marketing Manager
Christy M. Miller

Strategic Marketing Manager
Barry Pruett

Technical Editors
Matthew Brown
Steve Gershik
Dave Shinn

Technical Support Specialist
Nadeem Muhammed

Acquisitions Coordinator
Jane K. Brownlow

Software Relations Coordinator
Patty Brooks

Editorial Assistant
Andrea Duvall

Book Designer
Ruth Harvey

Cover Designer
Kim Scott

Production Team
Debra Bolhuis, Kevin Cliburn, Jason Hand, Daniel Harris, Bobbi Satterfield, Amy Gornik, Erin M. Danielson, Kay Hoskin, Paul Wilson, Christine Tyner, Bob LaRoche

Indexer
Tim Tate

About the Authors

Perry Board attended Taylor University as an art major with varied career intentions ranging from graphic arts to teaching. After graduating, he went to New York City as an intern at *Blender* magazine, the first magazine to be published as an interactive CD-ROM. He has taken various graphic arts jobs and presently works for Phillips Design Group, a leader in interactive media. He now lives in Indianapolis, Indiana, with his wife, Theresa, who is a high school English teacher.

Rick Luna earned his BFA in Graphic Design from Ball State University in 1993. Upon graduation, he worked for a local LDIP that was just starting. His knowledge of HTML and the Internet came from searching the Internet for information and applications to build pages for the new company. Still doing freelance print work, it was a project for his current employer (Phillips Design Group, Inc.) that got him hired. Since joining PDG, he has created sites for Zipp Speed Weaponry, The Finish Line, and others, as well as having sites used as demos in Internet trade shows.

Derek O'Dell has been working in multimedia design and development for approximately five years. With a degree in Computer Systems Engineering from Purdue University, Derek has completed the programming and design of several interactive projects. Using Authorware Professional, Derek was the lead programmer for interactive CD-ROMs for Software Artistry, The Finish Line, and Zipp Speed Weaponry. Derek has trained employees of many major corporations on Authorware, Photoshop, and Premiere. Derek works for Phillips Design Group of Indianapolis. Derek may be reached at 317-297-9164 or e-mailed at derek@pdgroup.com.

PDG, Inc. is a leader in cutting edge interactive media design and development based in Indianapolis, Indiana. PDG's award-winning designs have been displayed in New York, San Francisco, and around the world in design publications, books, cover art, galleries, and exhibits. PDG has extensive recognition in the industry, as authors and consultants for published articles and books. PDG's current project portfolio includes design and development of interactive CD-ROMs, Kiosk, Intranet, Special Effects, 3-D modeling/ animation, Graphic Design, and development of multimedia Internet Web Sites.

Contact Phillips Design Group at:

URL	**http://www.pdgroup.com**
E-Mail	**pdg@pdgroup.com**
CompuServe	**102363,372**
Phone	(317) 297-9164
Fax	(317) 297-9486
Address	Phillips Design Group, Inc.
	6350 Westhaven Drive, Suite C
	Indianapolis, IN 46254

Acknowledgments

We'd Like to Hear from You!

As part of our continuing effort to produce books of the highest possible quality, Que would like to hear your comments. To stay competitive, we *really* want you, as a computer book reader and user, to let us know what you like or dislike most about this book or other Que products.

You can mail comments, ideas, or suggestions for improving future editions to the address below, or send us a fax at (317) 581-4663. Our staff and authors are available for questions and comments through our Internet site, at **http://www.mcp.com/que**, and Macmillan Computer Publishing also has a forum on CompuServe (type **GO QUEBOOKS** at any prompt).

In addition to exploring our forum, please feel free to contact me personally to discuss your opinions of this book: I'm **bmilstead@que.mcp.com** on the Internet, and I'm **102121,1324** on CompuServe.

Thank you in advance—your comments will help us to continue publishing the best books available on new computer technologies in today's market.

Benjamin Milstead
Product Development Specialist
Que Corporation
201 W. 103rd Street
Indianapolis, Indiana 46290
USA

Contents at a Glance

Shockwave and the Web

Creating Basic Animations

Adding Interactivity

Putting It All Together

Using Lingo

Other Shockwave Products

Contents

VIII Appendixes   291

B Shockwave Toolkit Reference   293

C Glossary   297

Index   303

Introduction

Hopefully, you are reading this Introduction before you buy this book so you'll know what you can expect from it. Too often, I have picked up software instruction books that turn out to be something different than the cover led me to believe. Titles like "An Easy Guide to…" or "A Complete Resource for…" often turn out to be a big letdown. The "easy guide" ends up presupposing me to be a master already and the "complete resource" turns out to only cover basic material. Of course, this isn't always the author's fault; it is merely written with a different audience in mind. For your reference and convenience, this Introduction starts by explaining exactly who should read this book and what to expect from it.

Who Is This Book For?

The person who will get the most from this book is someone who is already familiar with the Internet and who already has a Web page that he or she would like to enhance through Shockwave. This book demonstrates the HTML code needed to put Shockwave elements on your page, but other Web page programming techniques will not be discussed.

Programs Used

Shockwave is only available for products created by Macromedia applications (Director, Authorware, Freehand). Therefore, this book assumes you have access to and a general knowledge of at least one of these products. Some of the examples in this book may be used as Shockwave "clip art" to be put directly on your Web page, but you must understand that to create new Shockwave elements, you must have Director, Authorware, or Freehand.

What You Learn in This Book

Most of this book focuses on Shockwave for Director to put multimedia on the Internet. To show a variety of examples, you are given a brief overview of the creation of the Director movie. Special attention will be given to the actual embedding of the movie into the Web page and other Internet-specific information. If you need to know more about creating graphics and advanced Director programming, other books can give more thorough information.

Creating Shockwave Web Pages can help you accomplish the following:

- Decide what tools you need to create Shockwave Web pages.
- Decide what you and your viewers need to see the Shockwave movies.
- Create basic animations in Director.
- Embed Shockwave movies in your Web page.
- Keep your movies small for fast downloading.
- Add interactivity to your movies.
- Match backgrounds with your Web page.
- Use Lingo for more advanced Shockwave concepts.
- Use new network Lingo for navigation and other Internet functions.
- Decide when to use alternatives to Shockwave.

How This Book Helps You "Shock" Your Web Site

You will find that this book is easily divided into sections and chapters so that you may quickly find what you are looking for. It logically progresses through various elements of Shockwave should you decide to read straight through, or you may skip to certain sections to find information about a specific aspect of Shockwave.

Part I: Shockwave and the Web

Part I, "Shockwave and the Web," describes what Shockwave is and some general concepts surrounding it. You learn about the various tools needed or recommended in creating Shockwave Web pages. It covers the necessary steps for a Shocked site, from configuring the server to setting up your browser with the plug-in.

Part I also covers limitations of Shockwave, which mainly concern file size. You are offered suggestions for keeping movies small as you consider download time for the user. Certain limitations are the result of security and various other reasons. These are also mentioned in this part of the book.

Part II: Creating Basic Animations

Part II leads you through the process of creating a movie, compressing it for the Internet, uploading it, and embedding the file in the HTML document.

You start with some simple animations to liven up your Web page and give it some energy. But there are many applications of Shockwave. Other uses included are functional purposes for Shockwave—using it to demonstrate ideas or teach concepts.

This section also explains a few methods for integrating your movies into your Web page and how to match background colors and patterns.

Part III: Adding Interactivity

Part III describes the process of adding interactivity to your Shockwave movies. The real power of Shockwave is not simply the motion and sound that it can add to your Web page, but also the ability to respond to input by the user.

You can learn rollovers and basic button clicks to change aspects of your movie. In Part IV, you work with more advanced applications of interactivity using Lingo.

Part IV: Putting It All Together

Part IV works with Lingo, the programming language of Director. Using Lingo, you can perform advanced functions and add powerful interaction to your Shockwave movies.

Starting with a general discussion about Lingo, you progress through some more advanced topics. Chapters 13 and 14, "Internet Lingo for Shockwave" and "Further Use of Internet Lingo," respectively, illustrate additional Lingo that works only through Shockwave to allow you to interact with the Internet: switching Web pages, movies, retrieving text, preloading items, and so on.

Part V: Using Lingo

In Part V, you will create a multiple-page Web site from start to finish using several Shockwave movies. The example site is basically a framework to which more depth can be added. In fact, it uses general concepts that can be adapted to your own site.

You discover additional options for modifying existing material on your Web page, such as shrinking graphics, editing animation and sound, and cutting content. Some alternatives are given to show ways you can use animated GIFs and other techniques to achieve similar effects to Shockwave.

Part VI: Other Shockwave Products

In Part VI, you have the opportunity to explore using Shockwave for Authorware and Shockwave for Freehand. These applications are intended for different purposes than Shockwave for Director. Shockwave for Freehand allows vector-based images that can be scaled and panned with clickable links within the graphic. Shockwave for Authorware is used for large-scale Intranet multimedia projects.

Appendixes

Several appendixes offer valuable information—software tools that you may find useful, and a glossary of related terms. An example gallery gives short descriptions and tips for various Shockwave movies. The source code of each example is included for you to take apart and examine.

Appendix A, Example Gallery: This appendix contains descriptions and pictures of various Shockwave movies. Many of the examples used in the book are included in the appendix as well as several other examples not mentioned in the text. The code for each example is included on the CD-ROM for you to look at and take apart.

Appendix B, Shockwave Toolkit Reference: You will read in this appendix about a variety of programs that you may find useful in creating Shockwave movies and Web pages. Some of the software is included on the CD-ROM.

Appendix C, Glossary: Here you will find short descriptions of the vocabulary used throughout the book. As you read, if you come across a term you don't know, simply check the glossary.

What's on the CD-ROM?

Throughout the book, examples of Director movies, compressed Shockwave movies, HTML pages, and other files are used. All of these are included on the CD-ROM in the appropriate directory (organized by chapter). By including these source files, you can easily follow along with the provided examples.

The Shockwave plug-ins are on the CD-ROM so that you can quickly get up and running with Shockwave. More recent versions of the plug-ins may be available from Macromedia's Web site:

http://www.macromedia.com

Other tools are also included on the CD-ROM that may be helpful in creating a Shockwave Web page, such as HTML editors, media viewers, Afterburner for compressing movies, and other useful programs.

Conventions Used in This Book

This icon will appear in the margin when an example file or program can be found on the included CD-ROM. Examples will always be found in the directory named for the chapter.

On the CD

Note
Notes are additional information or anecdotal advice that pertains to the current topic. Sometimes you will want to know some background information or additional concepts that are not directly mentioned in the rest of the book.

Tip
Tips are included when there is a shortcut or trick that can be used. They can also be a specific application of an idea or technique that relates to the chapter section.

Caution
Cautions are provided to warn you of actions that may be irreversible or can cause problems. You'll definitely want to read any Cautions before proceeding with the chapter. Cautions are used when you need to be careful about something—perhaps a confusing idea or a risky use of a concept.

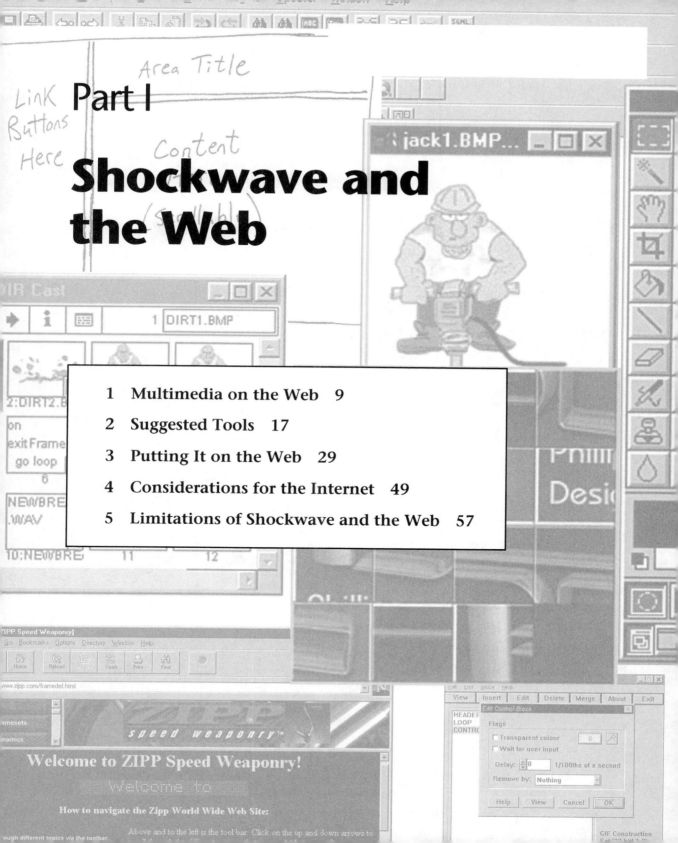

Part I

Shockwave and the Web

CHAPTER 1

Multimedia on the Web

Before getting to the actual details of Shockwave, you need some information about multimedia and the Internet. Here's what to expect in this chapter:

- Learn about the origins and ideas of the multimedia concept—reaching multiple senses simultaneously.

- Multimedia is relatively new to the Internet. Descriptions of Shockwave and how it provides interactive animation and sound to the Web are included.

- Alternatives and limitations are also discussed as they relate to multimedia on the Web.

Reaching Our Senses

A good roller coaster moves fast, goes high, and has lots of unexpected twists and hills. After a while, all the rides seem to be the same because they can't get bigger or faster or higher for safety reasons. What did the roller coaster creators do to distinguish the latest and greatest "Bloody Devil III" from the boring old "Fire Bomber"? They couldn't do much more with motion, so they added flashing lights and dark tunnels. Then they added music and screaming sound effects. Then they added water guns to spray the riders. Soon globs of blue slime ooze from the hand rails. The roller coasters affect the riders' senses through movement, but also through sight, sound, and touch.

Amusement parks aren't the only place where this has happened. Students don't write many papers anymore; they do presentations. Though writing still has a very important place in education, it can be limiting to certain people. By adding pictures, a whole new spectrum is added for individuals who learn better by seeing rather than reading. Presenting the information orally benefits those people who learn through listening. Adding tangible objects, sounds, video, diagrams, interaction, and other elements ensures that the presentation reaches every possible audience with the greatest impact.

This is true in business. Meetings may have overhead projectors, slides, video, computers, physical objects, and so on. By reaching more than one sense (sight, sound, touch, and so on), the presenter is sure that he or she is most effectively reaching the audience and holding its attention.

Of course, the driving force behind many of these enhancements is the advancement of technology—more options available to more people for less money. The point here is that technology has expanded our communication and experiences to reach more than one sense simultaneously. Instead of choosing to read, listen, or see, we have the option of doing all three at once. The buzzword referring to this is "*multimedia.*"

Multimedia in the computer sense most often refers to the development of the CD-ROM. A "multimedia computer" will have a CD-ROM player, sound card and speakers, and a color video display. The CD-ROMs often contain audio, video, pictures, text, and other elements that can be experienced. However, the computer has taken multimedia further than television or other presentation devices. It has made a very powerful addition: *interactivity*. By making software interactive, the user can make choices that affect the presentation. Instead of waiting through a series of videos, pictures, or text, the user can choose what to view. He or she can make decisions that affect how the information is presented. The multimedia viewer enters a completely different world that they control and experience.

Multimedia on the Internet

The Internet originally had very limited capabilities. Most computer terminals could display text in one color and had very little to offer in terms of graphics. However, the Internet has exploded in popularity and with its expansion has come technological developments to reach multiple senses over the vast network.

It wasn't that long ago that all one could expect from a Web page was a graphic here and there and a lot of text (see figure 1.1). I remember when it was a big deal when you could actually wrap text around an image! Within the past year, all this has changed even more dramatically than merely being able to flow text where you want it. It is now not an uncommon thing to run across multimedia Web pages—pages that have not only imagery but imagery with animation and audio (see figure 1.2). Suddenly, it isn't enough to know just HTML, the language of the Web. HTML programmers and designers are now required to know and be familiar with the wide array of new technologies that set their Web pages apart from the rest.

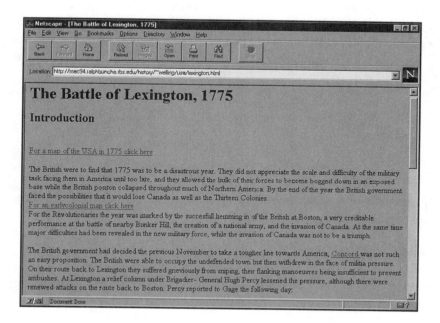

Figure 1.1
A standard Web site may use only text to convey information.

Figure 1.2
An enhanced site uses images, motion, sound, and other additions to stimulate the viewer.

The most popular way to add extra functionality to any Web site is through Shockwave. Introduced less than a year ago, Shockwave is responsible for almost single-handedly transforming the Internet from a text based information retrieval mechanism to a legitimate, full-fledged entertainment and advertising machine. Imagine having the whole world as your audience! Many have, and as the number of people with access to the Internet grows at an exponential rate, so do the number of companies wanting to take advantage of this untapped market.

How does one create a site that makes people want to visit and, more importantly, makes them want to come back? The answer: Shockwave. With it, a visitor to your site can be greeted with a spinning banner accompanied by music and animated text. When the user moves the mouse around the page, he or she can find user-triggered events to draw their attention to specific points of interest. Almost anything one can dream up is now possible, and those willing to take the time to use this new tool effectively will be creating sites that keep people coming back for more.

What is Shockwave?

Shockwave in itself is not the tool that creates multimedia content but rather it is the means by which that content is delivered to Web browsers. Shockwave compromises two components. One is the Shockwave plug-in, available at the time of this writing only for a few browsers, Netscape Navigator being the most popular. The other component is a utility called Afterburner.

The Shockwave plug-in, once installed, plays multimedia files in a Web browser such as Netscape Navigator or Microsoft Internet Explorer. The HTML for inserting the files into a Web page is a simple addition. The files must be created using Macromedia Director, which is a popular multimedia authoring tool. Once a Director movie is created, you will be the proud creator of a "Shocked" Web site in minutes!

The other half of Shockwave is a small program called Afterburner. Afterburner compresses Director movies at a ratio of greater than 2:1. It will compress both .DIR and .DXR Director movies to a format with the .DCR extension. This is a compressed Director movie that is then ready to be placed on any Web server along with the accompanying HTML documents. The compression process itself takes a few seconds, and as mentioned before, the HTML from there on out is quite simple.

For an in depth discussion on how to "Shock" a Web page, see chapter 3, "Putting It on the Web."

> **Note**
>
> It's important to realize that Shockwave is not a single software package that adds multimedia to the Web. It's a conversion process. The multimedia (motion, sound, and so on) is created in another software package, then can be viewed over the Internet using Shockwave as sort of a bridge. To create the multimedia files, you will need Macromedia Director, or a few other software packages as discussed in chapter 2, "Suggested Tools."

Shockwave

Thus far we have been referring to Shockwave for Director, but there are also several other applications that can be involved. Shockwave for Director is the most common form of multimedia over the Internet, but for Intranets and complex multimedia projects, you may also use Shockwave for Authorware. *Intranets* (as opposed to the *Internet*) are smaller, closed networks that large companies use to link computers in a restricted region. Because most Intranets use faster connections, Shockwave for Authorware can use much larger, more detailed multimedia files.

Need other Software to create Shockwave

A third form of Shockwave is Freehand, a vector graphics program. It allows the user to scale and pan a detailed image over the Web. Certain areas can also be defined as clickable links to other Web pages.

Shockwave versus Other Solutions

Chapter 17, "Alternatives to Shockwave," covers animated GIFs, Java, Real Audio, and movie file formats. There are various other ways to add advanced interactive multimedia to Web sites. If you are a C++ programmer for example, you can do advanced rollover functions and so forth in JAVA. However, if you are like the vast majority of HTML programmers, learning the C++ programming language just to make a button highlight when your cursor moves over it is not worth the months of programming and debugging that will invariably result when coupled with JAVA's learning curve. You could write a CGI script to perform a few simple functions, but each one would require a new HTML document to be loaded to see the result; and then, there is no way to include audio. Needless to say, most Web page creators don't know anything about Perl or CGI, let alone JAVA or C++ and probably prefer to keep it that way.

Creating a "Shocked" site is much easier to do than the alternative. A graphics background and a familiarity with various graphics packages are all that is necessary to create the components that will be part of a Director movie.

However, the key to creating good Shockwave Director movies is being able to create effective movies that are as small as possible to minimize download time.

Keep it small

Shockwave and the Web

A Director movie doesn't run as soon as a Web page is loaded. The entire movie loads and starts to run anywhere from a few seconds to three or four minutes (for a very large movie) *after* the HTML document has loaded. At that point, it behaves normally, with no pauses or additional wait times. The fact of the matter is that the average user is using a 14.4 modem. Even with a 28.8 modem, a movie that is 200K takes about 180 seconds to download.

Of course, there are other factors that can decrease performance even further such as Network congestion or, to a limited extent, the speed of the server you are currently downloading data from. The good news is that most movies aren't 200K in size and that there are ways to keep them from getting out of control, as discussed in chapter 4, "Considerations for the Internet."

Working within Limitations

It's amazing to see what people can do given certain limitations. People who make crafts, for example, are incredible at this. They can take a soup can, some string, a bottle cap, and a few tooth picks and transform them into a scale model of the Battle of Lexington and Concord.

Shockwave and the Internet in general contain many limitations, discussed further in chapters 4 and 5, "Limitations of Shockwave and the Web," and throughout the book. The main limitation is file size, but beware of cynicism! You might think that sub-200K files can never amount to anything great, but you will soon learn to work within the limitations to produce some excellent movies for the Internet.

I often compare some of the Shockwave games to the old Atari 2600 games—choppy, humble graphics, limited sound, fairly simple in design. Now, years later, Shockwave is new and exciting and people don't compare it to CD-ROMs or other software. This is a new development for the Internet and it will remain exciting as long as people work with it and make progress in putting interactive media on the Web.

This book cannot possibly cover everything with Shockwave, and it is not intended to. It shows you the basics, as well as tips and techniques, and gives you a broad background from which you can develop your own work. The best way to learn tricks and stimulate ideas is to get out there and start checking out some Shockwave sites. Go to Yahoo (**www.yahoo.com**) or another Web-searching site and uncover as many Shockwave locations as you can. You will constantly be finding things that amaze you and teach you to look past limitations for new creative solutions.

From Here...

The next few chapters get you started with Shockwave. The learning curve in creating Shockwave movies begins fairly easily. However, the potential for more advanced applications is limitless.

- Chapter 2, "Suggested Tools": Covers some of the suggested tools you will need in creating Shockwave Web pages.

- Chapter 3, "Putting It on the Web": Gives you the basic process that you follow for every Shockwave addition to your site.

- Chapter 4, "Considerations for the Internet": Offers various suggestions in designing your projects for the Internet with attention to file size and your intended audience.

- Chapter 5, "Limitations of Shockwave and the Web": Describes various limitations you need to work around. There are functions in Director that you may want to use, but will need to change for Shockwave.

- Part II, "Creating Basic Animations": Teaches you to create a few simple Shockwave enhancements for your site.

CHAPTER 2
Suggested Tools

As always, the more tools you have, the easier your work. But if you learn to use what you have to its full potential, you can get by with just a few tools. This chapter mentions only software. Multimedia for the Internet needs to remain relatively small so hardware requirements aren't very demanding. A video display in thousands or millions of colors is good to have, as well as a sound card. Other than that, you'll need to check with the individual software package vendors for system requirements.

This chapter covers:

- Which Internet browsers currently support Shockwave
- Where to get the Shockwave plug-ins and how they are used
- What Macromedia Products are needed to create your own original Shockwave files
- A few suggestions about graphics tools for creating graphics
- Audio utilities to edit sound for Shockwave

Working with Good Tools

A good tool makes a job easy, as any mechanic will tell you. The same holds true in the computer realm. In one of my first jobs in multimedia, I was hired to create images to be used as supplementary screens for a video production. Assuming the company had the necessary software to use, I went in on my first day and sat down at a computer. The project was explained to me, and my boss pointed to a clip art book for CorelDRAW! Version 3 (Version 6 had been released already). My heart sank as I thumbed through corny cartoon drawings and other useless clip art. I had no good tools to create with. In the end, I brought in my own version of Photoshop and scanned in some pictures to use, but I learned to find out ahead of time what tools I would have to work with.

The Essentials: Viewing Shockwave Files

Some tools are essential for you as the developer and also for anyone to view your Web site. The Shockwave essentials can be divided into three categories: the *Shockwave file*, the *Internet browser*, and the *Shockwave plug-in*. Think of the Shockwave file as a movie (in fact, this is the term that Director uses for its files). The browser is like a movie theater, the place where you are able to load and view items from the Internet. When the browser receives a Shockwave HTML command, it recognizes the Shockwave file type and calls the appropriate *plug-in*. The plug-in is like a projector that plays the movie from within the browser.

The Shockwave file itself is not a tool; it is an end product. Creating and implementing it is the focus of this book. The browser and plug-ins are the tools used to view the file.

> **Tip**
>
> The success of the Shockwave file depends not only on how it's placed on the Web page, but more importantly how it was created. Because download time is such an important consideration, a good Shockwave movie loads quickly and packs a big performance into a small file.

Web Browser

Netscape

A supporting browser is necessary to recognize the Shockwave file type and HTML code. Currently, Shockwave is best supported using Netscape Navigator 2.0 or later. Netscape is one of the most popular Internet browsers, so creating web pages with Netscape viewers in mind will be ideal.

Another popular browser is Microsoft's Internet Explorer. Support for Shockwave is currently limited, though installing Shockwave does give the option of using Internet Explorer by installing an ActiveX addition (figure 2.1). At the time this book was written, version 3 of Explorer was not yet released. I have tested Shockwave with a beta version and it appears to work, though certain network functions don't seem to be operating correctly (switching Web pages using Shockwave, retrieving text files from the Internet, and other network-related commands).

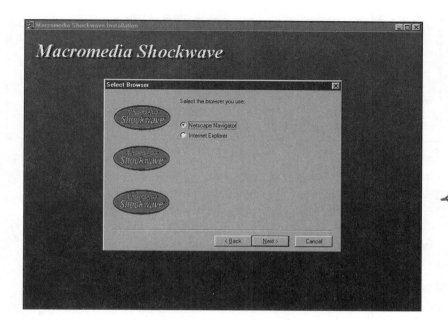

Figure 2.1
Shockwave's installation menu lets you select your browser.

Other browsers that Macromedia claims to support Shockwave are Netmanage's Websurfer and Attachmate's Emissary. Others are sure to follow, though hopefully we will see more standardization in Web browsers. If you have designed many Web sites, you know how difficult it is to predict the appearance of a Web page because different browsers respond differently to the HTML code. Our suggestion is to stick to Netscape Navigator due to its popularity.

You can find Netscape and Internet Explorer in stores if you like, or you can download them from their Web sites. The locations are listed below for your reference.

> Microsoft's Internet address:
>
> **http://www.microsoft.com**
>
> Netscape's Internet address:
>
> **http://www.netscape.com**

ON the CD
n32 z0006.exe

Duh! (handwritten annotation)

> **Note**
>
> You must have the appropriate browser and plug-in for your system. Windows 95 users will need a different program than Windows 3.1 users, because Windows 95 supports 32-bit software while Windows 3.1 uses only 16-bit programs. Be sure when you download a browser or a plug-in that you have chosen the correct one for your system.

Plug-Ins

To view the Shockwave movie, the browser must have a plug-in. Because Macromedia has developed Shockwave for Director, Authorware, and Freehand, there are three plug-ins to be installed. All three are automatically installed in the proper location when you run the Shockwave installation program.

The plug-ins are available for download at Macromedia's Web site and are also included on the CD-ROM with this book.

On the CD

Macromedia's Internet address is:

http://www.macromedia.com

Once the plug-ins are in the correct directory for your browser, they will automatically be available when you run the browser. The Shockwave installer will automatically put the plug-ins in their proper location. To install the plug-ins supplied on the CD-ROM, run one of the following programs:

W95 (handwritten annotation)

For Windows 95 or NT: N32Z0005.EXE, then run the extracted setup file.

For Windows 3.1: N16Z0005.EXE, then run the extracted setup file.

For Macintosh 68K: N68Z0005.SEA

For Power Macintosh: NPPZ0005.SEA

Your browser's preferences menu should give you an option for cache size, which must be at least 10M. A large cache size is to your benefit, anyway, because it allows you to leave a Web page and return to it without having to redownload everything. You'll soon see how file size and download time are major considerations with a Shocked Web site.

Recommendations: Creating Shockwave Files

A supporting browser and the plug-ins are all you really need to get started. You can put Shocked files on your Web site or view them on someone else's. However, to create original Shockwave files of your own, you need to use one of Macromedia's products, as well as a few other tools.

Macromedia Products

Macromedia products are high-end multimedia tools useful in creating CD-ROMs, kiosks, other interactive media, print, and of course, Shockwave. They are not free and are usually not available in your local neighborhood software or computer shop. You can order them through a Macromedia distributor. Contact Macromedia for more information on how to order **(800-457-1774)**. You can also order some products from Macromedia's online store: **http://www.macromall.com**.

Director

For Internet multimedia, you need Director 4.0 or 5.0 (see figure 2.2). Director is a powerful tool used in creating multimedia products. You may use it only for animation and sound, but it also includes a detailed programming language that can perform a variety of complex tasks. Many CD-ROM and kiosk projects are authored using Director. Graphics, sound, animation, video, and other elements are all brought together using an authoring tool such as Director.

Multimedia is the most common application of Shockwave on the Internet. If you want animation and sound on your Web site, this is the product to use. Note that you can create most Shockwave movies using Director 4, but you must have version 5 to use the compressed and streaming audio features.

The retail price of Director 5 is $929, or it's available in a package called the Director Multimedia Studio that includes other software packages such as Extreme 3D and SoundEdit 16 for $999. Director may sometimes be available through mail-order software catalogs.

Note

Many examples in this book were done in version 4 so that anyone can use them, but certain example files were done in version 5. Anyone can view the movies using a browser with Shockwave, but you will not be able to open version 5 files in Director 4.

Fig. 2.2
Macromedia
Director for
Windows.

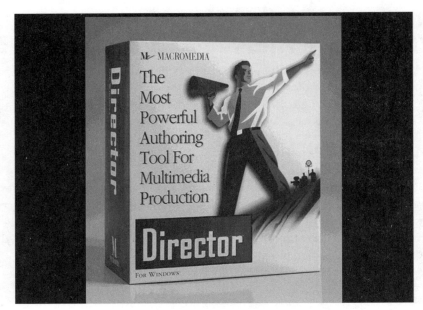

Authorware

For large-scale Intranet multimedia projects, Authorware 3.5 is the choice (figure 2.3). Authorware is a major multimedia production tool. It offers an easy-to-use interface for creating complex multimedia products. Authorware performs the same function as Director: compiling graphics, sound, video, and other pieces into a final interactive multimedia project. The advantage to Authorware is that it offers more organization and a faster, easier creation process for complex productions.

Shockwave for Authorware may be used on the Internet, but due to large file sizes, it is not as efficient as Director. Because Intranets have higher speed connections for their users, larger file sizes can be used. Shockwave for Authorware also supports *streaming*, which allows the user to download only certain parts at a time, as they are needed.

Authorware retails for around $4,800, putting it out of reach for most home users, though special offers are not uncommon. It is rarely seen in catalogs or stores, and usually is ordered through a Macromedia reseller.

FreeHand

For scalable images, use Freehand Version 5.0 or later (figure 2.4). Freehand is a vector graphics program that allows precise control in drawing an image. It is similar to other drawing programs such as Illustrator or CorelDRAW!.

Figure 2.3
Macromedia
Authorware for
Windows.

*only
$4,800*

Figure 2.4
Macromedia
Freehand for
Macintosh.

*only
$400*

Shockwave for Freehand is ideal for maps, charts, diagrams, and other detailed graphics that may be hard to see as a standard image file (GIF or JPEG). With Shockwave for Freehand, you can zoom, pan, and link to other Web sites with the Freehand graphics image.

Freehand sells for around $400, and is also available in package deals with other graphics programs. It is sometimes seen in mail-order software catalogs.

SoundEdit 16

SoundEdit 16 is the audio editing tool that is used for streaming audio using Shockwave (figure 2.5). You may or may not decide to edit your sounds using this software, but it is essential to use it for the final step: compressing the audio file. An Xtra is used with SoundEdit 16 to export a special file type (called an SWA file) that is used by Shockwave over the web. Unfortunately, SoundEdit 16 is only available for the Macintosh at this time. It retails for around $200 or can be found in package deals.

Figure 2.5
Macromedia
SoundEdit 16 for
Macintosh.

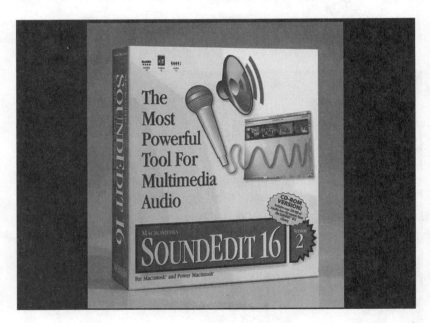

Compress

Afterburner

Afterburner is the tool created by Macromedia to turn a standard file into a compressed version to put on the Internet. It is included on the CD-ROM and is also available from Macromedia's Web site (http://www.macromedia.com). Using Afterburner is discussed more thoroughly in chapter 3, "Putting It on the Web." There are separate Afterburner programs for Director, Authorware, and Freehand. Director 5 offers support for Afterburner as an Xtra, so running a separate program is not needed.

> ### Note
>
> Shockwave will still recognize and load standard file types. Afterburner is a benefit to download time because it compresses the file, but it's not necessary. So a normal .DIR file created in Director can be viewed by Shockwave, though the same file might be half as big after being compressed with Afterburner into the .DCR format.

Graphics Creation Software

Creating graphics is a big part of multimedia and Shockwave. You could just use clip-art and other pre-created graphics all of the time, but you would be missing out on customizing your Shockwave graphics (and missing out on a lot of fun, too).

Computer graphics can be divided into two categories: bit-map and vector graphics, and it's essential to know the difference. If you buy a program that creates one type of graphic, you will be disappointed if you try to use it for a different purpose.

Bit-Map versus Vector Graphics

Bit map means just what it sounds like: a map of bits. Figure 2.6 shows a magnified view of a bit-map graphic. A bit-map image is divided into fragments, or single bits, each with color information. Each bit is called a *pixel*, from the term "picture element." The pixels are mapped horizontally and vertically. A bit map that is 400 pixels wide by 300 pixels high will contain 120,000 pixels, and each one has a color value. Color depth may vary for a bit-map image. An "8-bit" image contains 256 colors, so any particular pixel may be one of 256 colors. A 24-bit image contains over 16.7 million colors that each pixel may be. Obviously, the higher the color depth, the larger the file size. Scanned photographs are bit-map images. Most images intended to be viewed on a computer screen are bit-map images. Director and Authorware use mostly bit-map images.

Vector graphics, on the other hand, are a series of computer commands to "draw" an image. Vector graphics are broken down into circles, lines, arcs, boxes, color "fills," and other instructions (figure 2.7). The file size of a vector graphic is usually much smaller than a bit-map graphic because it does not keep track of thousands or millions of bits of information. Most vector graphics are intended to be used in printing because they are scalable. Shown large or small, the angles and measurements the computer uses are the same. If a bit-map image were blown up too large, it would become blurry or "pixelated" due to the pixel data being spread out too far. Vector

(continues)

.DIR

.DCR
↑
compress

(continued)

graphics are best used for crisp, hard-edged images, such as logos or diagrams. Shockwave for Freehand uses vector graphics.

Figure 2.6
A magnified view of a bit map.

Figure 2.7
Vector graphics use curves, lines, and other geometry.

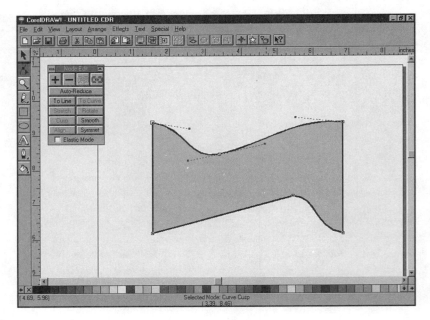

Bit-Map Graphics

A good image editing program is strongly recommended for creating or editing graphics. While Director has a paint window built into its interface that allows you to create and edit images, it is very limited compared to other products made with a focus on high quality graphics.

Adobe Photoshop is currently an industry standard in computer graphics. It sells for approximately $600, which is not too expensive considering its versatility and power. It's useful for everything from retouching scanned photos to creating completely original graphics. Various third party developers create filter plug-ins that work with Photoshop. Kai's Power Tools is an example of this.

The CD-ROM with this book contains a few public domain graphics programs that you may use in creating your Shockwave graphics. Paint Shop Pro and Graphics Workshop are two that you can try.

what! (handwritten)

use psp (handwritten)

Vector Graphics

Photoshop is ideal for bit-map image editing (see note on Bit-Map versus Vector Graphics). You may also want a vector graphics program, such as Adobe Illustrator, Macromedia Freehand, or CorelDRAW!. Usually, vector graphics programs are used for images intended for print, but they can also be useful for on-screen graphics, designing logos, maps, diagrams, and other precise drawings. You could even create a complex path in a vector graphics program, then import the path to a bit-map editor where detailed selections may be more difficult.

3-D Graphics

A 3-D graphics package can also be very useful, particularly if you want to animate an object moving or changing three-dimensionally. Kinetix 3D Studio Max, Macromedia Extreme 3D, and Caligari TrueSpace2 are a few examples. Animating three-dimensionally will increase file size because multiple angles are needed for an image; however, keeping physical size small can still offer reasonable file sizes for 3-D animation. Popularity of 3-D graphics is increasing rapidly, particularly in multimedia and video production.

Audio

To include sound in your multimedia, you may wish to have a sound editing utility. This will let you crop and reformat audio to fit your needs. Most audio cards come with some sort of sound utility, though some are more useful than others. To do intense sound editing, you'll want a good program, although this book doesn't go into detail on sound programs. Macromedia's multimedia bundle offers SoundEdit 16 and Deck II for the Macintosh, and SoundForge for Windows. Sound effects and music are available on various Web sites or from CD-ROM collections, or you may choose to record your own.

MIDI is not directly supported by Shockwave, though you may decide to create your own music using either built in MIDI instruments or an attached MIDI instrument. The audio will need to be recorded as a digital audio file. Several formats can be used, such as WAV or AIFF. For streaming audio, it will need to be compressed using a Shockwave Xtra for Macromedia's Sound-Edit 16.

From Here...

The software listed here can add up quickly to a big bill. You may decide to purchase only Director and use public domain software for graphics and sound. And while it's true that the more resources you have the better your end product will be, there is really no tool to substitute for your own creativity and adaptability.

The following chapters offer more on how to use these tools:

- Chapter 3, "Putting It on the Web,": A look at how to set up your movie.
- Chapter 4, Considerations for the Internet: What you should know about decreasing download time.
- Chapter 5, "Limitations of Shockwave and the Web": Tempo channels, what carries over from Director to Shockwave.

Putting It on the Web

[handwritten notes:]
1st. R.D\macromed\Freehand\Setup
2nd D\programs
3rd D\shockwave plugins\Win95

For Shockwave ⟶ N3220006

You have your Director movie all ready, and now you want to put it on your server for all the world to see. Here is what you need to do, and this chapter explains it all in the following:

- Install and then run Afterburner on your Director movie.
- Insert the burned Director movie into an HTML document.
- Install the Shockwave plug-in into your Web browser then preview your creation.
- Configure your server for the new MIME type.
- Upload the files to your Web server.
- Test your HTML document.
- Catering to Web browsers that cannot see Shockwave. *[handwritten: Can't Find this]*
- Match the backgrounds of your Web pages with your Shockwave movies: What is HEX?

Installing and Running Afterburner on Your Director Movie

[handwritten: what ↓ aftrbrnr.exe]

To install Afterburner, open the Shockwave folder, and double-click the file named *aftrbrnr.exe*. This installs Afterburner on your system. The process automatically installs all the Shockwave drivers (Freehand, Director, and Authorware) and asks if you're using the Netscape or Internet Explorer browsers.

Activate Afterburner by double-clicking it, then locate the Director movie that you want Afterburner to compress. When selected, click "OK" to save it along with the name you've chosen. The Afterburner process does not change the original movie but makes a compressed copy of it. Click "OK." You will then see a graphic representation of the progress Afterburner is making on compressing your movie. Then Afterburner closes.

Inserting the Burned Director Movie into an HTML Document: Typing in the HTML

There are a couple of software packages on the market that let users create Web pages without knowing HTML in a WYSIWYG (**W**hat **Y**ou **S**ee **I**s **W**hat **Y**ou **G**et) environment. One is Macromedia's Backstage Designer, and the other is SoftQuad's HoTMetaL Pro 3. A little later in this chapter, you will see examples of how to do this.

[handwritten note in margin: Hotmetal 3 Lite is on PDQ cd]

For now, this covers the HTML involved because these two programs do not support all the available options that can accompany your movie (none at the time of this writing do). This is easy for those of you who are familiar with the HTML language and editing HTML documents by hand. Those who aren't so familiar need not despair; the additional options aren't necessary for your movies to work, but they do give you more control as to how the end user interacts and sees the movie.

The markup for inserting a compressed Director movie (*.DCR) into a Web page is as follows:

```
<EMBED SRC="path/mymovie.dcr" WIDTH="n" HEIGHT="n"
➥TEXTFOCUS="n"></EMBED>
```

For the Width and Height parameters, enter the exact size of your movie. Entering a different size results in either a cropped movie, or a crashed or locked-up Web browser.

The TEXTFOCUS argument is optional. It is used to tell the browser with the installed Shockwave plug-in when to accept input from the user with respect to the Shockwave movie when the HTML document is being loaded. The available parameters for TEXTFOCUS are:

Table 3.1   Parameters for TEXTFOCUS

Command	Action
onMouse	This is the setting that Shockwave defaults to if the TEXTFOCUS argument is not used. This tells Shockwave not to accept input from the keyboard until the user clicks anywhere on the movie.
onStart	Shockwave responds to keyboard input as soon as the movie loads.
never	Shockwave ignores all input from the keyboard.

> **Note**
>
> These commands apply only to the movie being loaded and won't affect the Web page itself.

For example, suppose that you have a compressed Director movie named *header.dcr*. The movie is 200 by 45 pixels in size. Also, you want the movie to respond from user input as soon as it has finished loading. Finally, the movie is located in the same directory that the document it's embedded into resides. The HTML for what has just been described looks like this:

```
<EMBED SRC="header.dcr" WIDTH="200" HEIGHT="45"
➥TEXTFOCUS="onStart"></EMBED>
```

In another example, suppose that you have the same movie with the same dimensions. This time, however, you want to put the movie in a directory called "shockedstuff" that is one directory up from the directory where the HTML document it is a part of resides. Also, you want to use a TEXTFOCUS setting of "onMouse." The HTML would look like this:

```
<EMBED SRC="shockedstuff/header.dcr" WIDTH="200" HEIGHT="45">
➥</EMBED>
```

Note the absence of the TEXTFOCUS argument. If TEXTFOCUS is absent, Shockwave will assume the default parameter for that argument, which is "onMouse."

You may even control which palette the movie uses, either its own or the system palette via HTML. This is something that should be used with caution, though, because forcing the Shockwave movie to use its own palette maps the entire display to that palette, thereby disrupting the display if a custom palette is being used.

The HTML for controlling the palette is a simple argument added within the <EMBED> tag. Here is an example:

```
<EMBED SRC="header.dcr" HEIGHT="200" WIDTH="45"
➥PALETTE="background"></EMBED>
```

Specifying PALETTE to equal "background" runs the Shockwave movie using the system's palette. Replacing "background" with "foreground" forces the movie to use its own palette and consequently forces the entire display to use the movie's palette as well. If you plan on using multiple Director movies within a single HTML document, you're better off not playing with the PALETTE argument. In the absence of the PALETTE argument, Shockwave assumes the default setting, which is "background."

Using WYSIWYG Web Page Creation Software that Supports Shockwave

There are a few packages on the market that allow for the integration of Shockwave and other multimedia objects within the program itself, instead of creating a Web page, then firing up a text editor to add the specific HTML. It seems only natural, then, to talk about Macromedia's Backstage Designer. Backstage Designer allows for the creation of Web pages in a WYSIWYG environment, without the need to view your Web site in an external viewer.

See PDQ cd for Hotmetal 3

Another application, from SoftQuad, is HoTMetaL Pro 3. This package offers the same feature set as Backstage Designer but with added support for Netscape Extensions that are Netscape-specific HTML. It even supports Netscape Frames, an impressive feature. This is noteworthy because it is possible to have a Director movie with a number of links targeting any number of frames through Director's Net-specific Lingo, discussed in chapter 13, "Internet Lingo for Shockwave."

Along with running through Backstage Designer and HoTMetaL Pro, you'll also learn what to do if someone uses a browser that doesn't recognize Shockwave. This is referred to as "Catering to other browsers."

Integrating Shockwave Movies with Backstage Designer

D:\macromedia\ backstg\ setup

On the CD

A demo copy of Macromedia's Backstage Designer is on the CD-ROM in the folder entitled, "Backstage." Double-click the *Setup.exe* file to begin the installation process and follow the directions.

Now Backstage Designer is booted up (Figure 3.1).

Click the "Insert Netscape Plug-In" icon (figure 3.2).

Backstage then displays an image that *represents* a plug-in that you wish to add to your Web page. Double-clicking the icon gives you the Netscape Plug-In Properties dialog box, as shown in figure 3.3, which is where you specify the kind of plug-in you wish to use. This image will always be present even after you embed your Shocked movie because Backstage Designer is incapable of displaying embedded objects. Actually, there are no editors available that can display Shockwave movies, but after you are done, the image that represents the Shocked file will be the same dimensions as the file itself so that you at least have an idea of its placement. Figure 3.3 shows what the representative image looks like.

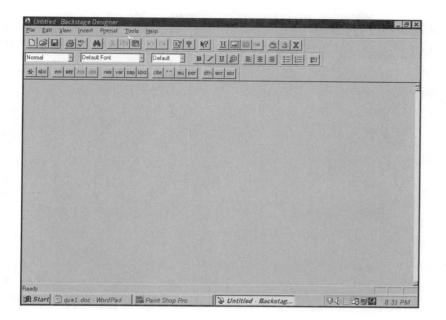

Figure 3.1
Backstage
Designer.

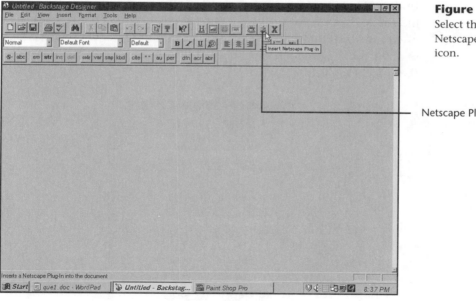

Figure 3.2
Select the "Insert
Netscape Plug-in"
icon.

Netscape Plug-in icon

Figure 3.3
Backstage Designer
inserts an image
that represents the
movie that you
want to embed.

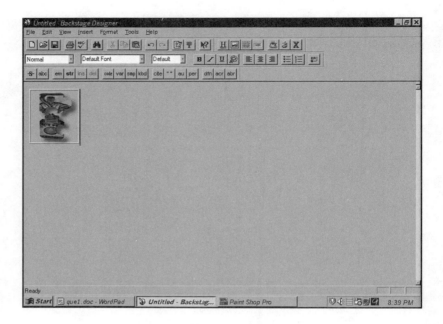

Under "Plug-In Source" (figure 3.4), select "Browser" and locate the *.DCR
file you wish to use (your Director file that you have compressed with
Afterburner and that will have the DCR extension). After your file has been
selected, Backstage automatically inserts the dimensions of the movie into
the appropriate fields.

Figure 3.4
The "Netscape
Plug-In Properties"
dialog, where you
can select the
Shockwave movie
to use as well
as additional
options.

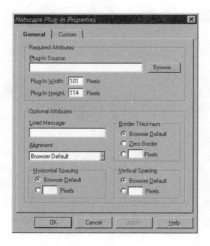

Next, click the Custom tab, as shown previously in figure 3.4. Look at the
"Alternate Content" section (figure 3.5) and click in the "Image Source" box.

Locate the file you want to use as the alternate image for your movie, should someone happen to view your site without support for the Shockwave plug-in. The appropriate dimensions for your alternate image are placed automatically into your Web page, even though Backstage does not show you the information. You can ignore the rest of the parameters in the Netscape Plug-In Properties dialog box.

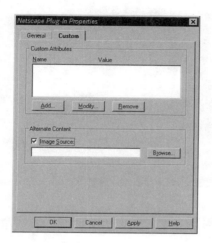

Figure 3.5
The "Alternate Content" area allows the insertion of an alternate image in the event that a non-compatible browser is used to view a Web page using Shockwave.

Shockwave and the Web

Integrating Shockwave Movies with HoTMetaL Pro Version 3

Open HoTMetaL Pro by double-clicking its icon. To start on a new document, select "FILE" then "NEW." Next, save the new document in the directory that contains the Shockwave movie that you wish to add (figure 3.6).

The first thing you may notice is that HoTMetaL displays icons on the screen that represent HTML tags. As your work progresses, you may wish, at some point, to turn off this feature. To do so, simply press "CTRL+W." Repeating this action toggles the screen back and forth. If you wish, you may continue editing with the "View Tags" (also available from the "VIEW" drop-down list) option off. It is much easier to insert markup, though, with "View Tags" on.

Next, let's insert the <EMBED> tag so that we can insert a Shockwave movie into our Web page. To do so, select the PARAGRAPH element icon from the tool bar. Then, while the cursor is within the <P></P> tags, select either "Markup," then "Insert Element" or press "CTRL+I." You are greeted with HoTMetaL's Insert Element dialogue box. Scroll down the list and locate the element called "EMBED" (Figure 3.7).

Figure 3.6
HoTMetaL Pro
Version 3.0.

Figure 3.7
HotMetaL Pro's
Insert Element
dialog box.

Double-clicking the "EMBED" element inserts it.

Next, you need to select the director movie to use. To do so, right-click the
<EMBED> tags and select "Element Attributes."

ROYAL Consumer Business Products   Product Registration Card   **ORGANIZERS**

PLEASE PRINT

Name: _____

Address: _____

City: _____ State: _____ Zip: _____

Company: _____

Date of Purchase: _____ Model: _____

Email: _____

Store where purchased: _____ Product was a gift. ☐

Purchase Influence Factors

☐ Price of Product   ☐ Product Size   ☐ Telephone Memory

☐ Product Appearance   ☐ LCD Display Size   ☐ Additional Functions

☐ **In-Store Promotion** ☐ Memory Capacity   ☐ Optional PC Link

ROYAL®
Consumer Business Products
P.O. Box 121
Jamison, PA 18929-0121

Tip

Right-clicking any element in HoTMetaL Pro gives you a number of options associated with that element.

The resulting dialog box has a number of options relating to embedded objects (Figure 3.8). You need only concern yourself with the "SRC" (source), "HEIGHT," and "WIDTH," as these are required parameters.

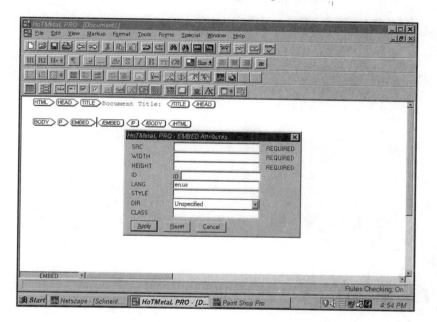

Figure 3.8
Embed Attributes.

At this point, because you already saved the document in the same directory as the Shockwave movie you are about to insert, you need only type in the name of the movie in the "SRC" field. Type the "**Height**" and "**Width**" parameters into their respective fields, then select "OK."

Unlike Backstage Designer, HoTMetaL does not insert an icon that represents the Shockwave movie. Instead it does something that is a little more practical. Because it's considered to be good form to cater to browsers that do not support Shockwave, HoTMetaL Pro places the alternate image, when you specify one, where the Shockwave movie would be. At that point, you may apply a Server-Side and/or a Client-Side Image map to the alternate image using HoTMetaL's Image Mapping option (available by right-clicking any image).

To specify an alternate image for your movie, you must first insert the <NOEMBED></NOEMBED> tags by placing the cursor to the right of the <EMBED> </EMBED> icons and then pressing "CTRL+I." The "Insert Element" dialog will then pop up, allowing you to scroll down to locate the "NOEMBED" tag. Insert it by double-clicking. Your screen should now look like figure 3.9.

Figure 3.9
The EMBED and NOEMBED tags.

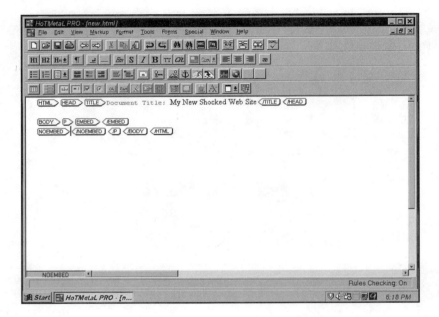

Place the cursor in between the <NOEMBED></NOEMBED> tags, if it is not already there, and then select the "Image" button from the tool bar (figure 3.10).

If your alternate image is in the same directory as your HTML document and Shockwave movie, you need only insert the name of the image in the "Image Field." You may also insert alternate text, height, and width information for the image into the appropriate fields as well. When you are done, select "OK."

Now that your alternate image is in place, you may add a Clickable Image Map in the form of either a Client-Side or Server-Side Image Map (both are ideal). If your Shockwave movie is being used as a navigation tool, then your alternate image, which could be a screen capture of the movie, needs to have these image maps applied to it.

HoTMetaL Pro 3 makes it very easy to add image maps. Merely right-click your image, then select "Image Mappings" (Figure 3.11).

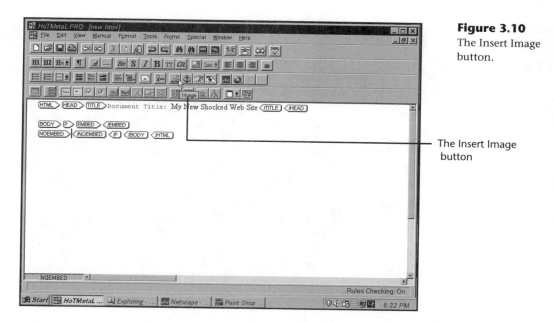

Figure 3.10
The Insert Image button.

The Insert Image button

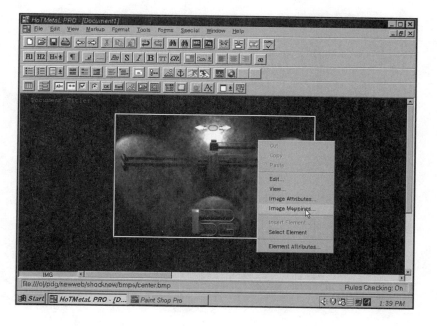

Figure 3.11
Right-click your image and then select "Image Mappings" to bring up the image-map editor.

An image map editor then appears (figure 3.12).

Figure 3.12
HoTMetaL Pro's
integrated image
map editor.

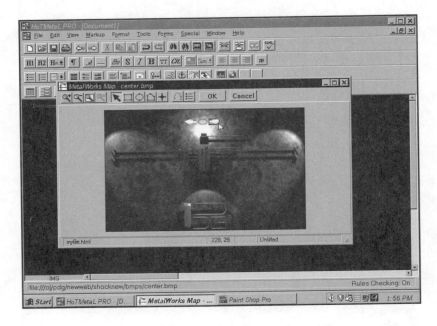

Simply click an area tool such as the rectangle tool and click and drag an area
(figure 3.13) that you would like to be a link.

Figure 3.13
Select the rect-
angle tool then
click and drag on
the area that you
wish to be defined
as a link.

When you let go of the mouse button, you will be given an opportunity to insert the destination of the link in the form of an absolute or relative URL, as shown in Figure 3.14.

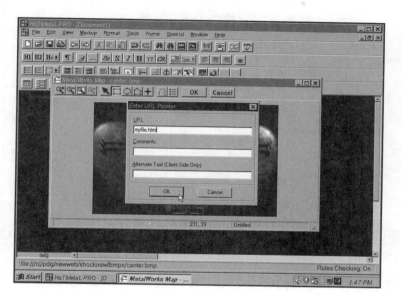

Figure 3.14
After you have defined an area, a dialogue box will automatically appear so that you may enter the destination for your link.

Click "OK" and then select whether you wish to use a Server-Side Image Map (ISMAP), a Client-Side Image Map (USEMAP), or both. In this example, as illustrated in figure 3.15, we are using a Client-Side Image Map. Deselect the ISMAP option so that's the case. That's it, you're done!

When using Server-Side Image Maps, check with your server administrator about what format the generated *.map files need to be in (CERN or NCSA) and where the CGI (Common Gateway Interface) program is that takes care of image mapping.

Also, older browsers do not recognize the "USEMAP" attribute (Client-Side Image Maps) so if you wish to define multiple hot areas on your image, definitely use "ISMAP" (a Server-Side Image Map). Netscape 2 and above, Enhanced Mosaic, and Internet Explorer are a few that do.

Figure 3.15

After pressing "OK" in HoTMetaL's image-map editor, you can select either a Server-Side (ISMAP) or a Client-Side (USEMAP) clickable image map for your image.

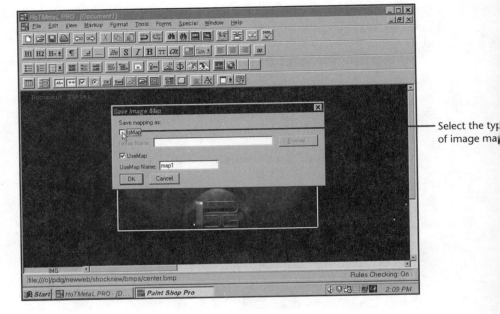

Select the typ of image ma

Installing the Shockwave Plug-In on Your Web Browser

The plug-in for Shockwave for Director is included on the CD-ROM. To install the plug-in, open the Shockwave folder and double-click the file entitled *sw1b2b32.exe* and follow the directions. If you're running Netscape, you have to restart the program for the changes to take effect.

Even though you've been through a couple of examples of how to Shock a Web page, I'm sure you've noticed that in both cases, an icon representing your Director movie was placed in your Web page and not the actual Director movie itself. This may seem odd in a supposedly WYSIWYG environment. These packages are unable to play Director movies and are meant solely as a tool to make it easier to Shock a page without the need to do so through a text editor. So, in order to see how it actually works, you need to preview your Web page in Netscape. At this point, it is not necessary to upload your files to a server to preview them. Simply boot Netscape, click "File" and then "Open File," and locate the document that has the embedded movie in it.

It is a good rule of thumb to view all your HTML documents in an actual Web browser no matter what method of creating them you end up using. The programs mentioned will give you a good idea of what your page will look like, but they are not exact. Different Web browsers put different amounts of space between different HTML elements. A Web page in Backstage Designer will look slightly different than in Netscape, which will in turn look slightly different in Mosaic and in Microsoft's Internet Explorer.

MIME Types—Configuring Your Server

Before you can view a Shocked site from your server, you must first be sure that the *MIME* (**M**ultipurpose **I**nternet **M**ail **E**xtensions) type has been set for the compressed Director file so that the server will handle it properly when it is called. If you are unfamiliar with how to proceed or are not familiar with UNIX or your server in general, let the server administrator do the following for you.

Configuring UNIX Servers

For UNIX-based Web servers, the following MIME types need to be added:

> **application/x-director dcr**
>
> **application/x-director dir**
>
> **application/x-director dxr**

Alternatively, if there is an application on the server that registers MIME types, the following information is required:

> **mime type:** application
>
> **sub type:** x-director
>
> **extensions:** dcr, dir, dxr

You may have noticed that two of the extensions in the preceding paragraphs were DIR and DXR. DIR, being the native Director format, can be opened in Director and edited. The DXR format is a protected movie that can be played, but not opened in Director. These file types, once the proper MIME types have been set, will work exactly like the compressed DCRs except that they will not benefit from Afterburner compression and will consequently take longer to download.

Configuring Mac Servers

For Macintosh-based Web servers, the *MacHTTP.config* file needs to have the following lines added:

> **BINARY .DXR TEXT * application/x-director**
>
> **BINARY .DCR TEXT * application/x-director**

Configuring WebSTAR Servers

If you're using WebSTAR server software on a Macintosh server, do the following:

1. Run WebSTAR Admin.
2. In the Pick A Server Window, Select your server.
3. Choose Suffix Mapping from the Configure menu.
4. Choose the following settings:

> **Action:** BINARY
>
> **File Suffix:** .DCR
>
> **File Type:** TEXT
>
> **Creator:** *
>
> **MIME Type:** application/x-director

If you intend to provide uncompressed DIR or DXR Director files, repeat the process for each of the file extensions.

Upload the Files to Your Web Server

There are a variety of shareware FTP (**F**ile **T**ransfer **P**rotocol) packages on the Web that allow you to transfer files to your server. If your PC runs Windows 95 and you're familiar with a few simple UNIX commands, you may select Start, Run, and then type the following:

> **ftp www.myserver.com**

where `"myserver"` is your URL. Press Enter. You will then be asked for your user name and password. A DOS-like window will pop up. This is where you type in the commands for navigation, similar to DOS. From there, navigate your way to the directory where you would like to place your files and use the PUT command to begin transferring your files (remember to change the method of transfer to binary). Typing `help` gives you a list of UNIX commands (assuming your server is a UNIX box). If all this is unfamiliar territory, download something that has a *GUI* (**G**raphical **U**ser **I**nterface) such as the programs mentioned in the following paragraphs.

A really good FTP package for PCs can be downloaded via your Web browser from various sources, such as:

> **http://www.jtec.com/**
>
> **http://www.windows95.com/apps/ftp.html#wsftp**

You can download a shareware FTP package for the Mac called Fetch 3.0.1 from the following address:

http://wwwhost.ots.utexas.edu/mac/index-by-date.html

http://wwwhost.ots.utexas.edu/mac/internet-ftp.html#fetch-301

Whenever you transfer files to your Web server, be sure to send the files as binary. Sending as ASCII renders the files useless!

Test Your HTML Document

Now that your files are on your Web server, it's time to test the performance of the page. When evaluating the time that it takes to download the page, ask yourself if the average user would wait for your Director movie to come up. Does the movie need to be as large as it is? Can it serve its purpose if some elements are removed to make it smaller? Is there information on the page for visitors to look at while they are waiting? If the movie contains some kind of navigational links in it, are they replicated somewhere else in the page so they can go to another page on your site instead of leaving if they get impatient?

Of course, the average users are probably willing to wait a little longer for a game to download, or for something else just as interesting, if they know that what they're waiting for is going to be worthwhile. So, in that respect, trying to decide whether or not something is going to take too long to download is a subjective thing. Some people would wait, and others might not.

It also helps to test the page in a real-life situation. If you work for a company that has a super-fast T1 line to the Internet right in the office, then testing with that kind of connection would be pointless. Jump on a machine that has your everyday dial-up connection and hardware the average user might have.

Finally, some people don't realize that once they have viewed a Web site, it has been *cached* on their system. This means that the next time the site is viewed, it won't take as long because the Web browser looks on your computer for the images and such, instead of downloading them all over again from the Internet. This may seem obvious, but I have actually seen a person giving a demonstration on Shockwave without realizing this simple fact. He went on to inform the audience that his 170K movie took only three or four seconds to download when, in fact, it was cached on his computer, having been downloaded weeks before.

Catering to Web Browsers that Cannot See Shockwave

If there's one constant on the Internet, it's that it's always in a state of flux. Change is the norm as new technology and new markup appear. Therefore, Web-browser developers are constantly updating their software to take advantage of the latest and greatest, which is a time-consuming and costly task. As a result, there are many browsers in use that will undoubtedly be unable to view your Shockwave masterpiece. What they see, more often than not, though, is up to you.

The previous sections on using Backstage Designer and HoTMetaL Pro showed you how to place an image in place of a Shockwave movie in the event that the movie was not recognized by a browser. You've learned how to do this in a WYSIWYG environment, so let's see what the HTML looks like.

The <EMBED></EMBED> tags allow for <NOEMBED></NOEMBED> tags to be placed within them. Browsers that recognize <EMBED></EMBED> ignore any information that falls in between the start (<EMBED>) and end (</EMBED>) tags. For example, the following has a Director movie with an alternate image placed between the <NOEMBED></NOEMBED> tags:

```
<EMBED SRC="my.dcr" HEIGHT="20" WIDTH="20"><NOEMBED><IMG
➥SRC="my.gif></NOEMBED></EMBED>
```

In the preceding example, a browser that recognizes the markup for embedding an object ignores all the information except that which specifically deals with the embedded object in this case, the Shockwave movie. This includes the <NOEMBED></NOEMBED> and anything that is inside them.

A browser that does not recognize the tags for embedding objects, on the other hand, ignores them. This includes not only the "EMBED" but the "NOEMBED" markup as well. However, because the preceding example includes markup for an alternate image within the "NOEMBED" tags, this information will be displayed in place of the movie.

As it turns out, anything that is placed in between <NOEMBED></NOEMBED> will be displayed in place of your Shockwave movie when viewed with a non-supportive browser. If you want text to be displayed instead of an image that represents the movie, you can do so. More importantly, if your movie is meant to be a control panel of sorts for navigating your Web site, you may place the required HTML for a clickable image map along with your alternate image within <NOEMBED></NOEMBED> for the most seamless workaround possible!

Matching Backgrounds and Movies Using HEX

You may want the background of your Web page to match a color within your Shockwave movie. In the past, selecting a specific color meant being able to convert the RGB value of that color to Hexadecimal format. Netscape, and consequently all browsers that support background colors, requires that the color combination be in three sets of two, each set representing Red, Green, and Blue (RRGGBB).

How, then, do you get a two-digit value for any Red, Green, or Blue value that can be as high as 255, which is three digits? If you are on any Windows platform, the answer is simple. Fire up your trusty Windows calculator, type in the first value, then click "HEX." You are then greeted by the Hexadecimal value for that particular value. Next, do the same for the rest of the RGB values, once for Green and once for Blue. Conversely, you may first select HEX, type in the two-digit value from a HEX color, and select Dec (decimal) to receive the three-digit equivalent.

Macintosh users aren't so lucky; however, the Mac OS comes with a very basic calculator, unlike the scientific calculator on the PC side. This apparent shortcoming is easy to surmount because there are numerous sites available on the Internet that will convert your RGB values for you. You can find one excellent source here:

http://www.echonyc.com/~xixax/Mediarama/hex.html

Or you may elect to find a Mac-based program for converting RGB values to HEX. One such utility can be found at this address:

http://www.sci.kun.nl/thalia/guide/color/faq.html#color-pickers

Both Macromedia's Backstage Designer and SoftQuad's HoTMetaL Pro 3 offer easy solutions for selecting colors without the need to manually convert RGB values to HEX. They also take care of all the HTML coding for you so that it's simple to accomplish.

If you're a diehard HTML programmer, or you're curious as to what is involved on the programming side, you can find an excellent *FAQ (*Frequently **A**sked **Q**uestion*)* on using backgrounds in HTML documents at the following Web site:

http://www.sci.kun.nl/thalia/guide/color/faq.html

From Here...

In this chapter, you learned how to embed Shockwave movies into Web pages by using several different methods. Either of the programs used in this chapter are capable of accomplishing the tasks at hand.

Backstage Designer is designed for the novice. It completely isolates the user from HTML while giving an option to view the "source code" if you want to edit the page in a basic word processor-like environment. HoTMetaL Pro 3 is meant more for the advanced HTML programmer/designer who wants to see and is not confused by seeing all the HTML on the screen. It also offers increased functionality and much broader support for HTML 3.2 and Internet Explorer-specific extensions.

You also learned how to cater to Shockwave-ignorant browsers, how to send files to your Web server, and what needs to be changed on a Web server before that server is capable of delivering Shocked movies (changing the MIME type):

- Chapter 4, "Considerations for the Internet": Covers everything you need to know about how to create your Shocked files, limitations of an end-user's system, and the Internet.

- Chapter 5, "Limitations of Shockwave and the Web": Delves into features of Director that have been disabled for security reasons.

- Chaper 6, "Liven Up a Page: Animations for Fun": Explores applications of Shockwave.

Considerations for the Internet

A certain Web site I've visited occasionally gives me two options: enhanced with Shockwave and nonenhanced. I always choose nonenhanced. Why? Because I am looking for fast information. Shockwave takes time, and if the user is there only for quick information, he or she will not be willing to wait for fancy stuff. To decrease download time, you will need to be careful in how you construct your Shockwave Web pages so that the user is not annoyed with too many enhancements.

This chapter contains a few suggestions for limiting the size of your director movie:

- Limiting graphics size and color depth
- Keeping file size down with features of Director
- Adding efficient audio to Shockwave files
- Testing your movie at the lowest level

Thinking about Your Intended Audience

You may have already created a Director movie that you would like Shocked on your Web page. If it's already a relatively small file, this may be no problem. But if you're like me and love to add every detail and feature possible, you end up with a 5M Director movie. Even after it's compressed, it's ridiculously large. So it's best to keep the Internet in mind as you create.

Are your viewers really interested in fancy stuff, or will it be more of a bother than an enhancement? Are they visiting your page to find information or to be entertained? A balance between aesthetics, excitement, and functionalism is necessary.

Download time was discussed in chapter 1, "Multimedia on the Web." You'll soon realize that file size will consume your thoughts as you create. The more you can pack into a small file, the better off you'll be. Of course, certain people will be willing to wait longer than others, but the last thing you want is someone going to your Web page, seeing "`13% downloaded of 300k`" at the bottom of the screen, and not being willing to wait for your fantastic work of art to arrive. To ease this download time, you might consider having a very compact Shockwave movie come up immediately to mesmerize the viewer with some text or a special effect while the final Shockwave movie downloads in the background. See chapter 13, "Internet Lingo for Shockwave," for more on how to do this by using network Lingo commands.

Graphics

Obviously, smaller physical size means smaller file size. You may want your logo to dominate the screen as it spins, dances, or sings, but if it means the viewer has to wait five minutes just to see a silly animation, it's not worth it. Use the minimalist ideal: Less is more.

Color Depth

We mentioned color depth of bit-map images in chapter 2, "Suggested Tools." Afterburner compresses 8-bit and 1-bit images the best, so it's good to stick to those two in your Director movie, though you may experiment with other depths. As you can see in table 4.1, as you increase bit depth, the number of possible colors for each pixel increases—and more possibilities mean bigger file size.

Table 4.1   Color Depth Chart

Bit Depth	Number of Colors
1-bit	2 colors
2-bit	4 colors
4-bit	16 colors
8-bit	256 colors
16-bit	65.5 thousand colors
24-bit	16.7 million colors

The more 1-bit images you can use, the better. Consider this example: A 100-pixel square image in Director that is 1-bit is only 1.2K, while the same size image that's 8-bits is 19.5K! That's quite a difference. It's also easier to get away with 1-bit images when they are animated because the motion can hide their simplicity.

Not only is 8-bit the highest depth you should use due to file size, it also includes the largest audience on the Internet. Many Internet viewers may have video cards that can display only 8-bit color, so even if you created something in high color, they could not see it. Their computers would automatically *dither* the image down to 8-bits.

> **Note**
>
> *Dithering* is the process the computer uses to simulate colors that aren't in its palette. For example, you create an image in 24-bits that uses a particular hue of orange. When you convert it to 8-bits, the palette may not contain that exact color. If you choose the option of dithering colors, the computer will simulate that orange hue by speckling pixels that are similar in color next to each other (perhaps pixels of red and yellow). Just like in Neoimpressionist Georges Seurat's pointillistic (divisionistic) paintings, your eye mixes the actual colors it sees to appear as the intended color, like an optical illusion. Sometimes an image dithers beautifully, and you can hardly tell a difference from the original high-color image. Other times you get speckles of ugly colors that may look awful. If the latter occurs, you may decide to go back and adjust the colors of the original until the dithered image looks good.

Images with large areas of flat colors will compress much better than images with areas of various dithered colors. You may choose not to dither the image when you convert it; you can remap the colors to the nearest hue in the palette.

Palettes

High-color images (16- and 24-bit) have no palette. They use a system that defines the properties of the actual color. Eight-bit images and lower use a color palette. Each pixel in an 8-bit image has a number associated with it that corresponds to a color location in the palette, so a certain hue of red may be number 137 in the palette.

In converting your high-color image to 8-bits, you can choose either the computer's system palette or an adaptive palette. The system palette is the same on any computer (though Windows and Macintosh have different palettes). The adaptive palette chooses only colors that are needed for the particular image and creates a custom palette, so it looks much better. Director has system palettes for Windows and Macintosh built in, as well as several other built-in palettes.

> **Caution**
>
> If the viewer's computer is running in 8-bit mode, your custom palette can override their system palette and cause the rest of the screen to sort of "go crazy." For example, an image on the screen accesses color #86. This may be green in the system palette, but your custom palette puts red into position #86, and all pixels that used to be green now show up as red. To protect against this, stick to a system palette. If you're ambitious, you can leave certain colors in the palette that are needed by the system and put your own into other positions; however, this chapter won't go into detail about doing that. If it's not important that you accommodate people with 8-bit displays, go ahead and make custom palettes.

Director Tools

Director contains various tools that can create graphics, buttons, text, and other elements. You may find that you want to create these things in other programs such as Photoshop, but Director's tools can often do the same thing and will use much less space in the movie's final file size.

Vector Graphics Tools

Consider using Director's tool buttons to create boxes, circles, and other simple graphics. To use the same example mentioned earlier, the 1-bit, 100-pixel square that was 1.2K could be drawn with the Director tool as a vector graphic and will only use up 64 bytes! Clicking the "i" in the cast member window will display the selected member's size within the movie. By selecting more than one cast member, the "i" button shows you the combined total.

Remember, vector graphics only need to define lines, angles, shapes, and other "drawing" features. This will almost always result in smaller file size than bitmap graphics that need to define every pixel of an image. Refer to the sidebar, Bit Map versus Vector Graphics, in chapter 2, "Suggested Tools," for more on the differences.

Tiling

Tiling is a useful feature in creating nice backgrounds using very little file space. If you have ever used the `<body background="filename">` tag, you are familiar with tiling, or repeating an image over and over throughout a certain area. Director comes with eight built-in tiles, most of which are fairly basic. But you can create your own tiles from a cast member. See the example in chapter 8, "Special Effects and Other Shockwave Techniques," for more information on the tile feature.

Text

Text compresses very nicely with Afterburner. You may be tempted to create text in your graphics program and import it as a bit map, but if this isn't essential, you can use Director's tool to create text. Version 5 of Director has improved the text features to offer anti-aliased text. When using the text tool in Director 5, the text is merged into the stage like a bit map so that the user does not need to have the same fonts installed on his or her system. However, the field tool (which allows text to be modified by lingo or by the user) leaves the text as a certain font, size, style, and so on. It's important to remember that the viewer may not (and probably doesn't) have the same fonts installed on his or her system. It's best to stick to the standard fonts available on most computers when you use fields. Shockwave will automatically select a similar font when the movie is created on one platform and played on another. Table 4.2 shows some common fonts for Windows and Macintosh.

Table 4.2 Standard Fonts	
Windows	**Macintosh**
Arial	Helvetica
Courier	Courier
MS Serif	New York
MS Sans Serif	Geneva
Symbol	Symbol
System	Chicago
Terminal	Monaco
Times New Roman	Times

Shockwave and the Web

Tip

If you're counting every kilobyte and want to reduce a few more, here's an easy way. Director has a default font mapping table that it uses (and that Afterburner uses) for every movie, whether it uses fonts or not. By specifying your own font map, one that is nearly empty, you can slim the final .DCR file by a few K.

1. First, create a simple text file with almost nothing in it. A semicolon indicates a comment, so one of these is fine.

2. Next, go to Movie Info in Director and declare this text file to be your font map.

3. Save your movie. That's all you have to do!

If you do use fonts, but want your own font mapping table, read the font map text file (*fontmap.txt* on Windows systems). It will explain more on how to do this. Then you can delete all of the Macromedia comments to have your own bare-bones font map.

Sound

Audio can be a great addition to your Director movie if it's used efficiently. A good sound effect can turn a dull animation into a fun enhancement. However, sounds take up a significant amount of space in the movie. Afterburner for Director 5 will compress the audio, but don't expect miracles. For lengthy audio, you may decide to stream the audio file separately. See chapter 18, "Shockwave for Audio," to learn how to do this.

Keep the length short. Every second of audio can rack up the Kilobytes of the final movie. If possible, use sounds that can be looped. Four beats of music can sound like a whole soundtrack if looped well. You may wish to choose sounds that are useful in more than one situation in the movie.

High sampling rates mean big file size. You may have a fantastic sound clip that is stereo, 16 bits, and 44.100 KHz; but a three-second sound at that rate would be 516K! Reducing to mono, 8- bit, 11.025 kHz is most space-conscious. If the audio sounds too awful at that rate, use 22.050 kHz. Though you may be able to reduce a sound to lower than 11.025 kHz, certain sound cards may have difficulty with this.

> **Note**
>
> Again, remember your viewers. I once worked with a guy who had a little "blip" sound every time he pressed a key on his keyboard. It was fine for him, but it would drive me crazy after ten minutes. If you loop a sound, give an option to turn it off or fade it out after a while. Just about every sound effect collection has the ever-popular vomiting, toilet-flushing, and slip-on-a-banana-peel slide whistle. But not everyone will love those sounds as much as you do.

Currently, Shockwave offers no support for MIDI. It could be very efficient in terms of file size, but may not be practical since there are so many different sound cards with different MIDI instruments either built in or connected. Unless a standard map were used, you could never be really sure if your piano sound ended up as a piano or a clarinet. But I've been surprised enough to know that I shouldn't say something is impossible. It could be that MIDI will soon join the Internet multimedia gang.

Testing Your Movies

Be sure to test your Shockwave creations at the lowest common denominator. You may have a 166 MHz Pentium with 64M of RAM and a 28.8 Kbps modem. However, your grandmother—old-fashioned as she may be—still has a 486 66 MHz computer with 8M of RAM and a 14.4 Kbps modem. To evaluate your movie, be sure to test it on the slowest system you think viewers may have. Testing on both Windows and Macintosh platforms is important, too, to be sure everything works for all viewers. You may decide to leave Grandma in the dust and make a 500K Shockwave file that runs only on high-performance machines, but the size of your audience will be limited.

From Here...

You're learning that there are a lot of things to keep in mind when creating Shockwave files for the Internet. The reward of the Internet is that so many people can all view the same information, but the limitation is that you have a large audience to consider.

- Chapter 5, "Limitations of Shockwave and the Web": Further limitations of Shockwave on the Web and ways of dealing with them.

- Part II, "Creating Basic Animations": Beginning with Shockwave, we'll start with a few basic animations to enhance your site.

- Chapter 6, "Liven Up a Page: Animations for Fun": From start to finish, you'll step through the process of creating and putting a Shockwave file on your Web page.

CHAPTER 5

Limitations of Shockwave and the Web

We've already talked about limitations due to size and download time, so let's talk about other types of limitations you will need to consider as you create your Shockwave movies. Actually, most things you can do in Director carry over to Shockwave, but there are a few things to keep in mind. This chapter covers the following:

- Linked media
- Xobjects and Xtras
- The tempo channel: a few workarounds using Lingo
- Director commands disabled for the Internet

External Files

The simplest form of a Director (or Shockwave) movie uses only one file. Everything needed is included in that one movie file. However, more complex movies may use external files in addition to the .DIR or .DCR file. Special consideration must be made for external files used by the movie or used by the Shockwave driver.

Linked Media

Linked media is like a cast member that is stored externally instead of within the movie. It can be a sound, video clip, or just about anything that you don't want stored within the Director movie. Director 5 even allows entire casts to be loaded as an external file. The movie would simply contain a reference to the name of the file, which would be retrieved and used as needed.

To use linked media, it needs to be downloaded ahead of time and stored on the end user's computer. The reason for this is the unreliability of transfer time on the Internet. If you have a sound or video file that you call from your Director movie, the user might end up waiting for an indeterminable period of time before it is ready. Any linked media files need to be already available in the same directory as the Shockwave plug-in.

Xobjects and Xtras

Xobjects are additions that Director users may use (or create) that allow Director to interact with external devices such as a CD-ROM or video card. They are separate files that the movie loads when it is played.

Xtras are new to Director 5. They are similar to Xobjects in that they may be developed by third parties to enhance the movie. Transition Xtras, Cast Member Xtras, and Lingo Xtras are three types of Xtras that may be used by the movie when it is played. See the Director manuals for more on using these.

Just like linked media, Xobjects and Xtras need to be on the viewer's computer in the plug-ins directory. Shockwave automatically looks in this directory, no matter what path is specified in your movie. For Xobjects, this ensures that the user intended it to be used, which prevents the risk of viewing a Shockwave file that might call hardware the user does not want it to call. Without this protection, a Shockwave movie could affect the user's hard disk or other devices without alerting the user.

Where to Put External Files

The directory for Xobjects and linked media is within the plug-ins directory of your browser. Shockwave will not look anywhere else for these files. Netscape Navigator's directory structure is used here as an example.

- Windows 95—the directory named NP32DSW. A default location example would be:

  C:\Program Files\Netscape\Navigator\Program\Plugins\NP32DSW

- Windows 3.1—the directory named NP16DSW. A default location example would be:

  C:\NETSCAPE\PLUGINS\NP16DSW

- Macintosh—the plug-ins folder. Default location is in the Netscape Navigator folder.

Tempo Controls

Another limitation is using the options in the tempo channel of the score in Director. Shockwave doesn't recognize commands from the tempo channel. A few simple Lingo scripts can accomplish the same tasks that may have been accomplished in the tempo channel.

Playback Rate

You can easily control the tempo using Lingo. To set the tempo to 30 frames per second, for example, use the following Lingo:

```
on startmovie
    puppetTempo 30
end
```

This could also be accomplished in a frame script, sprite script, or cast member script at any place throughout the movie.

Delays

To simulate a delay, you may use a loop. Note, however, that only one handler may execute at a time, so other activities may not occur concurrently. The following example delays for three seconds:

```
on enterframe
    startTimer
    repeat while the timer < 3 * 60
        nothing
    end repeat
end
```

The "startTimer" command resets Director's timer to 0. The timer counts in clock ticks, which are 1/60 of a second. The "repeat while…" loop continues until the timer reaches 180 clock ticks (three seconds times 60 ticks per second). "nothing" is not a call to another handler; it's a Lingo term to do simply what it says.

If you want to delay for a few seconds, but maintain user interaction, set up two frame scripts. In the first frame, use the following script:

```
on exitframe
        startTimer
    end
```

Then in the second frame, use:

```
on exitframe
        if the timer <3*60 then go to the frame
    end
```

The above method will loop in the second frame for three seconds, but will allow user interaction if you have buttons on the stage.

Wait for a Mouse Click or Key Press

To wait for a mouse click or key press, put a few simple handlers in the script channel of the frame you want to pause in. The first of these three handlers loops the playback head in the frame. The second two handlers respond to either a mouse click or key press to move into the next frame. Note that all three handlers are placed within the one frame script.

```
on exitframe
    go to the frame
end

on mousedown
    go to the frame + 1
end

on keydown
    go to the frame + 1
end
```

Director Features that Have Been Disabled

To protect the end user, Macromedia has disabled certain features of Director that could potentially be damaging or at least annoying to the viewer. Basically, anything that modifies or calls any of the hardware in the user's computer (hard disk, printer, and so on) has been disabled. This is different from Xobjects in that the commands are built into Director, not called from an external module.

You might think this is limiting your power as the movie creator, but the functions have been disabled for security purposes. You might be an honest Shockwave developer who uses the commands for good purposes, but there could be people who try to write or erase files, turn off the computer, print something, or perform other actions that the user did not agree to.

The following list (see table 5.1) was taken directly from Macromedia's Shockwave developer's information on their Web site. Most of these commands deal with reading and writing external files, running a movie in-a-window, or controlling the system resources. Limited file reading and writing can be done, though only within the Shockwave plug-in directory. See chapter 14, "Further Use of Internet Lingo," for more on how to do this.

Table 5.1   Director Features Disabled for Shockwave

Feature Disabled	Description
openResFile, closeResFile	Controls resource files located outside of the movie
open window, close window	Director movie in a window feature
importFileInto	Replaces file member with an external file
saveMovie	Saves the movie to a file
printFrom	Prints whatever is displayed on the stage
open, openDA, closeDA	Launches and closes specified applications
quit, restart, shutdown	Exits the movie, restarts or shuts down the computer
fileName of cast	Link to external files, paths, and so on
fileName of window	Link to external files, paths, and so on
getNthFileNameInFolder	Link to external files, paths, and so on
moviePath	Link to external files, paths, and so on
pathName	Link to external files, paths, and so on
searchCurrentFolder	Link to external files, paths, and so on
searchPaths	Link to external files, paths, and so on
mci	Passes strings to Windows media controller

From Here...

Well, the limitations are out of the way. You now know what you can and can't do. It's time to start creating! The next three sections take you through the process:

- Part II: Learn to create simple animations and embed them in your Web page.
- Part III: Add interactivity to the movies so the user does more than just watch something happen.
- Part IV: Learn more advanced Lingo to perform complex tasks and use Internet-specific commands.

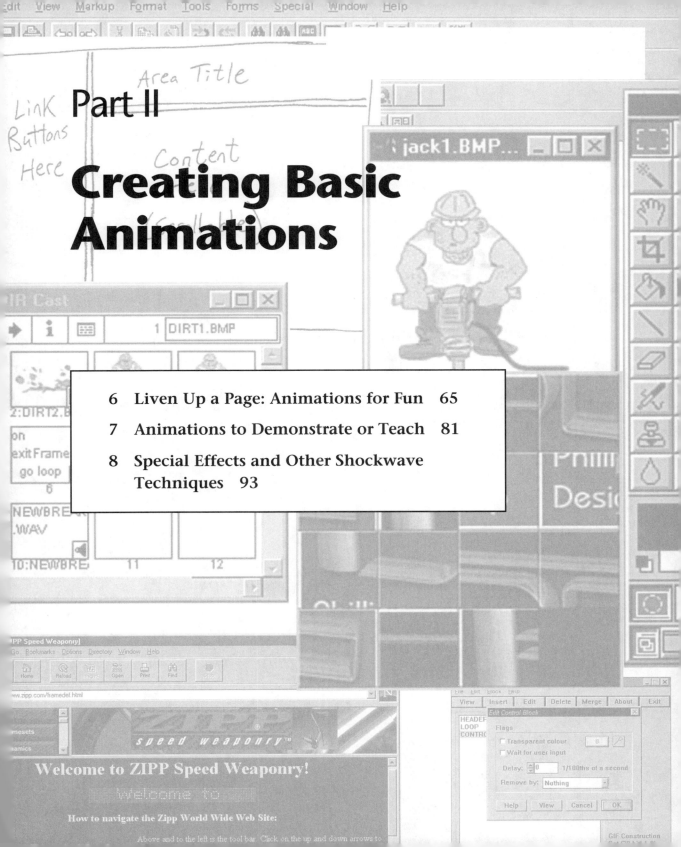

Part II

Creating Basic Animations

CHAPTER 6

Liven Up a Page: Animations for Fun

The easiest applications of Shockwave to a Web site are immediately apparent for the common Internet surfer who visits your page: motion and sound. Whereas previously multimedia such as this needed to be downloaded and viewed through other programs, movement and audio can now be presented immediately to the user.

This chapter begins with a few simple examples of Shocking your Web site. Interactivity and other more advanced features will be discussed in Parts III and IV. For now, we'll just focus on putting basic motion and sound on your page by doing three examples:

■ Make the word "NEW" flash repeatedly to draw attention to something on your Web page.

■ Create a "Home Page" title that zooms onto the screen.

■ Make an "Under Construction" animation for a page that isn't completed yet.

The Shockwave Process

The following are the four steps of the Shockwave creation process:

1. Creating or acquiring the graphics and sound.

2. Animating the graphics and sound in Director.

3. Compressing the file with Afterburner.

4. Uploading the file to the Web server and incorporating it into the HTML document.

This book focuses less on the actual graphics and animation processes and more on covering the concepts behind each example. This way, you can see more applications of Shockwave in a variety of circumstances. You'll soon see that the possibilities are endless!

Note

Many of the examples in this book are provided not only as learning tools, but are also useful clips for your Web site. They may be seen as templates to modify for your own purpose or to use as they are if you don't have access to Director or other software necessary in creating original movies for a Shocked Web page.

Example One: Flashing "New"

The word "New" is often seen on Web pages that are continually being changed and updated. To draw attention to a new link or new information, this example will cause the word "New" to flash repeatedly. With a final compressed file of only 5K, it is very efficient. With a 28.8 Kbps modem, it would take only a few seconds. This example is the most elementary of all Director movies. It involves alternating two images to achieve the flickering effect.

On the CD

The file new.dir in the chapter six folder of the CD-ROM contains the finished product. Here's how it was done.

Step One: Create the Graphics

Begin by creating a graphic of the word "New." I used Photoshop, though any bit-map graphics program may be used. To be versatile on any color background, be sure that what you create has an aliased edge with a white background. This way, you can later change the background color of the Director movie without seeing a rectangle around the "New" image.

Aliased versus Anti-Aliased Edges

Ever noticed a tiny white rim around the edge of an irregularly shaped image that was placed on a dark background? Chances are the designer had anti-aliased edges on the image, then tried to use a transparency feature (such as transparent GIFs or transparency in Director) to show the image on a different color background. *Anti-aliasing* is a way that the computer smooths rounded edges to make them appear less choppy from the low resolution of a computer screen. When the image is made

---

transparent, you are allowed to choose only one specific color to be removed. To eliminate a white background and see another color beneath it, a transparency feature may remove all white pixels. But it will hide only pixels that are *exactly* white. Anti-aliasing blurs edges to smooth them out, which means there are pixels that are nearly white but are shades of the edge of your image. These light pixels will not be made transparent, so they show up harshly on a dark background. To have a clean transparency, disable any features that will anti-alias the edges of your image. Note that this affects only images that are irregular in shape because the computer displays images in a rectangle. Graphics that are already rectangular have no need for transparency (unless you want an area within the borders to be made transparent).

Director 5 supports certain extra modules developed by third parties that support multiple levels of transparency, which will allow soft, feathered edges and transparent effects. The process of using these may vary and will not be covered in this book.

If the image was created in RGB color (24-bit), it needs to be converted to indexed color (8-bit) before being imported into Director. Wipe those tears away, all you who are spoiled by JPEG and other high-color formats! The average viewer will probably not even notice. For now, use a Windows system palette because most viewers will be capable of this. Director has the option of converting an image's color depth and palette, though I prefer to do this in Photoshop so that I can see the results and make changes if necessary.

You'll need two images to alternate for the flickering effect, so create a second image of the word "New" that is the same, exact size as the first one. To keep this example simple and compact, make this a 1-bit image (black-and-white). With the two graphic images created, you can now animate them. Figure 6.1 shows the two images.

Step Two: Animating in Director

The stage can be very small for this movie. Under Preferences, choose 48 pixels high by 48 pixels wide. Import the two graphics into Director as cast members one and two. Place the 8-bit image in channel one of the score and copy it from frame 1 to frame 2. Under the Ink menu, choose matte. This will make the white area around the edges disappear. In channel two, frame 2, place the 1-bit image so that the word "New" lines up with the word beneath it. Set this to be matte ink, also. The color chip on the control panel lets you choose a background color for the stage that will match your Web page.

Figure 6.1
The two "NEW"
graphic images.

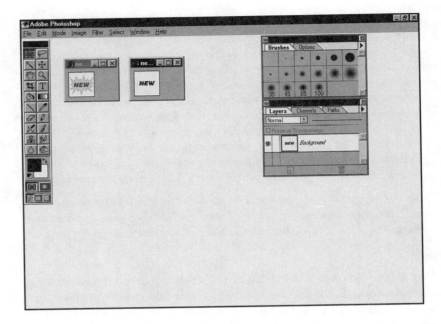

In the script channel of frame 2, set the playback head to loop to the previous frame:

```
On exitframe
      go to the frame - 1
end
```

Run the movie and see the word "New" flash. Choose Save and Compact from the File menu. Figure 6.2 shows the movie as seen in Director.

Step Three: Compressing the Director Movie

Compressing the movie is the easiest step because there's really nothing to think about. On the Macintosh, just drag the Director file onto the Afterburner icon. In Windows, run Afterburner and choose your .DIR file to be compressed. In Director 5, Afterburner is available as an Xtra. Figure 6.3 shows the Afterburner menu. The result: a compact .DCR file ready to be uploaded to your Web server—in this example, a slim 5K Shockbite.

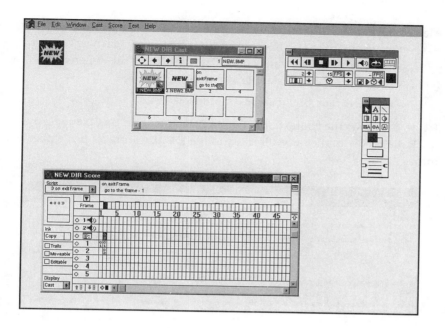

Figure 6.2
The finished "NEW" Director movie.

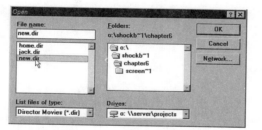

Figure 6.3
Using Afterburner to compress your Movie.

Step Four: Upload and Embed the File

If you already have an existing Web page, you probably know the procedure for uploading the file to your server using FTP or another method. The .DCR file can be treated just like any other .GIF or .JPEG image. As long as the browser can find the file, it will work. Remember that HTML documents are uploaded as text, but .DCR files need to be uploaded as binary.

Many Web page HTML editors do not support Shockwave, so you will most likely have to enter the HTML command in a text editor (such as Windows Notepad). Besides the file name, you will need to know the dimensions of the Shockwave movie. For our example, the HTML syntax is:

```
<embed src="new.dcr" height=48 width=48>
```

Figure 6.4 shows the context of our embed statement. In this example, the .DCR file resides in the same directory as the HTML document it is embedded into.

Figure 6.4

Put the embed statement in your HTML document.

To place the image exactly where you want it on the page may be tricky, but it's just like any other Web image. If you're using a WYSIWYG HTML editor that supports Shockwave, this may be easy. If it does not support Shockwave, you may wish to create a temporary .GIF image to use in the editor. Make it the same dimensions as the Shockwave movie. Then when it is in the position you want, edit the HTML code and replace the `<img src="temp.gif">` with the `<embed src="filename.dcr" height=n width=n>`.

Run your browser and test out your first Shockwave movie! (see figure 6.5.)

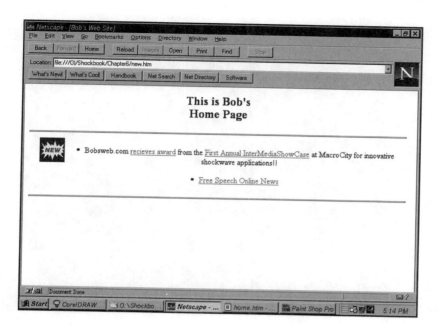

Figure 6.5
The finished
movie viewed
in Netscape
Navigator.

II

Creating Basic Animations

Example Two: Home Page Title

Because the title of a Web page is a focal point, you can distinguish it from
the rest of the page by adding a little motion. The following is an example of
a simple animation that moves the letters of the words "Home Page" onto
the screen and leaves them jiggling in place.

Step One: Create the Graphics

The first step is to create a graphic image of the words "Home Page." In this
case, I chose to have anti-aliased edges on my graphic because they look better. Because I won't be able to change my background color later with transparency, I created this image on black, the same color as the background of
the final Web page. This way, the Shockwave movie blends in with the rest of
the Web page. Remember to convert to 8-bit. Again, let's use a Windows system palette. The created graphic is seen in figure 6.6.

Step Two: Animating in Director

Set up the stage to be fairly small, but large enough to allow for some movement. Under Preferences, choose 400 pixels wide by 80 pixels high. Using the
color chip on the control panel, set the stage background to be black.

Figure 6.6
The Home Page
graphic.

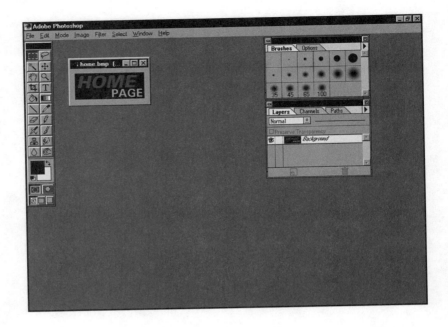

To animate each letter individually, they need to be broken apart. You may
have cropped each letter and saved each one as an individual file, but this is
unnecessary. After importing the image into Director, use the Duplicate Cast
Member command under the Cast menu to make four copies of the graphic
(I broke apart only the word "Home" and left "Page" as one graphic). Then,
using the paint window, erase part of each of the cast members until you are
left with "H" as cast member one, "O" as cast member two, and so on (see figure 6.7). If the part you leave unerased is a rectangle, it can be animated with
the copy ink, which is the fastest. If it is an irregular shape, you'll have to use
matte ink or background transparent ink; both animate more slowly to eliminate white areas.

Figure 6.7
The words
broken into five
cast members.

In the first five channels of frame 2, place each cast member in various positions around the edge of the stage (see figure 6.8). Frame 1 is blank, so they appear to come from off the stage. Then in frame 10, place the images in the center, as they would appear in their proper location for the title. Select all five sprites from frame 2 to frame 10 and use the in-between linear command (Control-B) to animate them across the eight frames. This gives the movement from off the screen to the final position.

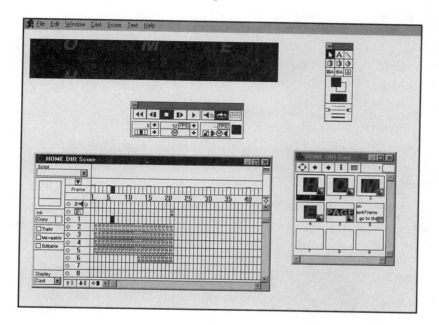

Figure 6.8
The images are placed around the edge of the stage.

II

Creating Basic Animations

To cause the letters to jiggle repeatedly, copy all five sprites from frame 10 to frame 11. Then adjust the position of each one slightly: one to the left a bit, one to the right, one up and to the right, and so on. In the script channel of frame 11, set the playback head to loop to the previous frame:

```
On exitframe
     go to the frame - 1
end
```

Play the movie, and you'll see the letters zoom in from off the stage, then shake in place.

Step Three: Afterburner

After saving the movie as a .DIR file, run Afterburner to compress it to a .DCR file. This one is still very small: only 6K. Remember, though, that as the browser loads the .DCR file on the Web page, it also needs to run the Shockwave plug-in to view the file. This may take a few seconds for each Shocked movie.

Step Four: Uploading and Embedding

In this example, you may want to center the Shockwave movie at the top of the page. Just like any other image on a Web page, you can use the alignment commands. In your HTML code, add the following lines at the beginning of the <body> section:

```
<center>
<embed src="home.dcr" height=80 width=400>
</center>
```

This will center your Shockwave movie on the Web page. To align it to the left or right, you can leave out the <center> codes and put a statement directly in the embed line:

```
<embed src="home.dcr" align=left height=80 width=400>
```

Test this using align=right to see how it works. Figure 6.9 shows the movie in a Web page.

Figure 6.9

The Home Page title as it appears on the Web page.

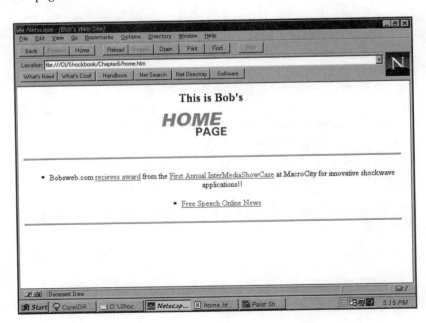

Example Three: Under Construction Animation

There may be times when you want people to know that a page exists, though you haven't completed it yet. Such pages usually say something like, "Page is under construction." This can be discouraging to visitors who think they have found what they are looking for, only to realize that the page isn't ready yet. To ease the pain, and to provide a taste of what may be to come, this example is an animated "Under Construction" scene. A cartoon man is shown with a jackhammer as a sign drops down from above. Sound effects help add to the fun of this Shockwave movie.

Step One: Collecting the Pieces

Five graphics are used in this example. You may re-create your own or examine the movie *jack.dir* in the chapter 6 folder on the CD-ROM. In figure 6.10, you see the following five graphics:

The man standing still

The man while he is jackhammering

Two images of dirt flying away from the jackhammer

The "Under Construction" sign

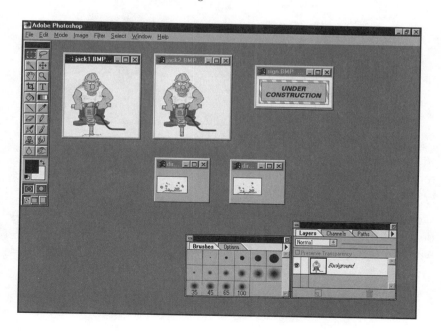

Figure 6.10
The five graphics that were created.

Two other elements must be gathered for this movie: a sound effect for the jackhammer and a sound for the sign dropping, both .WAV files in my example.

Step Two: Animating in Director

You can probably guess how to piece this one together. Import the five graphics and two sounds. The calm-looking man can be put into the first range of about 15 frames. Then put the wide-eyed man in frames 16 to 25. One by one, select every other frame (17, 19, 21, and so on) and move the man's position a few pixels in various directions. This gives the vibrating effect of the jackhammer. Also, in every other frame, alternate the two images of the dirt and gravel flying away from the hammer. Put the man in channel three and the dirt in channels one and two, then set the man's ink to matte. This way, the hammer is in a layer that overlaps the dirt, rather than the dirt overlapping the hammer.

In the sound channel, put the jackhamm.wav sound across the frames where the man is hammering. Figure 6.11 shows how the sound channel corresponds to the hammering sprites.

Figure 6.11
Aligning the jackhammer sound with the motion of the animation.

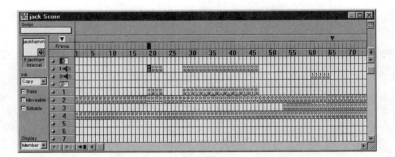

Next, animate the sign dropping from the top of the stage. As it lands, put the newbreak.wav sound in one of the sound channels. Notice how it appears to bounce a bit to give it some realism.

We could loop the entire movie; however, I thought the viewer might be annoyed with constant noises of jackhammering, so I set the man to continue hammering without the sound effects. Notice how I placed a marker (the triangle in the top row of the score window) in the frame I wanted to jump back to. Then in the last frame, I used the lingo "go loop" to move back to the last marker it encountered:

```
On exitframe
     go loop
end
```

Figure 6.12 shows the "Under Construction" movie as seen in Director.

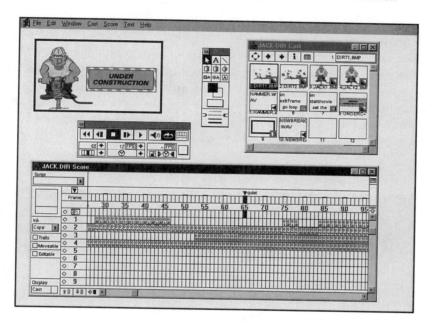

Figure 6.12
The Under Construction movie in Director.

II

Creating Basic Animations

Step Three: Afterburner

Compressing this file in the same way as the last two yields a DCR file of 39K—larger than the previous examples, but still quite manageable. With a 28.8 Kbps modem, it might take about 20 seconds; a 14.4 modem would take twice as long.

Step Four: Upload and Embed

You're probably getting the hang of this pretty well.

```
<embed src="jack.dcr" align=right height=150 width=256>
```

Perhaps you want to include an alternative image that will appear in case the viewer does not have a browser that supports Shockwave. It could be just a static image of the "Under Construction" sign. By adding a few additional lines to the HTML document, you can substitute a GIF or JPEG image for non-Shockwave browsers.

```
<embed src="jack.dcr" align=right height=150 width=256>
<noembed>
<img src="subst.gif">
</noembed>
```

The above additions to our embed statement allow a substitute image. How does it work? Netscape or a compatible browser understands all of the commands above. So it will embed the Director movie in the Web page, then will *not* embed the graphic substitute (it ignores anything within the <noembed> tags). Other browsers that do not recognize the <embed> or <noembed> tags will ignore them, but they *will* recognize the <img src="subst.gif"> statement and will then display the alternate image.

Figure 6.13 shows the movie in a Web page.

Figure 6.13
A Web page using the Under Construction movie.

From Here...

You have now been through the entire process of Shocking a Web site. From here onward, it is just a matter of learning to work with Director to create good movies for the Internet. Here's what you can look forward to next:

- Chapter 7, "Animations to Demonstrate or Teach": Using Shockwave animations to demonstrate or teach something that previously had to be a static image.
- Chapter 8, "Special Effects and Other Shockwave Techniques": Using special effects for your movies.
- Part III, "Adding Interactivity": Adding Interactivity to Shockwave.

II

Creating Basic Animations

CHAPTER 7

Animations to Demonstrate or Teach

Putting motion and sound on your Web page doesn't have to be for entertainment or for "energy" as many people see it. It may have a functional purpose. Imagine any situation where motion and sound can be used to demonstrate a concept that otherwise might be difficult to convey. This chapter gives you a few ideas and examples of Shockwave for useful purposes.

In any functional situation, you will need to consider whether or not the Shockwave addition is practical. If the purpose can be achieved through a static image, you might decide not to use an animation. Download time should be the main factor in your decision. If your viewers are willing to wait, Shockwave could be a valuable enhancement to your functional Web site. What you'll do in this chapter:

- Shows simple street maps with animated directions.
- Demonstrates a three-dimensional animation of the pieces of a bicycle tire with the material layers labeled.
- Demonstrates an advertising banner that could be placed on any Web page.
- Covers other possibilities for functional animations.

Form versus Function

As an art major in college, "form versus function" was a common topic in a ceramics course I took. The idea was to be aware of the balance between the usefulness of an object and its aesthetic appearance. Using the ceramics example, I could create a vase that looks beautiful: graceful shape, flawless construction, creative surface glaze. But perhaps my design incorporated a series of shapes cut from the side of the vase. The vase would lose quite a bit of functionality because it couldn't hold water. Depending on my intentions, this may work or this may be a problem.

Certain objects are best left on the functional side, while other objects have much more freedom to be artistic. For example, a fire extinguisher should remain functional. If it's not recognizable as a fire extinguisher and doesn't work exactly as a fire extinguisher should, it won't render its safety purpose in a dangerous situation. On the other hand, if a bowl were left purely functional, it would be fairly boring. There is much more freedom to be creative because the bowl can be various shapes, sizes, or colors.

How does this relate to Shockwave? Perhaps more generally, it has to do with your Web page design. The challenge is to create an Internet site that is both functional and visually pleasing. Shockwave applications can fit into both situations. Chapter 6, "Liven Up a Page: Animations for Fun," begins with a few simple animations with relatively limited functional purposes. The next two examples lean more heavily on the functional side.

Animated Street Map

Any school teacher will tell you that different people learn in different ways. Some learn best by reading directions, some learn by watching or listening, and some learn best by doing something. Through multimedia, Shockwave provides more opportunities for different learning methods.

This example is a street map with an animated dot that traces the path to our company. Words describe the steps while the dot moves. People who have difficulty with maps may find this to be valuable because it shows exactly how to get to the destination. The steps of this movie are fairly simple, and no fancy tricks are added because it's meant to be functional. In Internet terms, functional usually means easy to understand quickly and compact for fast downloading time.

The Map

Scanning an actual street map and using it for the Shocked map here is a possibility, but this isn't done for a couple of reasons. First, it includes a lot of unnecessary information (side streets and so on) that may cloud the simplicity necessary for this example. Second, the map here uses a plain, solid color background, which compresses very well. For more details about compression, see the following note entitled "Compression." Figure 7.1 shows the map in Photoshop.

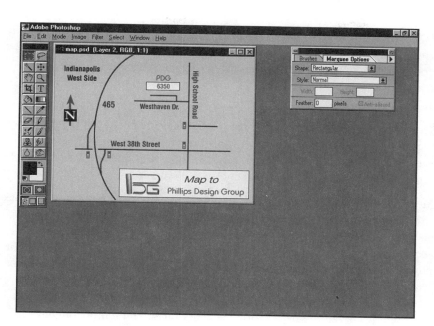

Figure 7.1
The map created
in Photoshop.

Compression

This chapter doesn't describe the exact process of *compression*, but here's the concept behind it. There is a lot of repetitive information stored in a normal uncompressed file. The compression process takes that repetitive information and simplifies it. For example, a list of pixels might contain information that defines the first five pixels to be blue. Uncompressed, this would be: pixel one blue, pixel two blue, pixel three blue, pixel four blue, pixel five blue. Compression might reduce this to: pixels one through five blue. You can see, then, why areas of flat color compress much better than dithered areas with various pixel colors—because there is much more repetitive information that can be compressed.

So, when working in RGB (Red, Green, Blue), how do you select a color that will become a flat, undithered color when converted to 8-bit? My method is to open an 8-bit file in Photoshop, and then choose Color Table from the Mode menu. Pick a color from the palette that you would like to use and write down the RGB color information for it. The tan color I used in the map was Red-204, Green-204, Blue-153. Then, as you work in RGB mode, you can create a custom color swatch or just type in those numbers from the color picker any time you need the color.

Animating the Directions

The animation moves a small red dot along the streets while a short descrip-tion describes where to turn left and so on. To keep the file size small, use Director's vector tool and text tools so you won't need to create more bit maps.

The red dot is easy to create as a vector graphic using Director's filled circle tool. To animate it along the street was a bit tedious. Straight streets are simple. Put one dot at the beginning of the street and one at the end several frames later, then use the In-Between linear command.

But what about curved streets? Route 465 on this map curves around and has a little exit ramp that the red dot follows. Director offers an In-Between spe-cial command that can create curved paths, but it's difficult to be completely accurate with it. The procedure is to put red dots at key locations. You might put a dot every ten frames at a position on the street. Then, select all of the frames with the key positions and choose In-Between Special from the Score menu and select Location. By adjusting the slider in the path box, you can specify how curved the path should be. Good luck. You'll probably have to settle for a path that's close but not exact. Then go frame by frame and adjust the dot's position exactly on the path you want.

As the dot reaches different steps in the directions, I had text appear to de-scribe the event. You just use Director's text tool to create this text so there's no need for bit maps of the text (which would add file size).

The text tool in Director 4 creates aliased-edge text, which is not always pleasant to look at. However, Director 5 has solved this by offering anti-aliased text with its text tool. You should also be aware that Director 4's text tool must use a particular font installed on the system, so you will need to be careful in selecting which font you use. If the viewer's system does not have the same font installed, a different one will be substituted. Director 5's field tool works the same way, but the version 5 text tool does not require font in-formation from the end users system.

Compressing and Uploading

This is a relatively large image, but because the background color is flat, it gets crunched to a final size of 13K. Not too bad. One line to your HTML document, and it's ready to go.

```
<embed src="/shock/map.dcr" height=300 width=400>
```

Figure 7.2 shows the movie in a Web page. In the preceding example, the map.dcr file was put in a different directory than the HTML file. I could have put in the entire HTTP address if I wanted to, but because it was one directory below my HTML file, I didn't need the whole location. So my two file locations might look like this:

```
HTML file:  http://www.pdgroup.com/roadmap.html
.DCR file:  http://www.pdgroup.com/shock/map.dcr
```

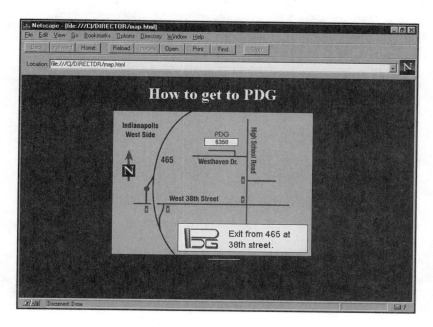

Figure 7.2
The finished map as seen by the browser.

Tire Peel-Away Diagram

This example shows the layers of a bicycle tire being peeled away with labels for the different materials. For now, the animation just waits for five seconds, then repeats. Chapter 9, "Rollovers and Button Clicks" talks more about using other methods for repeating using interaction.

The Tire Graphics

The tire animation is created in Autodesk 3D Studio. The tire is modeled three-dimensionally, and the layers are animated to peel away. Then 12 frames are exported. Due to the physical size of this particular image, any more than 10 or 12 frames would become too big for a Shockwave movie. Of course, "too big" is relative to each person. You might be willing to download a 500K file, while someone else might be willing to wait for only a 100K file. We could have used a smaller image and rendered more frames, but 12 is enough to show the animation (figure 7.3).

Figure 7.3
The individual
frames exported
from 3D Studio.

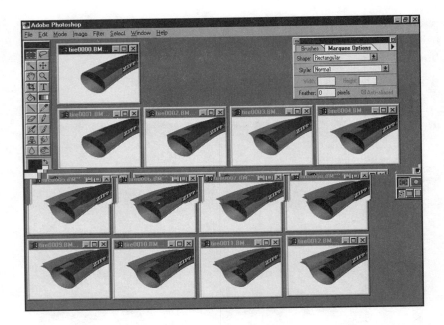

This example uses a custom palette. An adaptive palette is created in
Photoshop, and each frame uses the same palette. It's important that each
image uses the exact same palette. If each image had its own unique palette,
Director would need to load all 12 palettes and switch between them (which
would look awful as an animation, because palette changes usually cause a
screen flash). You'll get to see options in the HTML syntax to specify how the
browser should handle the custom palette if the user is in 256-color mode.

Animating the Peel-Away

The techniques of animating in 3D Studio won't be discussed here. Each
frame of the animation is exported from 3D Studio as bit-mapped images.
The actual process in Director is very simple, then, because each frame was
already created.

As you import the 12 images, Director asks if you also would like to import
the custom palette. In Director 4, this will happen only if you run Director
with your system set in 256 color mode. Director 5 will import the palette
while running in any color depth, though the cast members will be 16-bit if
you are running in high color and will need to be converted using the "transform bit map" command.

Text labels for the diagram were created and imported as bit-map cast members. The text could have also been created using Director's text tool.

If you align the 12 images in order in the cast window, you can easily move them to the score by selecting all 12 and holding the Alt key down while you drag them to the score window. This will place them in the first 12 frames in identical positions so you won't need to adjust each one to get them lined up exactly.

With only 12 frames in the animation, the tempo is set to 10 frames per second. A simple transition dissolves each of the text images onto the screen. Figure 7.4 shows the various parts in Director.

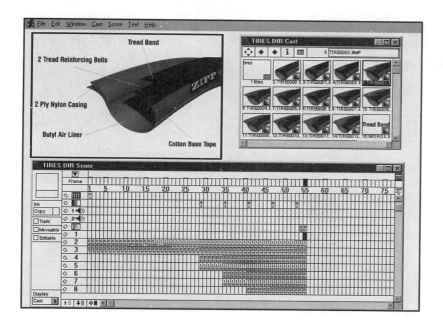

Figure 7.4
The tire movie in Director.

Posting the Tire Animation to the Web

After compressing the movie with Afterburner, enter the embed statement with the rest of your HTML document.

```
<embed src="tires.dcr" height=260 width=384>
```

Figure 7.5 shows the Shocked Web page with the tire animation.

You can also use the palette command in the embed statement to control how the browser handles the custom palette for a system running in 256 color mode. To ignore the custom palette and use the browser's system palette, set the movie palette to "background" as follows:

```
<embed src="tires.dcr" height=260 width=384 palette=background>
```

Figure 7.5
The Shocked tire
animation.

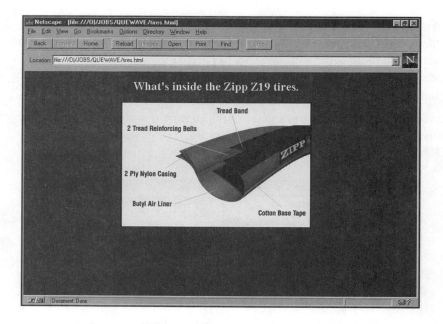

`Palette=background` is the default mode. If no palette statement is issued, the browser will use its palette to simulate the movie's colors. If you have specific colors that you absolutely want displayed with your own custom palette, you can specify the movie palette to be the active palette, as in the following example:

```
<embed src="tires.dcr" height=260 width=384 palette=foreground>
```

You should be aware that setting your custom palette to be the active palette will alter the rest of the screen for someone running in 256-color mode.

Advertising Banner

A current debate is trying to predict whether Web visitors will soon have to pay for access to certain Web sites, or if advertisers will cover costs for the developer by renting space on the Web page. If advertisement is the answer, this example could be quite common.

Many sites contain banners with advertisements for other Web sites, products, or services. Shockwave could easily be used for this functional purpose. Our example is a simple demonstration of how you could advertise your company or provide a place for other companies to advertise on your Web site.

Graphic Images

Our example has only two different "scenes" in the advertisement. One is an advertisement for the company PDG, and the other is a blank advertisement to show viewers that they may advertise their company in this space.

The PDG scene displays the logo and some text that was done in two steps that may be animated to draw attention to the banner. The second scene was also done in two parts to animate the advertisement. Figure 7.6 shows the graphics that were created. If you offered this space for other companies to advertise, they would probably supply you with graphics that they would like displayed.

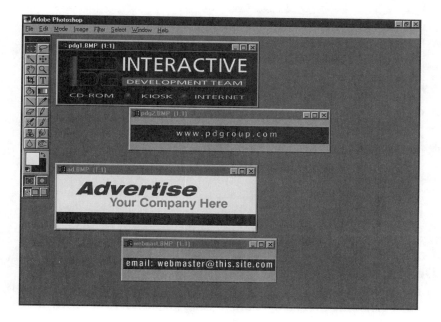

Figure 7.6

Graphics used in the advertisement banner.

Animating the Banner

You can be creative in how you animate the banner. In my example, I used a simple transition within the PDG scene to alternate between the Web address and the other text. You can see in the score how I put the Web address graphic on top of the PDG image and alternated on and off every ten frames. I used a horizontal transition at each changing point (see figure 7.7).

The second scene displays the graphic that says, "Advertise your company here." Over that, I animated the email address of the Web master so that it moves in from off the screen using an in-between linear process. These animations are not essential to the banner, but they add almost no file size and are worth using to draw attention to the advertisement.

Figure 7.7
Animating the graphics in Director.

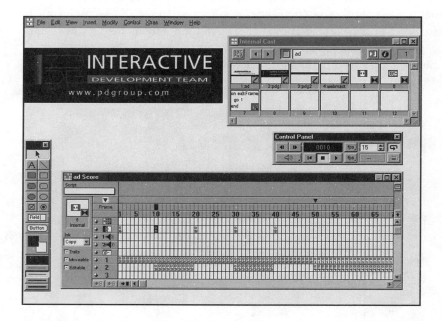

Compress, Upload, and Embed in the HTML Document

Figure 7.8 shows the banner as seen on a Web page. The DCR file size for this example is less than 15K, but it only contains graphics for two scenes. You might have ten companies wanting to advertise on your Web page, which could make the Shockwave movie too large. By reducing the physical size of the movie, you might solve this problem.

The HTML code is as follows:

```
<embed src="ad.dcr" height=112 width=400>
```

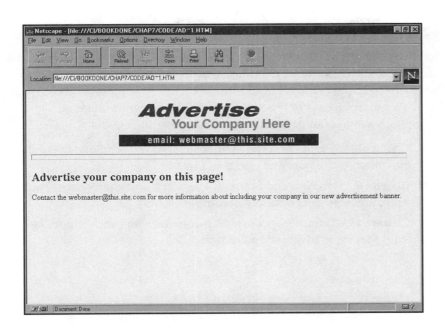

Figure 7.8
A Web page using
the advertising
banner.

II

Creating Basic Animations

Other Ideas

The compressed tire peel-away movie turned out to be 144K. Pretty big for something that doesn't do very much. The tire example can be understood almost as well by using a static image with the text labels. But you can see the potential for other, more complex diagrams—a technical drawing showing various pieces being put together or taken apart, an animation of an abstract process, and so on. Just about anything that's understood better using motion would be ideal for Shockwave.

These two examples don't use sound; however, you might find a way to use sound to help convey your ideas. A musical group would find sound very functional in demonstrating their songs over the Web. Or, audio may be just another enhancement that combines the educational movie with some fun elements.

So far, you've seen only noninteractive movies. In Part III, "Adding Interactivity" you learn the interactive aspects of Shockwave. The options for enhanced function then increase because the user can make decisions and see results. Chapter 11, "Using Shockwave for Data," takes functionality even further with Shockwave movies that perform advanced calculations and sort information.

From Here...

You may decide that your Web site should be entirely functional, or you may decide it should be solely for entertainment. Whatever your purpose is, you can adapt all of the examples from this book to meet your needs. What's next? One more chapter in this part will show a few more animation examples, then you can progress to more advanced topics, such as:

- Chapter 8, "Special Effects and Other Shockwave Techniques": More animation techniques and effects in Director.
- Chapter 9, "Rollovers and Button Clicks": Beginning interactivity and using rollovers and clicks to detect mouse action.
- Chapter 10, "Controlling Movie Elements with Puppets": Puppeting sprites for more advanced interaction.

Special Effects and Other Shockwave Techniques

Every computer graphics book has a chapter called "Special Effects" that usually leads readers to think they will soon know secrets that only Hollywood knows. Well, the best special effects are the ones you create yourself because no one else will be reading about them in a book somewhere. This chapter offers some Shockwave ideas that don't fall into any other categories. Some of the topics covered in this chapter are:

- Matching the background color of your Shockwave file to the Web page for irregularly shaped movies
- Using tiles to create a patterned background
- Using the BlendSprite command for smooth fades in Director
- Adding a music track to your Web page

No Rectangles, Please

Rectangular shapes have acquired the stereotype of being an unimpressive computer default. Graphic images are automatically set in a rectangle, so hard edges can be expected. Many designers have broken free of this restriction through various methods so that their work is not limited to boxy shapes. One method for the Internet is using transparent GIFs to drop out one color in the image so that the background can be seen. But Shockwave movies offer no way of leaving part of the stage transparent. Another method (and the solution for Shockwave) is to match the background of the image with the background of the Web page. In doing this, you no longer have to separate the Shockwave movie so distinctly from the rest of the page. It can be integrated seamlessly.

Matching the Background Color

Matching the background color of a Web page is fairly simple. All you need to do is make sure that the background color of your Director movie is exactly the same hue as the background color you specify in your HTML command. But first you need to know how color is specified.

HTML uses hexadecimal codes to identify colors. You learned earlier how Director uses a palette for its color identification. So how do you match them up? Easy.

First, decide what color you want the background to be. It doesn't matter if you use a standard system palette or a custom palette, but the background color must be in the palette for Director to use it as a background. The HTML can specify any color, but Director is limited to its own palette. When you have decided on a color, you need to convert the RGB information to hexadecimal to use in the HTML command.

For example, I have a custom palette loaded in Director, and the background color I want is a shade of green. In the palette window, I can double-click that color and see its RGB information. It turns out to be Red 102, Green 153, and Blue 102. Now I need a way to convert those decimal values to hexadecimal. Fortunately, Windows calculator has this feature built in, as would any good scientific calculator. Other utilities are available that will convert between hex and decimal. So the red value of 102 becomes 66 in hex, the green 153 becomes 99, and the blue 102 also becomes 66. The HTML command requires all three of these values stuck together as 669966. That is the hex value of my green color. So the HTML background command would look like this:

```
<body bgcolor=669966>
```

On the CD

Then I can choose the same color in Director to be the stage color, and the movie is no longer defined by a box shape. The examples *gallery.dir* and *gallery.html* on the CD-ROM both use this technique (figure 8.1).

Using a Patterned Background

The technique described in the preceding section is fine for solid color backgrounds, but what if you want to use a tiled background on your Web page? You can follow the same principle, but it may be trickier to line up the patterns properly.

There are two types of background tiles: with seams or seamless. Both are acceptable, depending on your intentions. A seamed tile is simply a rectangular shape repeated, while seamless tiles appear continuous so that the viewer can't tell where one seam begins and another ends.

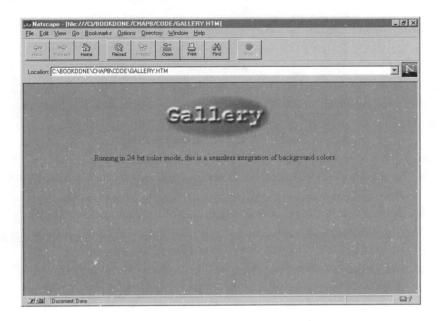

II

Creating Basic Animations

Figure 8.1
A seamless Shockwave movie that uses the same background color as the Web page.

> **Note**
>
> Achieving a seamless tile can be difficult and can look pretty lousy if not done properly. Lynda Weinman describes a good process for seamless tiles in her book, *Designing Web Graphics* (New Riders Publishing). To summarize the method, you use the offset filter in Photoshop to see your progress as you create a tile. The offset filter has the option of wrapping the pixel information. This allows you to see if your tile has spots that will show seams or empty areas that may need to be filled.

To use a tiled background, you'll need to use the same file for your tile in Director and for your tile in the HTML document. Follow these steps:

1. In Director, import the tile image as a cast member.
2. Then, from the Paint window, choose Tile Settings. Select the cast member you imported and adjust the size and position of the tile until it looks good in the preview window (figure 8.2).

Figure 8.2
Creating a custom
tile in Director.

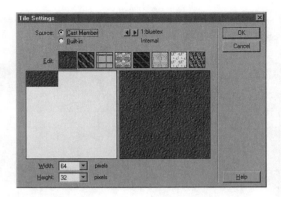

3. To use the tile for a background, you will need to create a filled box that covers the stage.

4. Then choose your custom tile from the pattern chip on the tool box.

5. Now, keep that filled box as the bottom layer of your whole animation (in Sprite 1).

6. Next, in your HTML document, you can issue a command to use your image as a tiled background. The following statement uses the "bluetex.gif" image and repeats it as a background pattern:

```
<body background="bluetex.gif">
```

Aligning your tiled Shockwave movie above a tiled HTML page can be tricky. A simple textured tile offers more freedom for misalignment than recognizable images on a tile. Often a texture can be placed anywhere, and it will appear to blend in. If your tile has images that need to be lined up, you need to use other techniques for lining up the movie. The methods would be the same as if you were going to position any image in a specific spot on a Web page—using spacer images, hspace and vspace tags, and so on. A book describing Web page design would cover this process better.

On the CD-ROM, the movie *shlogo.dir* and the HTML page *shockex.html* use the same textured background to appear seamless. A JPEG image (*example.jpg*) also uses the same background so all three blend together. Figure 8.3 shows the patterned Web page in Netscape Navigator.

The tile feature in Director is a great way of enhancing a boring background without using up a lot of space with a big cast member. This is an excellent shortcut as you work to keep your file size small.

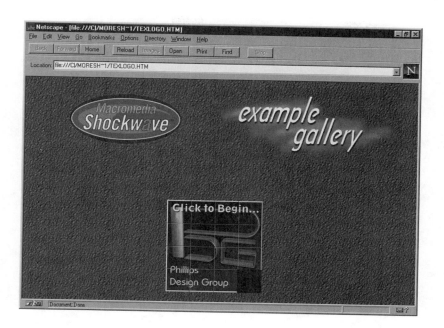

Figure 8.3
Tiled backgrounds
on the HTML
page, Shockwave
movie, and a
JPEG image.

Sprite Blends

Fade-ins and fade-outs are often desirable over other transitions. Director offers wipes, dissolves, and others, but standard Director transitions halt the playback head. A *sprite blend* can fade over a course of frames while other action is occurring. The previous example using the Shockwave logo *shlogo.dir* uses a sprite blend to fade one image while the rest of the animation continues.

Using a sprite blend is simple. Put the cast member to be faded in one frame and choose Set Sprite Blend from the Score menu (or Sprite Properties from the Modify menu in Director 5). The range between 1 and 100 selects how much to fade the sprite. To fade from nothing, choose 0 for the first frame. Then copy the sprite to another frame—for example, frame 10—and set the new sprite blend value (100 to be completely visible). Select the range of cells, choose In-Between Special, and select Blend. Just like that, the sprite fades from nothing to full view.

Sprite blends are great for enhancing a simple movie without adding extra cast members. It is also the only way to create a smooth fade, rather than individual pixels disappearing through a standard Director transition (figures 8.4 and 8.5).

Figure 8.4
A standard
Director transition
dissolves
individual pixels.

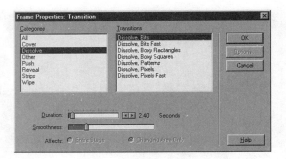

Figure 8.5
A sprite blend
fades the image
smoothly.

Audio as a Background Soundtrack

Looped audio can be used as background music for your Web page. This example uses a small graphic image that lets the user click between "Sound on" and "Sound off" because looped sounds can quickly become annoying.

> **Caution**
>
> If you put multiple Shockwave movies on one Web page, you should use audio in only one of them. Otherwise, you will have more than one element attempting to access the computer's sound hardware, which may be unpredictable.

The file *mloop.wav* on the CD-ROM is the sound that was used (*mloop.dir* is the finished Director movie). If you load it into a sound utility and play it back, it goes through eight beats of music on one chord, then eight beats on another chord. When set in Director to loop, it smoothly repeats. Note that this example is not streaming audio, it is simply downloading and playing it. Chapter 18, "Shockwave for Audio," covers the process of streaming an audio file.

Only a few frames are needed in Director. Set up a marker in one frame called "On." This will be where the music is playing. Put the sound in a sound channel and set the playback head to repeat using the "go to the frame" Lingo statement. In a sprite channel, put the graphic of the button to turn the sound off. We haven't discussed interaction yet, but this will give you a preview if you haven't done this before. Attach a Lingo script to the sprite with the "Sound Off" button that looks like this:

```
on mouseup
    sound stop 1
    go "off"
end
```

When the user clicks the button, it turns the sound off and goes to a second marker called "Off." In the frame with the "Off" marker, put the graphic of the "Sound On" button and attach a Lingo script to go back to the "On" marker. Figure 8.6 shows the example as seen in Director.

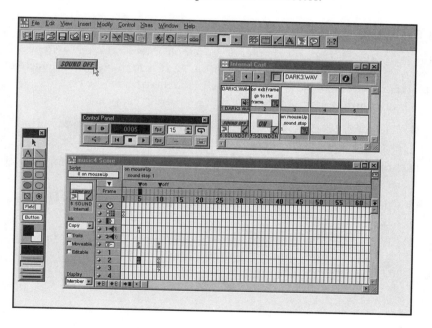

Figure 8.6
The Looping Sound Movie in Director.

Now you have two frames that the movie can jump between. "On" contains the looping music and the button to turn it off. "Off" contains no music, but has a button to jump back to "On" if the user wants.

> **Note**
>
> You're probably thinking, "Audio files are so large, why would I want to have the viewer download a huge Director movie just to hear some dumb music?" Well, you may be right. This example is 95K. Pretty big just for background music. But this is just to demonstrate the possibilities of Shockwave. Maybe you have a looping sound that is much smaller, and you don't mind the download time for it. If it's the last thing the HTML page loads, it may be all right because the viewers can read the rest of the page while the sound loads. Or maybe you're a musician and you have a demo of a song on your page that you want available for people to hear—or even just a short announcement sound that says, "Welcome to (whatever)" when the page loads.

From Here...

The last example from this chapter uses a simple interaction that switches between frames when the user clicks a button. Next, you move into interactive Director movies that allow the user much more involvement with Shockwave, rather than simply watching something happen.

- Chapter 9, "Rollovers and Button Clicks": Using rollovers and button clicks for user interaction.
- Chapter 10, "Controlling Movie Elements with Puppets": Using puppets to control Director functions with Lingo.
- Chapter 11, "Using Shockwave for Data": Working with Shockwave for data.
- Chapter 12, "Working with Lingo": Completely "Shocking" your site.

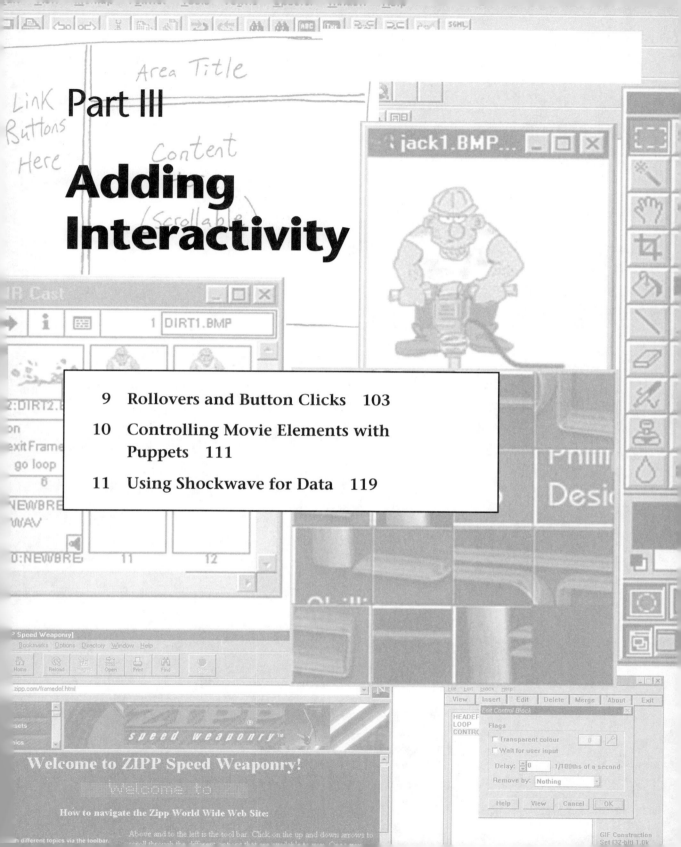

Part III

Adding
Interactivity

CHAPTER 9

Rollovers and Button Clicks

About ten years ago, a friend of mine bought a mouse for his computer. I thought he was crazy. Neither of us used any software that supported a mouse. I couldn't imagine that moving a hectic little dot around the screen could be easier than selecting things using the keyboard. Of course, our main input device at that time was a joystick, but my point here is that mice have completely changed the way people interact with a computer. And in catering to the mouse-driven world, *rollovers* and *button-clicks* are the bread and butter of multimedia. Chapter 10, "Controlling Movie Elements with Puppets," covers more advanced functions by puppeting sprites. This chapter covers both through the following simple examples:

- Advancing a movie when the mouse is located over it and stopping the movie when the mouse leaves the stage area
- Using the `rollover` and `mousecast` functions to identify the mouse location
- Performing an action when the user clicks a button

Rollovers

What is a rollover? A *rollover* is simply a detection of the mouse location. When the mouse is located over something, something happens. A common use of rollovers is highlighting an area when the mouse travels over it so that the user knows it is a clickable area. A menu, for example, might have five buttons that are all a dim blue color when nothing is happening, but when the mouse moves over each button, it turns yellow. Then if the user clicks it, something else could happen.

In Director, the rollover feature is just a test, nothing more. You check if a certain rollover state is true or false and tell the computer what to do in either circumstance. Because Lingo is a programming language, you can have it perform one action or a list of actions. For a rollover, you can have the screen turn purple, make worms dance around, and play your favorite "Dueling Banjos" sound clip if you want to. Of course, that would be very annoying for the user to have to endure every time he or she moved the mouse over a particular area.

Using the Rollover Lingo

The Lingo test is easy. Suppose that you have a sprite in channel 5 that you want to test for a rollover. If the mouse is over it, you want to jump to a marker called "hilight" in another frame. If the mouse is not over it, you want to repeat the frame it's in. You would use the following Lingo in the frame script:

```
on exitframe
     if rollover (5)=true then go "hilight"
     else go to the frame
end
```

Remember that the number in parentheses is the *sprite* number, not the *cast* number. The wrong one can make for a confusing situation. My example used the else argument to loop in the frame, but it could have used another if test. The next statement does the same thing as the preceding Lingo:

```
on exitframe
     if rollover (5)=true then go "hilight"
     if rollover (5)=false then go to the frame
end
```

On the CD

Let's look at a simple example of this. The file *pdgwave.dir* on the CD-ROM uses an easy rollover test to advance the movie when the mouse rolls over it, and to stop the movie when the mouse is not over it. This is useful because a continually looping movie could tie up the viewer's system or become annoying; this provides some means of interaction for when the movie starts and stops. Figure 9.1 shows the movie in Director.

The movie is a series of frames exported from 3D Studio that shows the PDG company logo rippling while playing a looping sound effect. The cast members play in sequence in sprite channel 1. Every frame in the loop has the same frame script Lingo, except the last one, which sends the playback head to the "start" marker to repeat the effect. The rollover scripts look like this:

```
on exitFrame
  if rollover (1)=false then
    sound stop 1
    go 1
  end if
end
```

So if the mouse is not located over sprite 1 (which always contains the image), two things happen: The audio is stopped in sound channel 1 using the "sound stop 1" command, and the playback head jumps back to frame one, which contains the static PDG logo image.

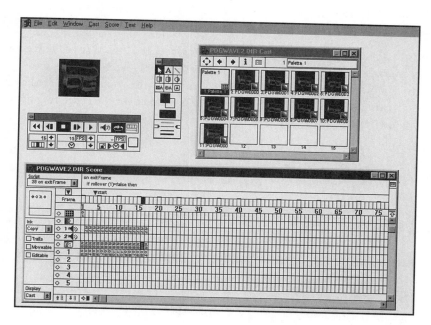

Figure 9.1
The rippling PDG logo.

Invisible "Hot Spots"

The rectangle that contains the sprite is the boundary of the rollover area. This is fine for rectangular shapes or areas that don't need to be exact, but what if you want to detect for a rollover in an area that is different from the bounding rectangle of the sprite?

One way is to create a second invisible shape above the sprite that will be seen as the rollover area (sometimes called a *hot spot*). So you might have a large bit-map image in sprite 3, and a small invisible shape in sprite 4. To create an invisible shape, use one of Director's hollow shape tools and select the dotted line for an outline (which means it has no outline). Then draw a shape over the area to be detected. Your Lingo would then use sprite 4 in the rollover command instead of sprite 3.

Using the Mousecast Lingo

A second way of having nonrectangular rollovers is the mousecast function. This Lingo command returns the number of the cast member that the mouse

III

Adding Interactivity

is over. If cast member 8 is in sprite channel 4 and the mouse is located over it, the `mousecast` function would return the number 8. If copy ink is used, then the bounding area is a rectangle just like the `rollover` function. But if matte or background transparent inks are used, the "hot" area is only the visible part of the cast member. So the area that becomes transparent will not register as part of the cast member.

On the CD-ROM, *arrows.dir* shows how the `mousecast` Lingo is used. There are three markers that the playback head jumps between. "None" is where the mouse is not located over anything. "Left" is where the mouse has rolled over the left arrow. "Right" is where the mouse has rolled over the right arrow. In the "None" frame, the Lingo is as follows:

```
on exitFrame
    if the mousecast=1 then go "left"
    if the mousecast=2 then go "right"
    go to the frame
end
```

You can see in the cast window that the left arrow is cast member 1, and the right arrow is cast member 2. The movie in Director is seen in figure 9.2.

Figure 9.2
Using the mousecast function.

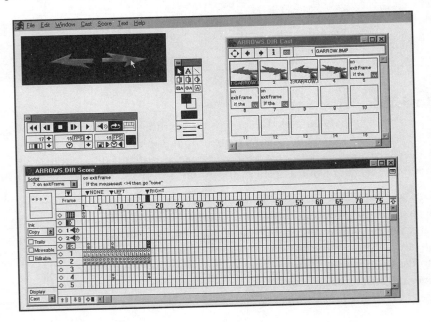

When the mouse is located over the left arrow, the `mousecast` function returns the value of 1 because the left arrow is cast member 1. The `if` statement causes the playback head to jump to the marker "left" where a different color arrow is used. In the new frame, there is a new Lingo statement to check the mouse position.

```
on exitFrame
  if the mousecast <>3 then go "none"
  else go to the frame
end
```

This statement checks if the mouse is still over the arrow. But the red arrow is cast member 3, not 1 like the first blue arrow. Now the statement must check if the mouse is over cast member 3. If it is, the frame loops; if not, it jumps back to the "None" marker. The right arrow performs the same way as the left arrow, but a new script checks for a different cast number.

Using the `mousecast` function can become confusing if you end up rearranging your cast members later on. To prevent confusion, you can make a simple change that uses a cast member's name instead of the number. Arrow2.dir shows the same movie using cast member names instead of numbers. The scripts look like this:

```
on exitFrame
  if the mousecast=the number of cast "blue left" then go "left"
  if the mousecast=the number of cast "blue right" then go "right"
  go to the frame
end
```

I named the blue left arrow "Blue Left" using the info button in the cast window. Similarly, I named the other arrows so that I could refer to them by name instead of by number. This way, you can move any cast members around without messing up your Lingo statements.

The `mousecast` function always returns a number, so you need to use the `number of cast…` statement for this argument to work. If you typed **if the mousecast = "blue left"** you would be comparing a number to a name, which would never be true. By using `the number of cast "blue left"` you are comparing two numbers, which will execute the test properly.

> **Note**
>
> To avoid confusion, Director 5 uses the term *number of member…* instead of *number of cast…* because multiple casts may be used. Lingo from Director 4 still works properly in version 5.

Button Clicks

Director offers no support for distinguishing right and left mouse buttons (on Macintosh, there is no right button, anyway). But it can perform two separate tests for the mouse button. One is if the button is pressed; the other is if the button is released. Respectively, these are mousedown and mouseup. Like rollovers, you can have the mouse button perform an action or list of actions that you want.

Mousedown

Here's a simple example of how the mousedown function could be used in a Shockwave movie. *Hats.dir* on the CD-ROM could be part of a Web page with information about products that you could purchase on-line. It contains a small button that, when clicked, shows a close-up of the product—hats, in this case.

We used two graphic images: one of the small button, and one with the close-up picture. Figures 9.3 and 9.4 show the two images in Director. The button is in one frame that loops continually. A Lingo script attached to the button looks like this:

```
On mousedown
    go "closeup"
end
```

Figure 9.3
Using mousedown to change frames.

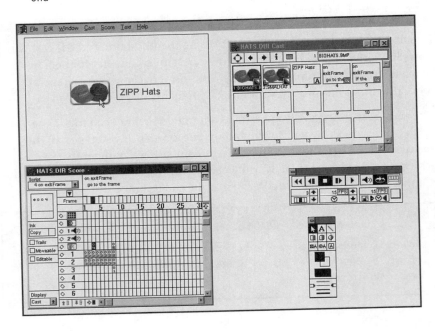

When the mouse is pressed, it jumps to the frame that contains the close-up. In the close-up frame, the script loops until the mouse button is no longer pressed. The Lingo in the frame script is as follows:

```
on exitframe
    if the mousedown=false then go "start"
    else go to the frame
end
```

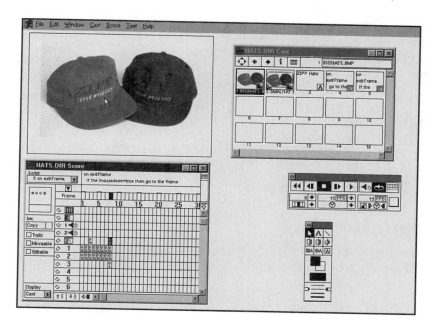

Figure 9.4
Repeating the frame while the mouse button is pressed.

Mouseup

Mouseup is used more often than mousedown because people usually click the button down and release it immediately. When attached to a cast member, a mouseup script will execute every time the mouse is clicked on that particular cast member. You should know that if a user clicks a sprite, then moves the mouse off the sprite before releasing the mouse button, the mouseup handler doesn't execute.

Using the example from chapter 7, "Animations to Demonstrate or Teach," you can repeat an animation using a button with a mouseup script. *Tires2.dir* on the CD-ROM shows this (see figure 9.5). A button in the last frame contains a script to return to frame 1 when pressed.

On the CD

```
on mouseup
    go 1
end
```

Figure 9.5
Using the mouseup
command for a
button to repeat
the animation.

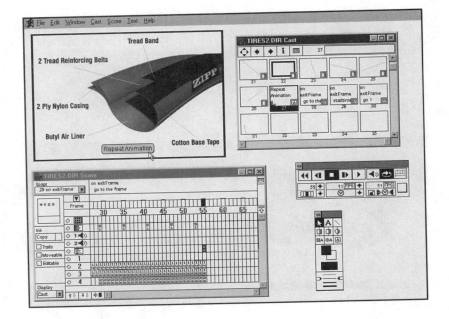

From Here...

You've started using interactivity in your movies, and no doubt you can find
many uses for rollovers and button clicks. Here is what to expect in chapters
to come:

- Chapter 10, "Controlling Movie Elements with Puppets": Puppeting
  sprites for Lingo-controlled screen changes.

- Chapter 11, "Using Shockwave for Data": Another purpose for
  Shockwave.

- Chapter 12, "Working with Lingo": Learn all about Director's
  programming language.

Controlling Movie Elements with Puppets

This chapter focuses on creating animations of famous puppet characters such as Kermit the Frog, Howdy Doody, and Oscar the Grouch. Hopefully, you didn't believe that last sentence.

Actually, "puppets" in this chapter refers to a technique in Director that allows you to control various elements of your movie by using Lingo. You learn about several uses of puppets to make your programming easier and more powerful.

This chapter covers the following:

- Puppeting sprites allows you to control cast number, location, and other properties of a sprite by using Lingo commands.
- A sound can be puppeted with a Lingo script to occur when the user triggers it.
- Other effects can also be controlled through Lingo using puppet statements.
- Specific examples are given so you can learn how to set up Shockwave movies that use puppets.

Using Puppets in Your Shockwave Movies

One definition of a "puppet" in Webster's dictionary is something that is "controlled by an outside force or influence." This fits well into the Lingo analogy of a puppet. You have learned to control various elements using the score—sprite location, sounds playing, and so on. By creating puppets of those elements, you are overriding the score using Lingo commands to control the elements.

The real strength of puppets is that they can be dependent on the user's actions. You don't want to have to create every possible situation in the score window and jump to different frames depending on the user's actions (actually, you may want to, but learning to use puppets is easier).

For example, you may want a specific sound effect to play when the user clicks a button. You can have the playback head jump to a separate frame that plays the sound, but by issuing a command to play a "puppetsound," you can control the entire effect within one frame using Lingo.

What is the advantage to the Web and Shockwave movies? Using puppets is merely a more advanced way of controlling elements. They may not shrink file size for downloading, but they make your job as the programmer much easier and give you more power to control the movie.

PuppetSprite

You should know that a sprite is a cast member in one of the 48 channels available in the Score window—possibly a bit map, vector graphic, text, button, and so on. You can choose any of the 48 sprite channels and turn it into a puppet. What you are doing in essence is telling the Score to ignore a certain sprite channel and let you control it through Lingo commands.

Controlling Button States with Puppets

On the CD

To start, here's a simple example of controlling the cast number of a sprite. On the CD-ROM, you will find *puppet.dir*, which is a simple movie that has three graphic images of a button. One image is the button in a normal state, one is the button you use in a rollover state, and the third is the button that's displayed when the user clicks it (see figure 10.1).

Figure 10.1
The three button states: normal, rollover, and clicked.

Without puppets, you need to have three separate frames for the different images. Whenever you roll over a certain area, it has to jump to the rollover frame; and, when you click it with the mouse, it again switches frames. By using puppets, you can do the same thing within one frame.

You start by putting the normal button image in channel 1. In a frame script, you will make this sprite a puppet.

```
On exitframe
    puppetsprite 1, true
end
```

As soon as you issue this command, the score releases the channel to be a puppet. Anything you put into channel 1 will now be ignored. You need to leave the button cast member in the score so that you will remember that it is a puppet.

The syntax for "puppetsprite" requires a channel number and either "true" or "false." You can use 1 for true and 0 for false if you like. "puppetsprite 1, false" would end the puppet and return control of channel 1 to the score.

Note

You must have something in the sprite channel in the score to initiate a puppet. You might think, "I'm going to control channel 3 using Lingo, so why should I even bother to put anything in the score?" Well, having something in the score gives your puppet a starting point. The puppet needs a cast number, location, size, ink type, and so on. With nothing in the score, there is nothing to turn into a puppet. Once you have initiated the puppet, you don't need to keep anything in the channel, because the movie will remember what the puppet's characteristics are. I often keep something in the channel anyway to help me remember that I can't use it for something else.

In the next frame, you are ready to work with your puppet. A script checks whether the mouse is rolled over the button. Whenever you want to refer to your puppet, you need to refer to sprite 1.

```
on exitframe
    if rollover (1) then set the castnum of sprite 1 to 2
    else set the castnum of sprite 1 to 1
    go to the frame
end
```

If the mouse is rolled over sprite 1, the script changes the cast number of our puppet to 2, which is the rollover image. Otherwise, the cast number is set to 1 (the normal button). The frame loops to check continually.

That was easy. Now add the click state of your button. Because the user must be rolled over the button to click it, you can attach a script to cast member 2, the rollover image.

III

Adding Interactivity

```
On mousedown
   set the castnum of sprite 1 to 3
   updatestage
end
```

Now, when the user clicks the rollover button, the Lingo script switches cast members again—this time to number 3, the clicked image. The "updatestage" command is used when you want an immediate change in the stage appearance; in this case, the playback head enters a new frame (or repeats within the same frame). In this example, you don't really need to update the stage because your loop repeats the frame very quickly, but in other cases you might not enter a new frame immediately.

Whoa, you're not done yet! Because the frame does loop continually, the button only stays clicked for a brief moment. Then the frame script detects a rollover and changes the cast number to the rollover image. This gives the appearance of a very fast click, but you want the button to stay down until the user releases the mouse button. So, you can modify your frame script like this:

```
on exitframe
   if the mousedown=false then
      if rollover (1) then set the castnum of sprite 1 to 2
      else set the castnum of sprite 1 to 1
   end if
   go to the frame
end
```

Now your rollover test only occurs when the mouse button is not pressed. The clicked image stays visible while the button is held down. Figure 10.2 shows this example in Director.

Changing a PuppetSprite's Location

Here's another simple example of using a puppetsprite. You may know that you can create custom cursors in Director. But you are limited to a 1-bit image that is 16×16 pixels. By using a puppetsprite, you can make any cast member into a cursor. However, this example doesn't need to be for cursors only. There may be other situations when you want the mouse to drag a sprite around the stage.

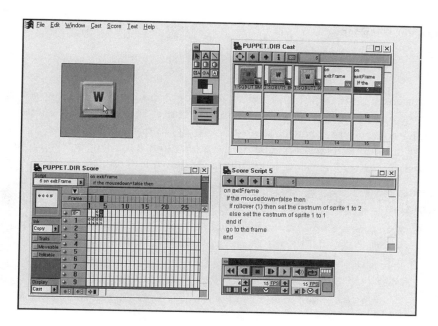

Figure 10.2
Using a puppet
to control the
button state.

Open the file *cursor.dir*, on the CD-ROM to see your sample. The first thing I
did was to create an image to be used as the cursor. Mine is a circle shape
with an arrow through it. I placed it in sprite channel 3. I will set up the
puppet in one frame, then control it in a second frame. The first script looks
like this:

On the CD

```
on exitframe
    puppetsprite 3, true
    cursor 200
end
```

The first line you remember from the other example; it turns channel 3 into a
puppet. The second command, "cursor 200," turns the standard cursor invisible. You are not really replacing the normal pointer icon. You're just making
it invisible and putting your puppetsprite in the same location. See the Lingo
Dictionary included with Director for more on the "cursor" statement. The
next frame has this script:

III

Adding Interactivity

```
on exitframe
    set the loch of sprite 3 to the mouseh
    set the locv of sprite 3 to the mousev
    go to the frame
end
```

These commands are straightforward. The "loch" and "locv." are Lingo terms for the horizontal and vertical locations of a sprite. The mouseh and mousev are Lingo terms for the horizontal and vertical locations of the mouse. By setting your puppet's location equal to the mouse location, it appears you have a custom cursor. The example in Director is shown in figure 10.3.

On the CD

Tip

Can you think of a way to animate your custom cursor? For a simple example, look at *cursor2.dir* on the CD-ROM. The Lingo script adds a statement to look like this:

```
on exitframe
set the loch of sprite 3 to the mouseh
set the locv of sprite 3 to the mousev
if the castnum of sprite 3=1 then set the castnum of sprite 3
to 2
else set the castnum of sprite 3 to 1
go to the frame
end
```

All this example does is switch between two cast members, but you could step through ten cast members by incrementing the cast number of your puppet every frame. Then when the cast number equals 10, set it to start again at one.

Figure 10.3

Creating a custom cursor using a puppetsprite.

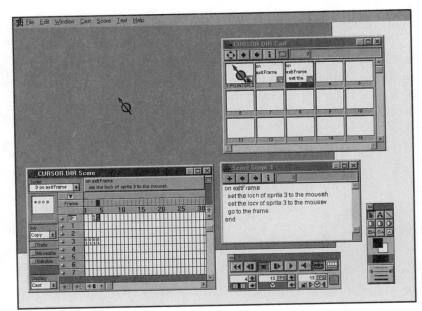

PuppetSound

PuppetSound is an easy command that enables you to play an audio cast member without putting it into the sound channel of the score. How is this useful? Say you have a 50-frame animation and you want to play a sound effect exactly when the user clicks the mouse button. You can't predict which frame the playback head will be in, and you want your animation to continue without jumping to a new frame, so you need a way of playing the sound through Lingo.

Look at your first example again—changing button states with puppets, but this time use *pupsound.dir* on the CD-ROM. You have now added a sound effect when the button is pressed. The script of cast member 2 looks like this now:

```
on mousedown
    puppetsound "newclick.wav"
    set the castnum of sprite 1 to 3
    updatestage
end
```

The syntax of puppetsound requires the name of the sound, not the cast number. My sound was called "newclick.wav."

Using puppetsound overrides any audio in sound channel 1 of the score, though channel 2 still plays sounds. To stop a puppetsound and return control to the score, use the statement:

```
puppetsound 0
```

> **Note**
>
> PuppetSound plays the sound once, then stops, but the sound channel is still a puppet, even after the sound is finished. To enable the sound channel of the score after a puppetsound, you need to use "puppetsound 0."
>
> Using the PuppetSound command with a looped sound causes it to play repeatedly until you stop it by using the "puppetsound 0" command.

Other Puppet Effects

Other score functions can be controlled through puppets. The tempo can be controlled by using the PuppetTempo command—this was mentioned in chapter 5, "Limitations of Shockwave and the Web," because Shockwave does not

III

Adding Interactivity

recognize the tempo channel. Other puppet effects include changing palettes using `puppetpalette` and performing transitions using `puppettransition`.

See the Lingo Dictionary included with Director for more on how to use these functions.

From Here...

You've now learned some basics about puppets. Hopefully you can see many uses for controlling elements through Lingo. Additionally, there are a few more chapters covering Lingo techniques:

- Chapter 11, "Using Shockwave for Data": You learn how your movies can store, sort, and manipulate information.
- Chapter 12, "Working with Lingo": This chapter offers some basics of the Lingo programming language for new users.
- Chapter 13, "Internet Lingo for Shockwave": Describes the new Lingo commands available for Shockwave to interact with the Internet.

Using Shockwave for Data

Data. It usually means boring information compiled into lists and columns with lots of numbers, letters, and codes for other numbers and letters that can be put together into other lists. It conjures up images of long printouts on continuous-form paper and tedious statements from the days of BASIC.

Actually, computers are used more for information than they are for graphics, games, presentations, and other functions that are more interesting to some of us. You'll see how Lingo can be used as a powerful programming language to sort and display data. This chapter shows you the following:

- Learn how to use lists to store, sort, and retrieve information.
- Takes a series of numbers and plots a line graph for you to see.
- Lists and describes lingo terms related to data functions.
- Offers other suggestions for using Shockwave with data.

Linear and Property Lists

Despite the dry nature of data, many people actually kind of like lists—grocery lists, to-do lists, Christmas lists, any kind of list. It feels good to organize things. "Lists" in Lingo allow you to organize a series of items. You might be familiar with the term "array" in other programming languages. This is the same idea—having one variable name with multiple "slots" where you can put information.

Here's an example. Let's say you have 15 names to keep track of. You could store the names by creating lots of variables. You might call them name1, name2, name3, all the way up to name15. But this is like having 15 pieces of paper with one name written on each. Wouldn't it be more practical to have all 15 names written on one piece of paper (figure 11.1)? In Lingo, you can have one list variable that can store all of the names in different positions. They can be retrieved, deleted, added to, sorted, and so on.

Figure 11.1
Lists help organize information.

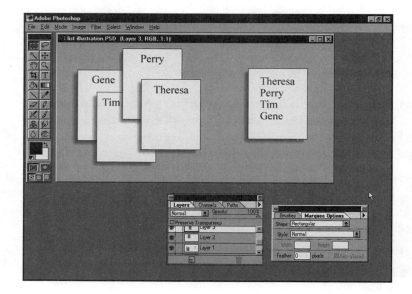

Linear Lists

Linear lists consist of a series of single items. The syntax separates the items by commas and encloses them in brackets. The items may be numbers or strings; strings must be surrounded by quotes. For example, the following Lingo statement creates a linear list called *shortlist*:

```
set shortlist=[345, 12, "banana", 465.8]
```

There are four items in the above list (three numbers and a string). Later, to retrieve one of the items, you can identify it by its position in the list. If you want to put the third item into a text field called "screentext" you could use this statement:

```
put getat(shortlist,3) into field "screentext")
```

・

The getat statement requires the name of the list and the position number of the item. In this case, the previous statement would have retrieved item 3, which is "banana," and put it into the specified text field.

To change a specific value within a list, use the setat command. The syntax is:

```
setat listname, position, newvalue
```

So in our previous example, to change the second value from 12 to 45, we could use this statement:

```
setat shortlist, 2, 45
```

What if you have a list with only four items, but you want to add more to it? Easy. There are several ways of doing so. For now we'll show you the append command, which adds an item to the end of a list.

```
Append listname, newitem
```

If I wanted to add the string "blah" to my above *shortlist*, I would type:

```
append shortlist, "blah"
```

Other commands used with lists are "listed" (pardon the pun!) at the end of this chapter.

Property Lists

Property lists are similar to linear lists, but contain two pieces of information for each item: a property and a value for that property. For example, a list variable called "boxlist" contains a series of properties that you can later retrieve:

```
set boxlist=[height:80, width:125, color:34]
```

Then when you want to know a certain property of "boxlist," you can phrase this nice Lingo sentence:

```
set newvariable=the width of boxlist
```

The above statement sets a new local variable equal to 125, the value of the property "width" of the list "boxlist."

Changing a property is just as easy. To change the color from 34 to 80:

```
set the color of boxlist to 80
```

To add a new property to the list, you can use the addprop command.

```
Addprop listname,#newpropname,value
```

So, in our example, to add a property called "spblend" to "boxlist," you could use the following Lingo statement. Note that you must have a pound sign (#) before the property name or Lingo thinks you are specifying a variable. If there is no such variable, a void entry is added to the list.

```
Addprop boxlist,#spblend,50
```

Graphing Information

This section will offer an example using a list to graph information. Open the file *graph.dir* from the CD-ROM. The movie accepts a series of values and puts them into a list. The user can add and change up to 30 values that will be plotted as a line graph.

The basic structure uses a linear list. You enter a value into an editable text field (figure 11.2). You may step forward or backward in the list and view your entries. Every time you step forward, if there is no entry already in the list, a new one is created.

When you have finished entering values, a script processes the information and turns the values into positions on a graph and connects segments between them.

Figure 11.2

Accepting values in a list for a line graph.

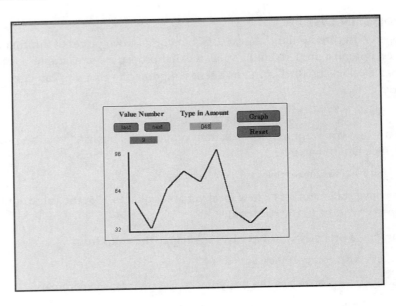

Setting Up the Stage

There are a variety of parts that need to be set up for this graphing movie. Some parts are visible, some are invisible.

Two text fields are placed on the stage—one that's editable for the user to enter values, and one that specifies the number of the entry in the list. Two buttons are available to move forward or backward in the list of entries. If the user wants to enter eight values to be graphed, he or she can move up and down from one to eight in the list to view or change the values.

At the bottom of the screen are horizontal and vertical axes. Labels on the vertical side show 0, 50, and 100. This is only temporary. The text fields are titled "high," "low," and "mid." When the program graphs the information, it puts the highest value in the "high" field, the lowest value in the "low" field, and the median value in the "mid" field. This way the user can enter any values and the graph will be scaled appropriately.

Puppets

To have an actual line for each value in the list, you need to use puppet-sprites. The cast member used is a segment created with Director's line tool. To set up the score for puppets, I put the same cast member in the same position for sprites 10 through 40; this allows for 30 possible entries in the list. The position is off the stage so that they are not seen before they are plotted. Your Lingo script will later move each one into its proper position.

Entering Values in the List

The list is initiated in a movie script. It starts out with only one value, zero. There are two global variables—the list itself and a second variable that keeps track of the position in the list. The movie script looks like this:

```
on startmovie
  global graphlist, gnum
  set graphlist=[0]
  set gnum=1
  put gnum into field "valnum"
  put getat(graphlist,gnum) into field "amount"
end
```

The two fields are called "valnum" and "amount." The position number (gnum) is always displayed in "valnum" and the actual value is displayed in the field "amount."

A frame script loops while the user enters a value into the "amount" field. The value is not added until one of the buttons is pressed. So, to enter a value and move to the next position in the list, a cast member script looks like this:

```
on mouseUp
  global graphlist, gnum
  setat graphlist,gnum, integer(field "amount")
  set gnum=gnum+1
  if gnum=31 then set gnum=30
  if gnum>count(graphlist) then setat graphlist,gnum,0
  put getat(graphlist,gnum) into field "amount"
  put gnum into field "valnum"
end
```

The setat command takes the number from "amount" and puts it into the list at the position specified by "gnum," which is the current position in the list. Then "gnum" is incremented by one, but it can't go past 30 because that is the maximum number of puppets prepared. The fifth line in the script checks the number of entries in the list. If this is a new entry ("gnum" is greater than the total number of entries), it creates a position and sets the value to zero until the user enters a new one. If the position already exists ("gnum" is not greater than the total number of entries), a new entry is not made. Finally the amount and position number are updated in their appropriate fields on the stage.

The "back" button works the same way, but decreases "gnum" by one and doesn't check for a new entry, because the user would be backtracking over values already entered. You can view the script on your own to see how it's written. Figure 11.3 shows the screen where the user enters values.

The "graph" button contains the following script:

```
on mouseUp
  global graphlist, gnum
  setat graphlist,gnum,integer(field"amount")
  if count(graphlist)<>1 then go "graph"
  else
    put "Cannot graph only 1 item." into field "message"
    starttimer
    repeat while the timer<60*2
      nothing
    end repeat
    put "" into field "message"
  end if
end
```

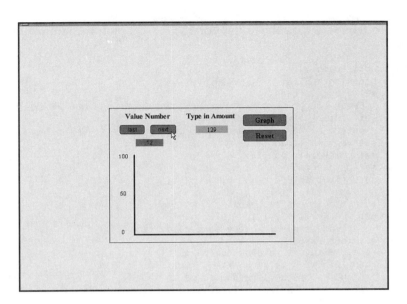

Figure 11.3
Moving forwards
and backwards in
the list of values.

The script sets the last value entered in the list at the current position. It checks to make sure there is more than one value in the list, then jumps to the frame marked "graph" where the information is processed and plotted. If only one value is in the list, a message alerts the user and the frame stays the same.

Graphing the Data

The first frame in the graphing section sets up the correct number of puppets. Here is the frame script:

```
on exitFrame
  global graphlist
  set x=count(graphlist)
  repeat with n=10 to (10+x)
    puppetsprite n, true
  end repeat
end
```

Using the function "count(graphlist)" you put the total number of entries into a local variable, x. Set up a repeat loop to puppet the correct number of sprites, starting at 10, because that is the channel number in which you began putting segment cast members.

III

Adding Interactivity

The next frame contains the real monster script that plots the information. It looks like this:

```
on exitFrame
  global graphlist
  set x=count(graphlist)
  --determine how wide each segment should be on horizontal scale
  set width=integer(325/x)
  --determine max value and pixel percentage for vertical scale
  set vmax=max(graphlist)
  set vmin=min(graphlist)
  set pixpercent=175.0/(vmax-vmin)
  set offset=integer(vmin*pixpercent)
  put vmax into field "high"
  put vmin into field "low"
  put (vmax+vmin)/2 into field "mid"
  --set each segment to the proper position
  set leftpos=65
  repeat with n=1 to count(graphlist)-1
    set rightpos=leftpos+width
    --checks if the line should go up
    if getat(graphlist,n+1)>getat(graphlist,n) then
      set the castnum of sprite n+10 to 14
      set botpos=275-integer(getat(graphlist,n)*pixpercent)+offset
      set toppos=275-integer(getat(graphlist,n+1)*pixpercent)+offset
    else  --the line must go down
      set the castnum of sprite n+10 to 15
      set toppos=275-integer(getat(graphlist,n)*pixpercent)+offset
      set botpos=275-integer(getat(graphlist,n+1)*pixpercent)+offset
    end if
    --in case the line is perfectly horizontal
    if getat(graphlist,n)=getat(graphlist,n+1) then
      set the castnum of sprite n+10 to 16
      set botpos=276-integer(getat(graphlist,n)*pixpercent)+offset
      set toppos=botpos-3
    end if
    --moves the puppetsprite into the proper position
    set the rect of sprite n+10 to rect(leftpos,toppos,rightpos,botpos)
    updatestage
    set leftpos=leftpos+width
  end repeat
end
```

Looks like a big mess, huh? I'm always impressed with how fancy a big script looks when its finished, although when you take it apart it's very logical in construction.

The first thing is to determine how wide each segment should be. If the user entered three values, the segments should be very wide; with 25 values, the segments need to be narrower. I decided ahead of time to make the total width of the graph 325 pixels. So, the width of each segment should be 325 divided by the number of segments, which is our variable x.

Next, you have to set the vertical scale. The max command will return the highest value in a list. Likewise, the min command returns the lowest value. I put the highest value in the field called "high," the lowest value in the field "low," and a median value in the field called "mid."

I created a variable called *pixpercent* that gives the proper percentage to scale the data to the graph. The height of the graph area would be 175 pixels. So by dividing 175 by the maximum value, you get a number to use later in scaling the data.

Note

If you want to know where this equation comes from, get out your algebra book. 175 is the highest pixel height of the graph. *Vmax* is the maximum value in the list, which you want to be the highest point on the graph. So what value can you multiply *vmax* by to get it to be 175 pixels?

> *Vmax * x=175*

Solving for x gives the equation: *x=175/vmax*

Once you know this value, you can use it to multiply with any item in the list to get the correct scaled value.

The *offset* variable is the pixel amount that each plotted point doesn't need. Because you're starting the vertical axis at the lowest value in the list instead of at zero, you have to offset each item by this amount.

Now you're ready to set the locations of each segment. You have to specify the left, top, right, and bottom positions in pixel coordinates. Left and right are easy. I started the left value at pixel 65. The right value just adds the *width* variable to the left value.

Top and bottom values are trickier. One value will be the height of the current number in the list, the other value will be the height of the next number in the list so that the segments connect. But depending on whether the next number is higher or lower, you need to use a different cast member. One member is a segment that goes upward, one is a segment that goes downward, a third cast member is a rectangle in case the numbers stay identical.

If the next item in the list is higher than the current one, then the line goes up, the bottom value is the current item and the top value is the next item. If the next item in the list is lower than the current one, then the line goes down, the top value is the current item and the bottom value is the next item.

The item is multiplied by the *pixpercent* variable and subtracted from 275, which is the vertical location of the bottom of the graph (pixels count with zero at the top of the screen and increase as they go down). Then the *offset* amount is readded to this value to take into consideration that the graph doesn't start at zero.

If this is confusing you, don't worry about it—it's a bit tough to hack through this programming situation. The more experience you have, the easier it is to understand.

Once the left, right, top, and bottom values are found, a puppetsprite is modified to show up on the graph. Then the left value is incremented and the loop repeats with the next item in the list.

The next frame waits for the user to change the data or reset the graph and start over with an empty list.

That's the end of the graphing movie. Fairly simple to look at, but it uses some tricky Lingo. The usefulness of this as a Shockwave movie may be limited, but what if you used a `getnettext` command to retrieve a text file from the Internet that contains graph data? Every day the information could change and a new graph could be displayed. Stock prices, sales information, just about anything could be graphed (see figure 11.4: URL isn't real). And this is just a small example. The power of Lingo as a programming language continues.

Figure 11.4
Using Shockwave to graph stock information.

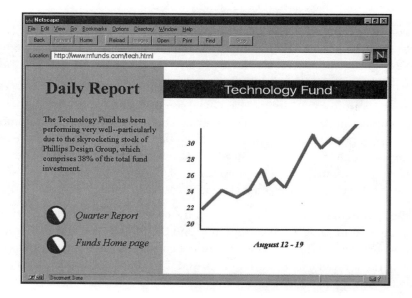

Other List Commands

There are many ways you can manipulate linear and property lists. Table 11.1 describes some of the basic commands used with lists.

Table 11.1 Commands Used with Lists	
Lingo Command	**Description**
append *listname, value*	Adds an item to the end of a list
add *listname, value*	Adds an item in proper sorted position
addprop *list, prop, value*	Adds an item to a property list
addat *list, position, value*	Adds an item in a particular position
count(*listname*)	Returns total number of items in list
deleteat *list, position*	Deletes an item from a linear list
deleteprop *list, prop*	Deletes an item from a property list
getat(*list, position*)	Returns an item from the list
getprop(*list,position*)	Returns value of a property in a list
getpropat(*list,position*)	Returns property name of position
min(*listname*)	Returns minimum value in list
max(*listname*)	Returns maximum value in list
sort(*listname*)	Sorts list in alphanumeric order
setat *list,pos,value*	Changes an item in a linear list
setprop *list,prop,value*	Changes an item in a property list

See the Lingo Dictionary and users guide for more about working with lists.

Further Ideas

Once you begin to work with advanced Lingo functions, you will see many opportunities to incorporate Shockwave movies to your Web site.

Perhaps you could have a large corporate telephone directory that lets the user search by name or department and displays phone, fax, e-mail, and other information (figure 11.5). Instead of using CGI scripts for searches and filling up Web pages with lists of information, you can create a Shockwave movie that stores and organizes it.

III

Adding Interactivity

Figure 11.5
Using Shockwave
to store and
display a company
directory.

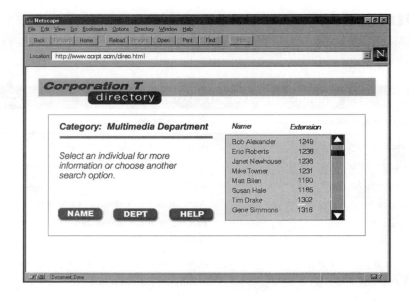

Another business application could be ordering products online. A Shockwave movie could display images of the products along with descriptions of
each. The user could select items and the movie could add their total bill and
compute the sales tax. When the whole shopping list is completed a CGI
script could be used to actually transmit the order to your company
(figure 11.6).

Figure 11.6
Using Shockwave
to order products
online.

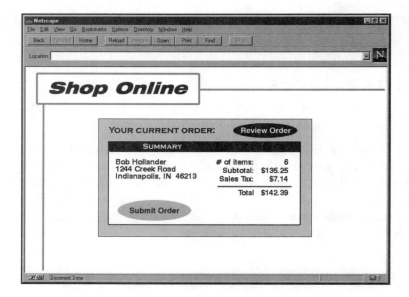

These suggestions are business oriented, since data functions tend to be related to business. But you could use Shockwave for just about any application. Your own imagination will be the limit of what Shockwave can do for you.

From Here...

Programming in Lingo allows you to use Shockwave for some very advanced data processing functions, if you are willing to learn to use it. Hopefully, you can think of a variety of other functional purposes for Shockwave movies involving data. The next few chapters focus more on Lingo, including some basics for beginners as well as new network Lingo for Shockwave.

- Chapter 12, "Working with Lingo": Shows some important basics of Lingo for new Shockwave developers.
- Chapter 13, "Internet Lingo for Shockwave": Internet Lingo that's new to Shockwave.
- Chapter 14, "Further Use of Internet Lingo": Shows you some more advanced functions using the new Internet Lingo.

III

Adding Interactivity

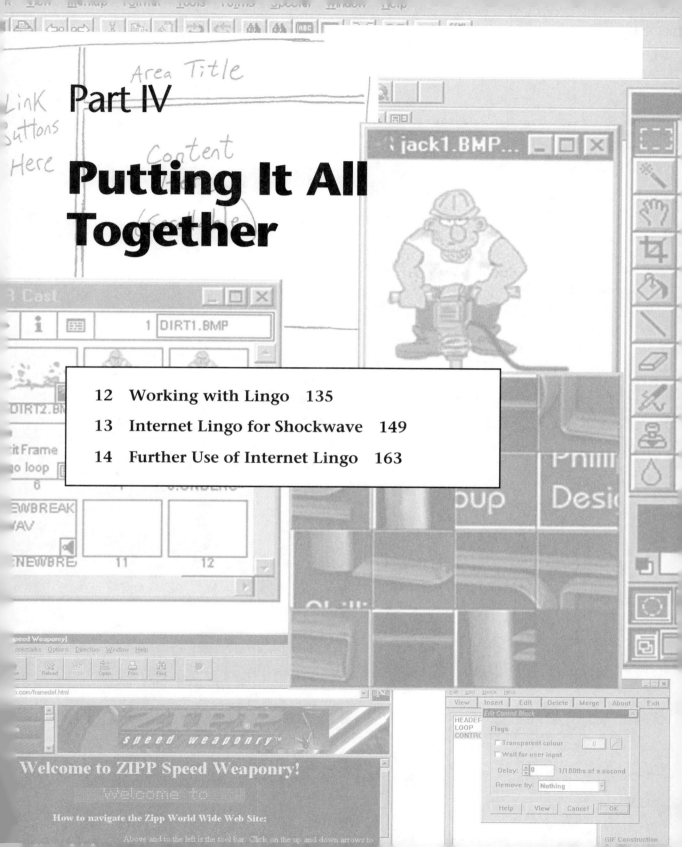

Part IV

Putting It All Together

CHAPTER 12
Working with Lingo

If you moved to Mexico, you would probably learn Spanish. You could get by with hand gestures and a lot of enchiladas you didn't mean to order, but sooner or later you'd probably want to speak the language.

Lingo is Director's programming language. You could make movies without knowing a word of Lingo, but it's definitely worth the effort to at least learn the basics. This chapter offers you just that—a crash course in working with Lingo.

Here are a few highlights:

- Covers the various types of scripts you can write so you'll know where to use each type.
- Defines global and local variables and shows you how to use them to keep track of information.
- Shows how to write handlers to organize and streamline your scripting.
- Covers some basic programming structures, such as setting values, testing for conditions, loops, and so on.
- Provides simple examples of how to write scripts to help you get started quickly.

Scripts

A *script* is a group of Lingo statements that performs a particular action. Scripts can contain one line of code or many lines. The Lingo code is organized and grouped into *handlers*. All handlers begin and end similarly:

```
on (event)
    (do this action)
end
```

Fortunately Lingo is very similar to the English language, so many Lingo terms relate well to the way we speak. The above handler format can be phrased almost like a sentence: "On a certain event, perform an action, then end."

Before you start writing actual scripts, the following defines the various types and when they occur.

Frame Scripts

Frame scripts are very common. You place them in the score in the frame script channel (figure 12.1). As the movie plays, anytime the playback head encounters a frame script, it will execute it. You may create two different types of handlers that respond in different ways:

```
on enterframe
    (lingo commands)
end

on exitframe
    (lingo commands)
end
```

Just like they sound, the "enterframe" handler executes when the playback head *enters* the frame; and the "exitframe" handler executes when the playback head *exits* the frame.

Note

Exitframe and enterframe do not necessarily refer to leaving one frame and entering a different one. If you create a loop that stays in frame 12, for example, the playback head is still entering and exiting the same frame repeatedly.

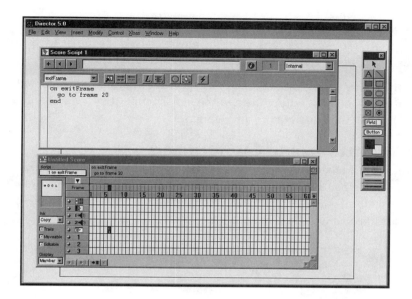

Figure 12.1
A frame script.

Movie Scripts

A movie script is available to the whole movie while it is playing (figure 12.2). Within a movie script you can place several types of handlers.

Figure 12.2
A movie script.

```
on startmovie
    (lingo commands)
end

on stopmovie
    (lingo commands)
end

on (customhandler)
    (lingo commands)
end
```

The "startmovie" handler runs immediately when the movie begins to play. Conversely, "stopmovie" runs when the movie ends. If the movie loops continually and never ends, the "stopmovie" handler never executes.

The third type is a custom handler that you create yourself. We'll talk more about these later. By putting them in the movie script, they are available anytime you call the handler from another script.

Scripts Attached to Cast Members

In the cast member window, you have the option of adding a Lingo script to any cast member that can be placed on the stage (figure 12.3). This could be buttons, bit-map images, text fields, vector graphics, and so on. Whenever the cast member is clicked, the script executes.

Figure 12.3
A cast member script.

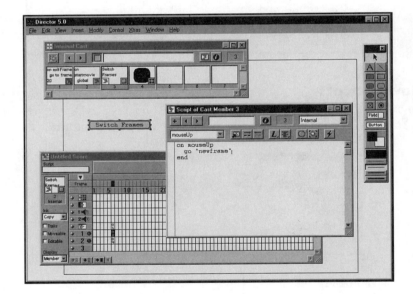

Two types of handlers can be used in cast member scripts:

```
on mousedown
    (lingo commands)
end

on mouseup
    (lingo commands)
end
```

When the mouse is over the top of the cast member on the stage and the mouse button is pressed, the "mousedown" handler executes; when the button is released, the "mouseup" handler executes. Usually, people press and release the mouse button immediately, so either handler can be used for a standard mouse click. You might want to use "mouseup" to control movie actions unless you have specific events that should occur while the button is held down.

Note

Two other types of handlers are available for editable text fields, but have no effect on other cast member types. "on keydown" and "on keyup" will respond when the user presses or releases a key. You can then check what key was pressed and have Lingo statements respond accordingly.

Sprite Scripts

In certain instances, you will want a script to execute when a sprite is clicked, but you won't want to attach a script to the cast member. Using a sprite script, you can attach a script that only executes in the frames that contain it (figure 12.4). The same cast member could have one sprite script attached in one frame, and a different sprite script attached in a different frame. This is useful for using the same button cast member to perform different actions when clicked in different frames of the movie.

To use a sprite script, select the sprite (or range of sprites) in the score and select "new" from the pull-down script menu in the score window (or click the script viewing bar at the top of the window). By selecting only certain frames that contain the sprite, you can attach the script only for specific positions in the score.

Sprite scripts operate in the same way that cast member scripts do, and require a mouse or keyboard input to execute. Note that sprite scripts will override any cast member scripts that are attached to the same item.

Figure 12.4
A sprite script.

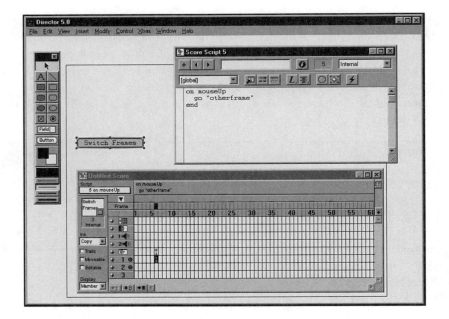

Variables

If you are familiar with any type of computer programming, you probably know what a variable is. It's an object in the computer's memory that is a substitute for a value that can change or vary. Variables are powerful because they allow your movie to perform differently in different circumstances, depending on the value of the variables.

Director uses two types of variables: *global* and *local*.

Global Variables

Global variables stay in the computer's memory for as long as the movie runs (or until you tell it to clear any global variables). They are used for information that must be available in different situations. For example, you may want to store information that the user enters and display it again later in the movie.

Any time you use a global variable, you need to first use the statement:

```
global variablename
```

For example, to create a global variable called "gpoints" to track points in a game, you could use the following Lingo:

```
global gpoints
set gpoints=0
```

The first statement shows that this is a global variable you're dealing with. The second statement sets your variable equal to zero. Later, if you want to change your global variable, you could use this handler:

```
on mousedown
   global gpoints
   set gpoints=gpoints + 5
end
```

Whenever this handler runs, it takes your gpoints variable and adds five to it.

Note

Many Lingo programmers put a "g" in front of the variable name they create to help them remember that it is a global variable. This is only optional. Your variable can be any word that is not already used by Lingo to mean something else.

Local Variables

Local variables are used within a handler and then are gone. Any variable used without the "global" term is created as a local variable. If you don't need the variable's information later in the movie, local variables are ideal.

Here's an example: There is an editable text field on the stage called "textfile." The user types the location and name of a text file into the field and the Shockwave movie loads the text using the getnettext command. The Lingo could look like this:

```
on exitframe
   set whattext=field "textfile"
   getnettext whattext
end
```

The getnettext command only needs the information once to perform its action, so we used a local variable called "whattext." When the handler finishes, "whattext" is no longer in memory.

Writing Your Own Handlers

You have seen various handlers that can be used: "on exitframe," "on mouseup," "on startmovie," and so on. But the real organizing power of handlers is in creating your own. By putting your own handlers in a movie script, you allow a common function to be called from anywhere else in the movie.

Plain Vanilla Handlers

When I say "plain vanilla handlers," I am referring to handlers that are called from another place in the movie and don't pass or return values. These are the most simple, but not at all less useful than handlers that pass values.

Here's a game example (stop taking your job so seriously and have some fun!). Every time the user clicks a space alien, you want to increase the score and put some text on the screen. You can make your own handler called "scorepoint" and put it in a movie script so it's always available.

```
on scorepoint
   global gpoints
   set gpoints=gpoints + 1
   put "Good Shot!" into field "response"
end
```

Now, in the sprite script of the space alien, you can call the handler:

```
on mousedown
   scorepoint
end
```

This example just shows the basics. All you're doing here is dividing the Lingo into two places. Instead of placing the statements in the scorepoint handler, you could place them in the sprite script and it would work the same way. But you might have many different situations where you want to score a point and put "Good shot!" on the stage. Instead of writing the whole segment over and over in different places, you can just call the scorepoint handler.

Passing and Returning Values in Handlers

Try to think of the various Lingo terms as parts of speech. The preceding handler is like a verb. The handler is even named to sound like a verb: "scorepoint." When you issue the command, you're telling Lingo to "score a point." Passing values can be done two ways: one is like a verb and one is like a noun.

Passing Values

Passing values to a handler is a verb. It's basically like the plain vanilla handler but with a few additional elements, called arguments. By specifying one or more values after the name of the handler, you can send information to the handler when you call it.

Going back to the space alien game, there might be several different types of aliens. One scores five points, one scores 10 points, and one scores 50 points. Instead of making three different handlers to add the points, you can pass a value to the same one.

```
on scorepoint howmuch
   global gpoints
   set gpoints=gpoints + howmuch
   put "You got "&howmuch&" points!" into field "response"
end
```

Then, when you call the handler, you add a parameter that passes the number of points to the handler.

```
on mousedown
   scorepoint 5
end
```

In another script on a different sprite, you might use "scorepoint 10" to add ten points. You can pass more than one parameter by separating them by commas.

Returning Values from Handlers

Using a handler to return a value makes it operate more like a noun instead of a verb. Instead of standing alone as a call to a handler, it is used as a part of another Lingo statement. With the return command, a value can be sent back to the script that called the handler.

For example, this handler (called "returnscore") adds the new points to the players current score and returns the total value. It looks like this:

```
on returnscore oldpoints, newpoints
   set newscore=oldpoints + newpoints
   return newscore
end
```

The script that calls the handler is:

```
on mousedown
   global gpoints
   put returnscore(gpoints,10) into field "points"
end
```

This script passes two values to the handler: the current score (gpoints) and the new points to add to it (10). The handler adds the two and returns the total score, which is put into a field called "points."

If a handler returns a value, the call to the handler must have parentheses—even if no values are passed to the handler. You can have a call to a handler that looks like this:

```
put returnscore() into field "points"
```

If the point value for the aliens were always the same, the handler could be:

```
on returnscore
    global gpoints
    set newpoints=gpoints + 10
    return newpoints
end
```

It's up to you to decide where to use handlers that return values, and where to use handlers that work on their own. It's just a matter of whether or not you want to continue working with that value in the script that calls the handler.

Simple Lingo Structures

You could learn specific words of Spanish using a dictionary, but you would still need to know how to phrase the words together in a sentence. This section shows just a few basic structures that are common to Lingo programming. They are fairly straightforward and logical.

Setting Values

A common command you will perform is setting one value equal to another value. Of course, this doesn't refer to constants; you can't set 8 equal to 14, but you will have variables that can be set and changed.

There are several ways of phrasing a Lingo statement to set a value.

```
set variable=new value

set variable to new value

put new value into variable
```

So the following Lingo statements would all set a variable called "gnumber" to 8:

```
set gnumber=8

set gnumber to 8

put 8 into gnumber
```

The phrasing is up to you. Sometimes one way sounds more natural than another, depending on your preference.

Testing Using If...Then...Else Structures

Often you will want to test for a certain condition, then respond depending on the outcome of the test. The "if...then...else" structure is very common and works like its name suggests.

```
If true condition then perform action
```

The "else" is optional; if you have one action for the "true" condition and one for the "false" condition, you can use this structure:

```
if true condition then perform action
else perform a different action
```

You also may have multiple lines of code for each of the parts of the structure. If you do have multiple lines, you need to end the test structure with an end if statement.

```
if true condition then
    perform action one
    perform action two
    perform action three
else
    perform other action one
    perform other action two
end if
```

Let's say you want to test for a rollover in sprite channel one; if it's true that there is a rollover, the cast number will be changed to eight. If there is not a rollover, the number will be set to five. The handler can look like the following. Note that in Director 5, the term "member" can replace the "castnum" Lingo from Director 4.

```
if rollover(1) then
    set the member of sprite 1 to 8
    updatestage
else
    set the member of sprite 1 to 5
    updatestage
end if
```

Repeat Loops

In many cases you will want to repeat the same Lingo statements over and over. You may have a certain number of loops, or you may loop continuously until a condition changes. Here are a few basic repeat structures you can use.

Repeat While...

"Repeat while..." continues the loop until a condition is false. If the condition is already false when the test is started, the Lingo within the repeat structure never occurs. If the condition is true and never becomes false, the loop will go on endlessly.

```
Repeat while true condition
    lingo statement
    lingo statement
    lingo statement
end repeat
```

For example, you want a sprite to be visible while the mouse button is held down and to turn invisible when it's released. Your script looks like this:

```
repeat while the mousedown=true
    set the visible of sprite 4 to true
    updatestage
end repeat
set the visible of sprite 4 to false
updatestage
```

The loop continues to repeat until the mouse button is not down, then the Lingo will progress outside the repeat loop.

Repeat With...

Here is a simple loop that repeats a specific number of times. It uses a variable that counts from one number to another number. These loops are particularly useful if you want to test a range of sprites for a condition.

```
Repeat with variable=firstnumber to secondnumber
    lingo statements
    lingo statements
end repeat
```

The above syntax is used if "firstnumber" is less than "secondnumber." If the reverse is true, the loop counts down by using the statement "repeat with firstnumber down to secondnumber."

For example, I want to check sprites four through nine for a rollover, and then go to a new frame if any one of them is true.

```
Repeat with n=4 to 9
   if rollover(n) then go "rollframe"
end repeat
```

The above example will progress through the loop five times testing for a rollover using the variable "n", which will be equal to 4, 5, 6, 7, 8, and 9.

From Here...

Of course, this chapter is only the tip of the iceberg when it comes to Lingo. It shows you some basic structures and scripts to get you started on understanding the language. The number of actual commands available through Lingo is enormous. To learn more, you will want to study the Director manuals or a third party Lingo book.

There are countless people who can use Director to make simple movies, but a good Lingo programmer is much less common. You can really set yourself apart if you learn to work with the programming aspect of Director.

- Chapter 13, "Internet Lingo for Shockwave": Begins with some Internet Lingo that is new for Shockwave. Functions are described to interact with the Web.

- Chapter 14, "Further Use of Internet Lingo": Carries the Internet Lingo a step further with some more advanced functions and applications.

- Chapter 15, "Putting It All Together: A Shocked Site": Puts much of your Shockwave knowledge together in a complete Shockwave Web site.

IV

Putting It All Together

CHAPTER 13

Internet Lingo for Shockwave

Animation and sound are excellent enhancements to a Web page, but Shockwave is not limited to those functions only. Your movies can also interact and respond to the Internet. This chapter offers applications of Shockwave that are exclusive to the Web. The main functions covered are:

- GoToNetMovie: Enables you to load new movies in the same Web page location.
- GoToNetPage: Can be used for Shockwave navigation through different Web pages.
- GetNetText: Loads an external text file from the Internet.
- PreLoadNetThing: Enables you to download files to the user's cache before they are needed.
- Other related functions are used in the preceding examples.

Using New Lingo

There has been much discussion through messages and Web pages about how to use the Internet Lingo commands. It is possible that Macromedia will document the new Lingo in upcoming versions of Director, but for the latest information at this time you should watch the developer's center of Macromedia's Web site:

http://www.macromedia.com/shockwave/developer.html

> **Note**
>
> The new Lingo commands used by Shockwave are not understood by Director. When you look at these examples or program your own, you won't be able to really test the commands. As you create your movie, leave the network Lingo commands out until you are ready to try it as a Shocked movie.

GoToNetMovie

The purpose of this function is to call and load a separate Shockwave movie to be played in the same location on the Web page. This could be useful for several reasons.

Suppose that you have a 200K movie that you want people to see. It would take several minutes to download it, during which they would normally just see a big, white square with the Macromedia logo in it. But by using the `GoToNetMovie` command, you can load a small Shockwave movie that comes up quickly and then calls the larger movie. So while the larger movie is downloading, the viewer sees the small movie (perhaps reading text or interacting somehow with it).

Or you may have five separate Shockwave movies that are available for viewers to see, and you want them to be able to switch between them without leaving the Web page. By using the `GoToNetMovie` command, you can switch movies easily without downloading all five as one big movie.

The syntax for the `GoToNetMovie` Lingo command is:

```
gotoNetMovie "moviename.dcr"
```

You may include the HTTP location as well as the file name, but it all must be within quotes because you are passing a string value to the command. You don't need quotes if you use a variable as a value for the command. Suppose that you have a variable called `whereto`. The following frame script would load a new movie using that variable:

```
on exitframe
    set whereto="http://www.pdgroup.com/shock/main.dcr"
    gotoNetMovie whereto
end
```

That example is useless because a local variable is just defined one line above the `GoToNetMovie` command. But in a larger context, the possibility of using a variable can be valuable.

Note

If you issue a second `GoToNetMovie` command before the first one is finished loading, it will cancel the first command and load the second movie.

Using an Introductory Movie to Call a Shockwave File

On the CD

Here's a simple example that uses `GoToNetMovie`. On the CD-ROM, the file *prepare.dcr* is a small movie that loads another larger movie, *pdgmain.dcr*, using the `GoToNetMovie` command. *Pdg.html* embeds the movie. Run it in your browser to see it work. From a CD-ROM or hard drive, it doesn't make much difference. But over the Internet, there would be a long delay before the second movie loads. So the small introductory movie loads quickly to get rid of the blank, white default box and to make the viewer aware of what's coming.

You can look at the *prepare.dir* file in Director to see how it is set up, though it won't run properly because Director can't understand the new Lingo. In frame 3, a script calls the new movie.

```
On exitframe
    gotoNetMovie "pdgmain.dcr"
end
```

In this case, the second movie is located in the same directory as the first movie. You could also specify the whole URL:

```
On exitframe
    gotoNetMovie "http://www.pdgroup.com/pdgmain.dcr"
end
```

Once you have issued the `GoToNetMovie` command, Shockwave starts to load the new movie. Because it can never be sure how long it will take, the current movie continues to run until the new movie is finished loading. So a looping frame keeps the viewer aware that something "cool" is loading. When the new movie is finished loading, the first one is automatically ended, and the second one begins. Figure 13.1 shows the introductory movie in a Web page.

Note

Usually, a Lingo command must finish executing before it can move on to a new frame or new command. But network Lingo is different. It only starts a process. This is called an asynchronous operation. `GoToNetMovie` will start loading a movie but doesn't need to wait until the movie is finished loading. In later examples, you will learn to use the `netdone()` command to determine if the operation is completed or not. For `GoToNetMovie`, the new movie automatically takes over when it is loaded, so you don't need to check.

Only the first movie is embedded in the HTML document. In our example, it looks like this:

```
<embed src="prepare.dcr" height=400 width=250>
```

The only thing to remember is that the second movie that is loaded must be the same dimensions as the first movie because it will be played in the same spot on the screen. A new movie that is too large will be cropped, and one too small will leave blank space around the edge.

Figure 13.1
Using a small pre-movie to show a Shockwave movie is loading.

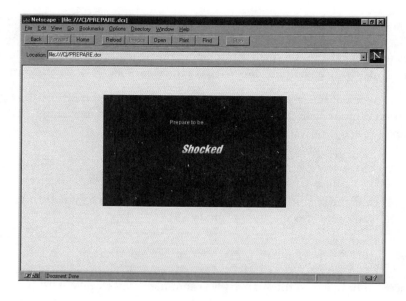

Moving Between Movies with *GoToNetMovie*

Perhaps you want to offer a choice of movies for the user to load. You could then use `GoToNetMovie` to navigate between movies. To show this, we have a basic example that switches between movies. This example uses three movies on the CD-ROM with this book: *blue.dir, red.dir,* and *green.dir.* The *gomovie.html* page uses the compressed .dcr versions of these files. They are very simple movies, but they show how you can jump between movies. Figure 13.2 shows the movie in Netscape Navigator.

Each movie in this example has two buttons that offer options of loading one of the other movies. So the red movie offers options to switch to the green or blue movies. The other two are similar.

The Lingo used was simple. I attached a script to the red button that looks like this:

```
On mouseup
    gotonetmovie "red.dcr"
end
```

The blue button and green button have similar scripts but use *blue.dcr* and *green.dcr* instead. These movies must all be in the same directory to work properly. If the movies were in different directories, you could specify the whole or partial location.

The `embed` statement uses one of the movies—the red one in our example:

```
<embed src="red.dcr" height=300 width=400>
```

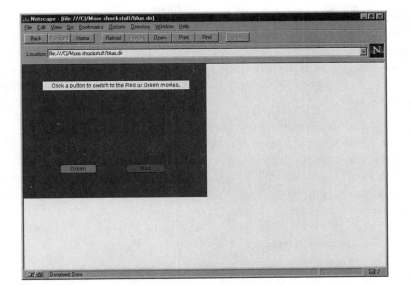

Figure 13.2
A simple
example using
`GoToNetMovie`.

We could have started with any of the three because they can all switch between each other. You might have one particular movie that you load first that contains an introduction and several options to load other movies.

GoToNetPage

You can also switch the entire Web page using Shockwave Lingo. The `GoToNetPage` command allows you to specify a new HTTP location to move to. The movie you are running will end, and the browser will switch to the new page. The syntax is just like `GoToNetMovie`:

```
gotonetpage "http://www.server.com/page.html"
```

If the new HTML file is located in the same directory as the Shocked movie, you don't need the whole location. You could use:

```
gotonetpage "page.html"
```

If you want to specify a specific location on the Web page, you can do so just as you would with a normal anchor:

```
gotonetpage "page.html#anchorname"
```

You can see how this command is useful as a navigation tool. You could have a main Shocked menu that lets the viewer select which section of your Web site to go to. You could even then have small Shockwave files throughout the site that let the viewer navigate to different areas.

A Menu Example Using *GoToNetPage*

On the CD-ROM, *pdgmain.dir* is a navigation tool that offers choices in an interactive, animated fashion and will go to the page the user clicks. *Pdgindex.html* embeds the .dcr version of the file. Sample HTML pages are included to show that the navigation works when *pdgindex.html* is loaded from the CD-ROM.

By looking at the *pdgmain.dir* file, you can see that there are seven possible options. The left arrow takes you to "CD-ROM," "Internet," and "Intranet." The right arrow takes you to "Kiosk," "Graphic Design," and "Animation." And the PDG company logo is always available as a link to the home page. So the cast member bit map that says "Graphic Design" contains a Lingo script that looks like this:

```
on mouseup
    gotonetpage "design.html"
end
```

By clicking "Graphic Design," the user is taken straight to the Graphic Design page of the Web site (figure 13.3).

Figure 13.3
The PDG navigation movie using GoToNetPage.

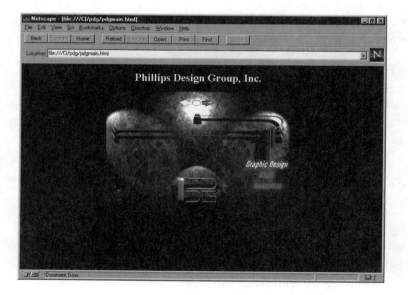

Using *GoToNetPage* to Detect for Shockwave

Many sites open their first page with a choice of Shockwave or non-Shockwave because they don't know if the user has the right browser and the plug-in. But you can detect this by creating a small Shockwave movie that jumps to a new page using GoToNetPage. If the user doesn't have Shockwave, the command is never issued, and the browser stays on that HTML page. If the viewer has Shockwave, he or she will be taken to a new page, which starts the Shockwave section of the site.

So you might create a Shockwave movie that has just one line of text that reads, "Shockwave detected. Entering the Shocked version of this site." Then in a frame script, you would have something like this:

```
on exitframe
    gotonetpage "shocked.html"
end
```

For your starting HTML document, you could use statements like this:

```
<embed src="shtest.dcr" height=64 width=256>
<noembed>
Shockwave not detected. Use the links below to navigate.
</noembed>
```

Someone with Shockwave would see the short movie and immediately jump to the Shocked page. Someone with a browser that doesn't recognize <embed> and <noembed> statements would see the text, "Shockwave not detected. Use the links below to navigate."

> **Note**
>
> Another situation is also possible. Someone with Netscape 2.0 or another browser that recognizes the <embed> and <noembed> statements but *doesn't* have the Shockwave plug-in would see a broken icon. This is because the browser understands <embed> but doesn't have the capabilities of playing the movie. The browser also understands the <noembed> statement, so it skips the line of text. This makes for a difficult situation because you can't have alternate images or text on a browser that understands the code but doesn't have the plug-in. Hopefully, if the viewer has Netscape 2.0 or a compatible browser, he or she has the Shockwave plug-in, also.

GetNetText

In certain situations, you may want to load a separate file into your Shockwave movie with text information. GetNetText allows you to do just that. It retrieves a text file from the Internet.

Suppose that you have some information that is continually changing—statistics, for example. And every day you want the Shockwave movie to display the updated information. Instead of creating a new Shockwave movie every day with updated information, you can just upload a new text file to your server every day and have the same movie load the text file. You could even have a CGI script automatically update the text file periodically, though how to write CGI scripts isn't covered in this book. For more information on CGI, try *Special Edition Using CGI*, by Que Publishing.

The syntax for the Lingo command is:

```
getnettext "http://www.server.com/file.txt"
```

Again, you need only specify the file name if it's in the same path of files as the Shockwave movie.

> ### Caution
>
> GetNetText works only over the Internet. You will be very frustrated if you can't get it to work off of your local hard disk. The command is intended to load information from an HTTP URL and will *not* load local files. The Shockwave movie can be played from a local disk, but the text files that are loaded using GetNetText must be on the Internet; and, in that case, you would need to specify the whole HTTP location because your movie is not in the same directory as the text file.

NetDone()

GoToNetMovie and GoToNetPage end the current movie when they're finished loading, but GetNetText stays within the same movie. You need a way of determining when the text file is finished loading; You can't just delay the movie for ten seconds and hope that it was enough time to get the information from the Internet. Downloading is too irregular for that. To test if the operation is finished, you can use another Lingo command new to Shockwave: NetDone().

You can use NetDone() in an if statement, and it will be either true (1) or false (0). After you have started the GetNetText operation, if NetDone() returns true, the operation is finished and you can proceed to use the information. If NetDone() returns false, then the file is still loading and you will need to wait longer before using the information.

Here are two simple Lingo statements that use GetNetText and NetDone(). For now, put nothing in between the parentheses; they will be explained later.

```
On exitframe
    getnettext "http://www.pdgroup.com/file1.txt"
end

On exitframe
    if netdone()=false then go to the frame
end
```

You can't put these two statements into the same frame because the `NetDone()` command here is set to loop to the frame. You would be issuing a new `GetNetText` command repeatedly.

Caution

You might decide to use a test like this:

```
repeat while netdone()=false
    nothing
end repeat
```

But this is a bad idea. I have found that `NetDone()` never seems to return true in a case like that, so you get stuck in an endless loop. The `updatestage` command doesn't seem to help this, either. Apparently, you need to allow for at least a single frame loop. Lingo loops can be risky anyway because you lose interaction functions while the script repeatedly executes.

NetTextResult( )

The `NetTextResult()` statement is used to access the information you just downloaded using `GetNetText`. You can use `NetTextResult()` to put the information into a variable or text field or do whatever you like. I am wary about how long the movie will remember the information, so I always put it into a global variable so it won't be lost (a new `GetNetText` statement can replace the `NetTextResult` information). You could use a script like this:

```
on exitframe
    global gresults
    put nettextresult() into gresults
end
```

A Sample Movie Loading Text from the Internet

From the CD-ROM, load the page called *gettext.html*. It will load the Shockwave file *gethttp.dcr*. For this example to work properly, you'll need to have a connection to the Internet. You can run the movie from the CD-ROM, and it will load text using the `GetNetText` command. It then tests if the operation is complete using `NetDone()` and displays the results using `NetTextResult()`.

On the CD

The movie allows you to type in an HTTP address and file name, and view the results. If you don't have any text files on your server to look at, you can call any HTML document anywhere on the Web. For example, you could look at the PDG index.HTML document by typing:

```
http://www.pdgroup.com/index.html
```

and pressing the Show HTTP button. Figure 13.4 shows the movie in a
Web page.

Figure 13.4
Using `GetNetText`
to view a text file.

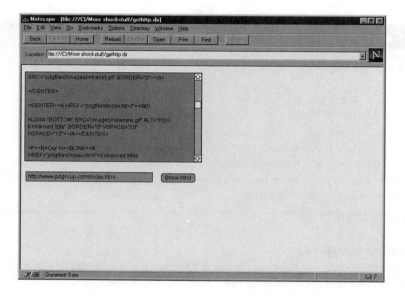

By looking at the Director file, *gethttp.dir*, you can see how this was put
together (see figure 13.5). A text field that can be edited was created to allow
you to type in the location and file name. Then, when you press the button,
a script executes:

```
on mouseup
    set x=field "where"
    getnettext x
    go "test"
end
```

This script sets a local variable *x* equal to the text field that contains the file
and location. Then it uses the `GetNetText` command to retrieve the item.
Finally, it sends the playback head to a frame marked "test."

In the "test" frame, a script looks like this:

```
on exitframe
    if netdone()=false then go to the frame
end
```

If the text file is not finished downloading, the frame loops. When the test
returns true, the playback head can go to the next frame, which has this script:

```
on exitframe
    put nettextresult() into field "results"
    go "start"
end
```

This script puts the text information into a scrollable text field that I named "results." Then it goes back to the frame marked "start" to allow a new text retrieval.

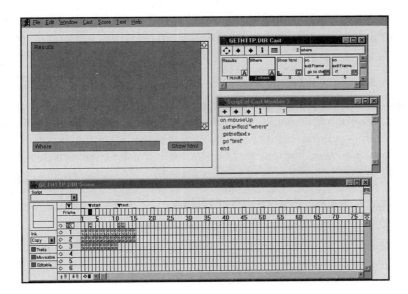

Figure 13.5
The *gethttp* movie in Director.

PreLoadNetThing

Preloading is the process of loading information that is not currently needed, but will soon be used. The purpose is to have the information available before it is required so that there is no waiting time to access the information.

The PreLoadNetThing command can be very useful, although it is currently limited. What it does is load any file item from the Internet to the user's disk cache. So, while they are interacting with the Shockwave movie, various items can be downloaded that will be used later. When it's time to use the items, they don't need to be downloaded from the Internet because they are already available on the user's local disk cache.

For example, you have a simple Shockwave movie that loads on one Web page. While the user reads the Web page or looks at the movie (game, text, whatever), the movie is preloading other items to the cache—a new HTML document, a GIF or JPEG image, another Shockwave movie, and so on. Then, when the user is ready to move to the next Web page, the items have already been loaded, so there's very little delay in seeing them.

The syntax is:

```
preloadnetthing "http://www.server.com/item.extension"
```

Suppose that I want to preload a JPEG image called *logo.jpg* while my Shockwave movie plays. In this example, the JPEG file is in the same directory on the server as the Shockwave file. In a frame script, you would put:

```
on exitframe
    preloadnetthing "logo.jpg"
end
```

Because Shockwave's network Lingo only starts the operation and lets it run in the background, the movie continues to play. Later, if you want to check whether the operation is finished, you can use a NetDone() test as you did with the GetNetText example. If the operation is finished, you can preload something else.

Limitations of *PreLoadNetThing*

There are a few limitations to using the PreLoadNetThing command:

There is a 64K limit. Anything larger appears to download, but will not be written to the cache. Hopefully, this will be different in future versions of Shockwave.

You have no way of knowing the size of the user's cache or when items will be removed from it. Most people have it set large enough to hold just about anything you want to preload—especially if you can only do it in 64K chunks. But if you plan on having the user navigate a variety of pages, you may not know if the preloaded items stay in the cache.

The system may slow down while the browser is downloading the items. It can affect your Shockwave movie's performance if you are continually loading things in the background.

It's difficult to offer an example of PreLoadNetThing because items currently on the Internet may not be there when you are reading this book. Hopefully, this chapter describes the process well enough so you can adapt it to your own purposes.

From Here...

This chapter has covered the main Shockwave network Lingo operations. You can find more advanced uses in upcoming chapters or in the gallery at the end of the book.

- Chapter 17, "Alternatives to Shockwave": More exciting options!
- Chapter 18, "Shockwave for Audio": "Hear" all about the use of streaming and other audio techniques.
- Chapter 19, "Shockwave for Authorware": Learn about the differences between Director and this high-end authoring package.

IV

Putting It All Together

CHAPTER 14

Further Use of Internet Lingo

The previous chapter introduced the main functions of Shockwave network Lingo. You learned how to navigate between movies and pages, how to retrieve text files from the Internet, and how to preload files to the user's cache. This chapter continues with those same functions, but expands them with a few additional commands.

- `GetLatestNetID` gives you a number to associate with a network operation. This allows you to perform more than one operation at a time.

- An additional parameter can target frames from a `GoToNetPage` command.

- External parameters can be passed to the movie from the embed tag.

- `SetPref` and `Getpref`—storing text information by writing to a file on the viewer's system.

- Use the `NetStatus` command to add a message to the browser status bar.

- `NetError()`, `NetMIME()`, and `NetLastModDate()` return more information about a recent network operation.

Multiple Operations

Shockwave allows you to initiate up to four network operations at one time. Obviously, this is not used for `GoToNetPage` or `GoToNetMovie` because you can't look at four pages or four movies at the same time. But for `GetNetText` or `PreloadNetThing`, you may want to do multiple operations: four text files to load, four graphic images to preload, and so on. When one of the four operations is finished, you have a free "spot" to perform another operation, so you can continually perform network commands; however, no more than four can be initiated at once.

> **Note**
>
> Even though you can initiate four operations at one time, this doesn't mean they will all occur simultaneously. Only one file can be downloaded at a time, and it will be going as fast as possible given the speed of the connection. Initiating four commands may just be simpler for you to do than initiating one at a time.

Identifying an Operation

Every time you issue a network command—`GetNetText` or `PreloadNetThing`—the operation is given a unique identifier. Fortunately, it's not a cryptic twelve-digit code number; instead, it starts at 1 and progresses up. Your first command is 1, your second command is 2, and so on. The number is reset to zero only when a new movie starts.

Remember those parentheses after `NetDone` and `NetTextResult`? Earlier examples left them empty. What goes into the parentheses is the identifying number for the operation. If you leave the parentheses empty, Shockwave assumes you are interested in the latest command, so if you are performing only one operation, you won't need a number. But if you are loading four text files, you need to be able to access all four, not just the last one.

By putting the identifier into those parentheses, you can access any of the last four operations. Suppose that you have initiated four `GetNetText` commands and you want to find out when they are all completed. You could use the following Lingo to check each one:

```
on exitframe
➥if netdone(1)=true then put nettextresult(1) into field "textone"
➥if netdone(2)=true then put nettextresult(2) into field "texttwo"
➥if netdone(3)=true then put nettextresult(3) into field "textthree"
➥if netdone(4)=true then put nettextresult(4) into field "textfour"
go to the frame
end
```

In the preceding example, if the particular operation is finished, the results are put into four different text fields. Note that the frame will continually loop, even after all four operations are finished, so you need a button that can jump to another part of the movie.

> **Caution**
>
> Remember, each operation has a unique identifier. The previous Lingo example will work only once! Any operations after the first four will have higher ID numbers, so your next four commands issued will have identifiers of 5, 6, 7, and 8. You'll soon learn how to determine the latest ID number by using `GetLatestNetID`.
>
> Also note that information for network operations will be discarded when new operations are started. Only the last four operations remain in memory, so when six operations have been completed, only ID numbers 3, 4, 5, and 6 will be able to return information.

GetLatestNetID()

You may decide to keep track of the operation identifiers yourself, perhaps by using a global variable that you set to increment with every network command. But a better way to keep track of the current operation number is to use the `GetLatestNetID()` function.

> **Note**
>
> You will notice that there are parentheses after the `GetLatestNetID()` command, but the command doesn't take a parameter because it always returns the *last* operation number. The parentheses are necessary for Shockwave to understand that it's a network command, but it ignores anything you put into them.

Suppose that I want to set a local variable, x, equal to the last operation number. Then I want to check to see if the last operation is finished. Perhaps this is put into a handler named "checkdone" that I call periodically from another part of the movie. It could look like this:

```
on checkdone
    set x=getlatestnetid()
    if netdone(x) then put nettextresult(x) into field "results"
end checkdone
```

The preceding example isn't really useful because I could have just used `netdone()` with nothing in the parentheses to check the latest operation. But maybe you have issued four operations and want to check the last four. Instead of using specific numbers, you can use a variable. Your handler might look like this:

```
on checkdone
    set x=getlatestnetid()
        if netdone(x) then put nettextresult(x) into field "fourth"
```

```
      if netdone(x-1) then put nettextresult(x-1) into field "third"
    ➥if netdone(x-2) then put nettextresult(x-2) into field "second"
    ➥if netdone(x-3) then put nettextresult(x-3) into field "first"
    ➥ end checkdone
```

This is a bit more complex. If the last operation ID is 12, then the four state-ments will check using 12 (x), 11 (x-1), 10 (x-2), and 9 (x-3). If each is done, it will put the results into four separate text fields. This same handler could then be used no matter what the latest ID number is.

Note

You use only two commands in multiple operations: `GetNetText` and `PreloadNetThing`. They work slightly differently. When `PreloadNetThing` is fin-ished downloading, you can issue another preload command immediately. But `GetNetText` requires that you use the `NetTextResult()` command before it re-leases its "spot" for a new operation. So if you issue four `GetNetText` commands but don't retrieve the text using `NetTextResult`, your four operations are still consid-ered active. By issuing *another* `GetNetText` command, you will cause the latest ID number to increase; however, the operation will not occur. Therefore, you will have unretrieved information in ID locations 1, 2, 3, and 4, and your latest ID number will be 5. This can throw off your Lingo scripts and can be confusing. Be sure you use `NetTextResult` to retrieve the text information and allow a new operation.

Targeting Frames with *GoToNetPage*

Certain browsers that allow separate scrollable windows on the same page use frames. You may have incorporated into your Web page design frames that you want to use with Shockwave's `GoToNetPage` command.

`GoToNetPage "url"` will leave your current page and load a new one. But with an extra parameter, you can target one particular frame on the page. So, your Shockwave movie could stay in one frame, while `GoToNetPage` switches the URL of another frame. Here is the syntax:

```
      gotonetpage "http://www.server.com/page.html", framename
```

Let's look at an example from the CD-ROM. In Netscape or another frames-capable browser, load *framed.html*. In the left frame, there is an embedded Shockwave movie with three options. When you choose one, it causes a new HTML page to load into the right frame. The Shockwave movie stays in the left frame without changing. This is very useful for navigation movies so that you always have certain options in one frame, and the Web page content can change in a different frame.

Figure 14.1 shows the framed HTML document. You can see that we have named our two frames "left" and "right."

The movie is embedded into the HTML document called "left.html" that is put into the frame called "left."

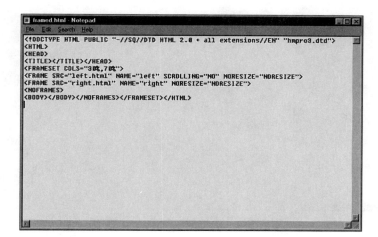

Figure 14.1
The HTML setting up our framed page.

In Director, we set up three buttons with Lingo scripts to call a new HTML page in the right frame. The second button, for example, looks like this:

```
on mouseup
    gotonetpage "two.html", "right"
end
```

This button will load the HTML document called "two.html" and it will target the frame named "right." Our movie continues to run because the HTML document in the left frame has not changed. Figure 14.2 shows this example in the browser.

Note

Targeting frames with GoToNetPage is only recognized by the Shockwave version 5 plug-in. The version 4 plug-in will ignore the target and load the new page in the same frame that the movie is playing in.

Figure 14.2

Targeting a different frame using `GoTo NetPage`.

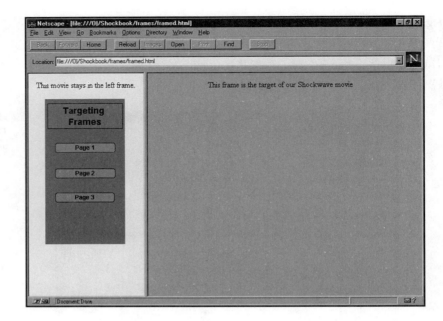

External Parameters

External parameters are strings of information that are passed to the Shockwave movie from the embed tag in the HTML document. External parameters were not an original feature of Shockwave, but are a valuable addition.

How are they used? Let's say you have a movie that uses the `GoToNetPage` command to switch Web pages. When you created the movie, your Web page to be loaded was named *page2.html* so you wrote the Lingo command as `GoToNetPage` *"page2.html."* However, you later changed your mind and re-named the HTML document for the second page to be *newp2.html.* Your Shockwave movie now does not work because the Lingo script uses the wrong file name for the new Web page. You have to go back into Director, change the Lingo command, save and Afterburn the movie, then upload the new version to your server.

Using external parameters, you can avoid problems like this that result from changing information. The solution to the above example would include an external parameter that is specified in the embed tag of the HTML document. You would pass a string to the movie that names the second Web page. Lingo reads the external parameter, knows what the name of the page is, and consequently puts the name into a variable used in the `GoToNetPage` command. By changing the name in the embed tag, the same Lingo script always uses the correct file name in the `GoToNetPage` command.

Specifying the Parameters in the Embed Tag

External parameters are listed just like the file name, height, width, and other information about the movie. For example, to use an external parameter named "sw1" that contains a string of information, you could use the following embed statement in your HTML document:

```
<embed src="movie.dcr" height=250 width=125 sw1="External
➥information goes here.">
```

The information contained in the *sw1* parameter could then be used within the Shockwave movie. Perhaps you want to put it into a variable or display it in a text field. The next section describes the Lingo used to retrieve the information.

Accessing the External Parameters

To access an external parameter in the movie, use the Lingo command `externalParamValue(n)`, where n is the name of the parameter. Continuing the example from above, the following Lingo handler would put the value of parameter *sw1* into a text field named "mywords."

```
on getx
    put externalParamValue("sw1") into field "mywords"
end
```

In the `externalParamValue(n)` statement, n could also be an integer instead of a string. As an integer, it returns the value associated with the *nth* parameter. So `externalParamValue(3)` would return the value of the third parameter.

Determining the Name of a Parameter

If you're not sure what parameters the embed tag uses, you can determine the name of a particular parameter by using another Lingo command: `externalParamName(n)`. So the following statement would put the name of the fifth parameter into a variable called "name5":

```
set name5=externalParamName(5)
```

If the embed tag had a fifth parameter called "swText," the above Lingo statement would set the variable "name5" equal to the string "swText."

Counting the Total Number of Parameters

To find out how many total parameters the embed tag contains, use the Lingo `externalParamCount()`. The parentheses are needed, though nothing is put in them. The following Lingo statement would set a variable called "ptotal" equal to the total number of parameters in the embed tag:

```
Set ptotal=externalParamCount()
```

Valid Parameter Names

Macromedia has issued a list of possible parameter names that you may use. These are simply suggestions for useful parameters. You can make up any name for a parameter as long as it does not have another purpose (the "src" parameter for example). Here is the list Macromedia provides:

swURL

swText

swForeColor

swBackColor

swFrame

swColor

swName

swPassword

swBanner

swSound

swVolume

swPreloadTime

swAudio

swList

sw1

sw2

sw3

sw4

sw5

sw6

sw7

sw8

sw9

> **Note**
>
> The above parameter names are merely names. You can pass any value you want using those parameters. If you want to use the *swVolume* parameter name to pass the URL of a Web page, that choice is up to you. The names were created by Macromedia to easily correspond to information you might be using.

You can use as many of the above parameters as you like. A possible embed tag could look like this:

```
<embed src="movie.dcr" height=300 width=400 swURL="http://www
➥.pdgroup.com/" swName="audio.sw1" swText="A really great song."
sw1="85" sw4="1">
```

Chapter 18, "Shockwave for Audio," uses external parameters in an example that plays streaming audio files. External parameters are ideal for situations where the same Shockwave movie could be used on different Web pages but performs differently—such as using the same movie to play different audio files depending on what Web page the user is viewing.

Storing User Preferences

This is quite a powerful feature of Shockwave. Macromedia calls it storing "preferences," but it's basically just writing a text file to the user's hard disk. It's useful for storing information that can be retrieved by a different Shockwave movie or the same movie after the user has left and returned to the Web page. You could store information that the user enters the first time he or she loads the movie, then simply load that information automatically for subsequent visits to the Web page.

> **Note**
>
> The text file is not written to the Web server, it's written to the user's computer. You can never be sure how long it will remain there and it is always placed in the *prefs* folder within the Shockwave plug-in directory.

Two Lingo commands are used, one to store the information and one to retrieve it. To store the info use:

```
setpref filename, value
```

The file name is recommended by Macromedia to be eight characters or less. It can have the extension .txt and will automatically be given that extension if none is specified. For example, if I wanted to store the phrase "I like snakes" in a file named "reptile" I could use the following Lingo:

```
setPref "reptile", "I like snakes"
```

The above statement would create a text file named *reptile.txt* and place it in a directory named *prefs* within the Shockwave plug-in folder of their browser.

To retrieve the file name, use the Lingo `getpref(prefname)`. To retrieve the example from above and put it into a text field, you could use:

```
put getpref("reptile.txt") into field "presults"
```

On the CD-ROM, load *pref.html* to see an example of how this works. If it is the first time loading the Shockwave movie (*prefs.dir*), it will ask you a few questions. The responses will be stored in a text file within the plug-ins folder. When the movie is loaded again later, it will retrieve the file and display a message showing the information. Figures 14.3 and 14.4 show the two possible options of the sample movie.

Figure 14.3
Questions are asked the first time the movie is played.

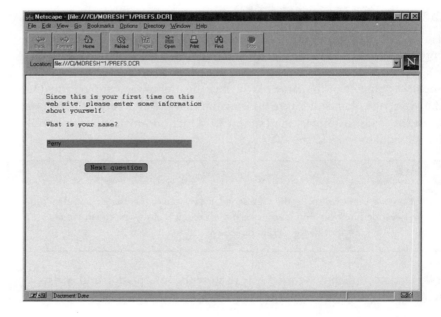

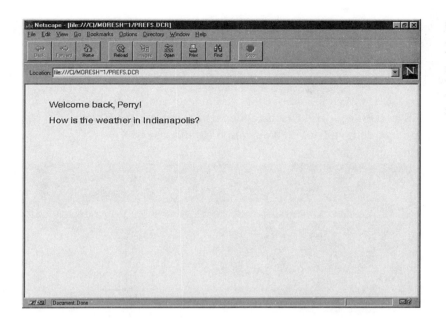

Figure 14.4
At any later time
when the movie
is loaded, the
text file retrieves
the stored
information.

Putting a Message in the Status Bar

The netStatus command is a simple Lingo function that puts a single line of
text into the status bar at the bottom of the browser window. The syntax is:

```
netstatus msg
```

For example, to display "This site is Shocked!" in the status bar, you could use
the following script:

```
on exitframe
    netstatus "This site is Shocked!"
end
```

Currently, this function does not work with Internet Explorer, though it may
change in future versions.

More Information about Network Operations

You can use three other commands to retrieve information about recent operations. These commands probably will not be used as often as NetDone() or

NetTextResult() but may be useful in certain cases. On the CD-ROM, load *GetNet.dir* or *GetNet.dcr* to see some of these commands used. Of course, it won't run from Director, but you can see how it is set up. You can load the HTML document, *Getnet.html,* to view the Shockwave movie also.

Getnet.dir is the same as the *gethttp.dir* file from chapter 16, but it not only loads a text file (or HTML source file), it also displays the ID number, date, error, and done state of each operation (see figure 14.5).

Figure 14.5
A simple Shockwave movie using various network Lingo commands.

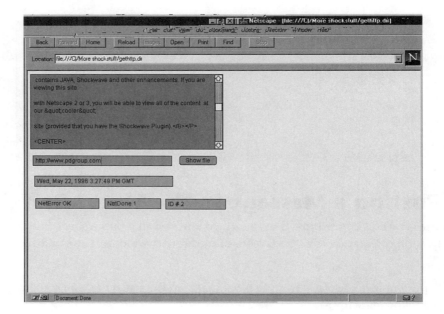

NetError()

NetError() allows you to check whether an operation was successful or not. There are several different responses you can receive from this command as seen in table 14.1.

Table 14.1 *NetError()* Responses	
NetError Response	**Meaning**
None	No operation has been started.
OK	Operation completed successfully.
(nothing)	Operation is not finished yet.
Error	Particular error is identified if the operation fails.

The syntax is just like `NetDone()`. The following Lingo handler puts the error response into a field called "`error`."

```
On checkerror
    put neterror() into field "error"
end checkerror
```

You could also specify a parameter in the parentheses to identify one of the four last operation ID numbers.

> **Note**
>
> You may be expecting an error message if a file is not found on the server. However, many servers send a message that says something like "file [file name] could not be found..." This is sent as an HTML document, so your `GetNetText` command will receive this and think it is the text that you requested. `NetError()` will return "OK" thinking the file was loaded properly. But when you use `NetTextResult` to view the results, you will see the HTML code for the message "`<body>The file could not be found...`"and so on.

NetMIME()

The `NetMIME()` function is used to identify the MIME type of a recent operation. *MIME* stands for *Multipurpose Internet Mail Extension*. Every file type has its own extension: Graphics can be .GIF or .JPEG, Shockwave files can be .DCR or .DIR, text might be .TXT, and so on. The server and browser need to know how to view or use each MIME type. So for Shockwave, any file that has the extension .DCR or .DIR has the MIME type of "Application X / Director."

You may wish to check with Macromedia on using this function. At the time this book was published, `NetMIME` continually reported "`Application X / Director`" as a MIME type for any operation, whether it was loading a Shockwave file or another file type. This could be a bug, or it could simply be reporting the MIME type of the movie that is playing, which will always be "Application X / Director."

NetLastModDate()

Each file on the server has a date and time attached to it when it was last modified. By using `NetLastModDate()`, you can view the last modified time of a file used in a recent network operation.

For example, if you were loading a text file using `GetNetText` that contained information that changed daily, you could have the Shockwave movie display the date and time that the text file was updated so users would know how recent the information is.

The syntax follows the same pattern as NetDone(), NetError, and the others. An identifier can be put in the parentheses or left out for the most recent operation. To put the date into a global variable called "lastdate," you could use the following script:

```
On exitframe
    global lastdate
    set lastdate=netlastmoddate()
end
```

As an example, the returned value put into the variable, "lastdate" could be "Tue, Jun 25, 1996 6:31:44 PM GMT." GMT means the time was converted to Greenwich Mean Time.

From Here...

You have now learned how to use multiple operations, external parameters, and several other Internet Lingo functions. Be sure to watch for updates and new information about Shockwave development on Macromedia's Web site (**http://www.macromedia.com**).

- Chapter 18, "Shockwave for Audio": The basics of using Shockwave Audio.

- Chapter 19, "Shockwave for Authorware": Learn all about Authorware versus Director.

- Chapter 20, "Shockwave for Freehand": Find out about using high-quality vector graphics on your Web Pages.

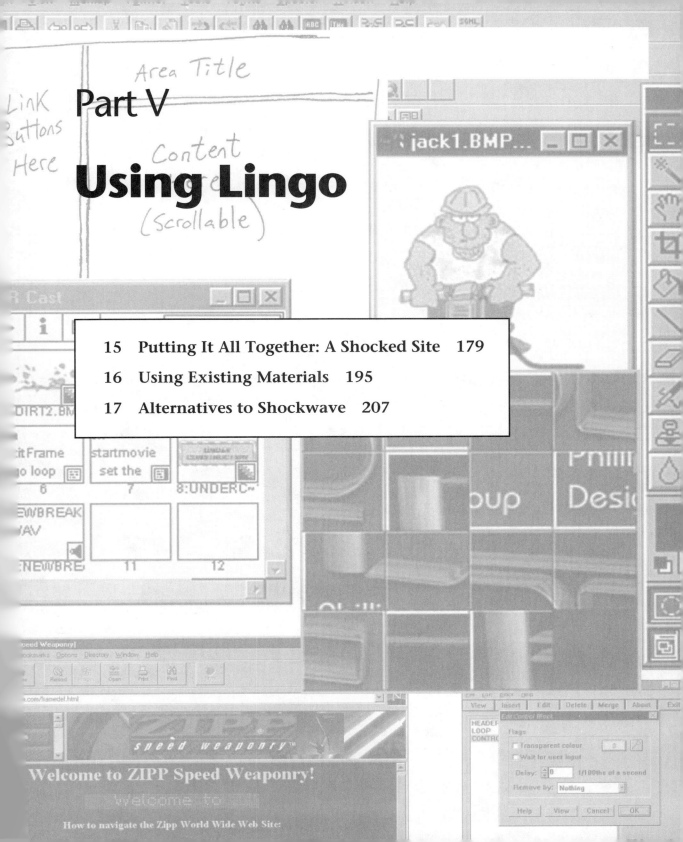

Part V
Using Lingo

Putting It All Together: A Shocked Site

Other chapters have described simple animations for fun, animations to demonstrate a concept, navigation tools, Internet Lingo, advanced Lingo concepts, alternatives to Shockwave, and many other topics.

This chapter takes you through the complete steps of creating a Shocked Web site. It won't describe every step in detail, just enough information to illuminate the process and review some important concepts. You should be able to follow the steps and easily adapt some of the basic ideas to your own site. To look at the example, load the HTML file, *shocked.html* from the chapter 15 directory on the CD-ROM. All of the pieces that go along with this HTML document are in the directory called *site1* within the chapter 15 directory.

What this chapter covers:

- Describes a few example sites that companies are currently using.
- You start with a storyboard—a plan for how the site will be laid out.
- The basic structure is set up. This site divides the page into frames. All of the individual HTML pages are started.
- The Shockwave movies are created and embedded into their proper places.
- The rest of the content is added, though for this site you won't include much detailed information because this is just an example.
- With the basic framework created, you can see how the site could grow deeper.

Current Example Sites

This chapter starts by going through a few example Shockwave sites that are currently out on the Web. You might continually check a variety of sites to get ideas and to see what other developers are creating.

And what better place to start than Macromedia's Web site **(http://www. macromedia.com)**. As the creator of Shockwave, it usually has various Shockwave movies on its site as well as links to other notable Shockwave Web sites.

Figure 15.1 shows Macromedia's opening Web page, which contains a Shockwave movie. It is basically a navigation tool with rollovers for the various areas of the Web site. An animation continually runs while waiting for the user to interact. Notice that Macromedia displays small text links at the bottom of the page to allow the user to quickly locate an area without waiting for the Shockwave movie (or for users who don't have the Shockwave plug-in or a supporting browser).

Figure 15.1

Macromedia's beginning Web page.

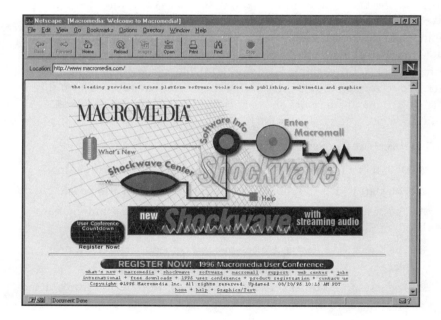

Figure 15.2 is a Shockwave Web site that uses audio streaming. It is promoting the music of Eric Johnson and allows the user to select a song from his

latest CD and listen to it. The Shockwave movie is a sort of "digital stereo" somewhat similar to the one you will find in Chapter 18, "Shockwave for Audio." The digital stereo idea is fast becoming a cliché on Shockwave Web sites, but there is nothing wrong with using it. This Web site uses two frames: one on the left with two navigation buttons and one on the right with the Shockwave movie and some text with other links.

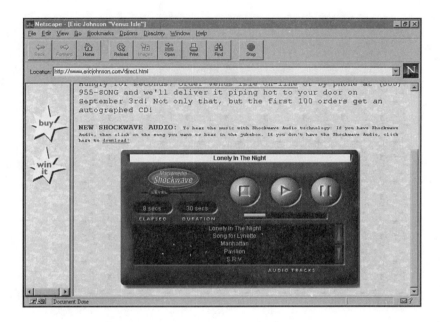

Figure 15.2
A Shockwave for Audio Web site.

V

Using Lingo

Apple Computers use a Quicktime VR effect in their Shockwave home page (figure 15.3). Quicktime VR was developed by Apple as a type of virtual reality interface. The user clicks left and right on an image and it seems to scroll three-dimensionally. The image here is very small, because a larger image would require a longer download time. This Shockwave movie also has buttons on one side to navigate through the Web site.

Campbell's Soup has a few simple animations in the form of Shockwave movies on its Web site (figure 15.4). The images are static until the user rolls the mouse over them, resulting in some elementary motion. Not extremely thrilling in comparison to some other Shockwave Web sites, but still an added dimension to what could be a fairly plain site.

Figure 15.3
Apple's home
page.

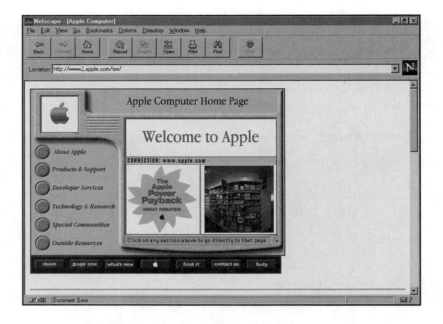

Figure 15.4
Campbell Soup
uses Shockwave as
a navigation tool.

Figure 15.5 shows GM's Shockwave Web site. Using highlighted rollovers, the user knows that the top text items are clickable links. Other Shockwave movies are found throughout the site with animation and sound, while the link rollovers are always available. The Shockwave movies are fairly conservative with more emphasis placed on information and ease of navigation.

Figure 15.5
GM's Shockwave site.

The Storyboard

Storyboards were originally (and still are) used to visualize important scenes in a film, television show, play, and so on. Rough sketches depict key events and basic ideas of the plot. Adopted by the business world, the word "storyboard" can now mean just about any plan for a finished product.

Back to the Old Drawing Board

Good ideas are more valuable than all the RAM chips in the world. Creation of your Web site begins the moment you visualize it in your head. A graphic designer once told me that he wouldn't sit at the computer until he had his ideas worked out on paper. I don't know if I completely agree, because the computer can be an excellent tool to spark ideas, but it is true that you need a plan before you can begin.

V

Using Lingo

To create a Web site, you need to plan the structure and key elements of the site ahead of time. Don't be afraid to get a big pad of paper and a sharp number two pencil and sketch ideas. You may find that your first idea often sounds good, but if you continue to think about more ideas, you come up with something even better than your original concept.

> **Note**
>
> Creating a good Web site takes much hard work, planning, and time. Companies pay thousands of dollars to have their sites created. The sample here is really only the beginning—an example to help you understand the process. By no means is this the "best" Shockwave site, it is merely a tool to demonstrate, help you learn, and give you some ideas of your own.

For this example Web site, it was decided to divide the page into three frames—one on the left with the navigation buttons (home, links, e-mail, and so on), one on the top right with the area title, and a large one below that with the main Web pages containing the actual site content. By using three frames, the user always has access to the links in the left frame and always can see the title of the Web page he or she is viewing. The content in the bottom frame can be scrolled without losing the links and the title. It's easy to go crazy with frames and divide the screen into a maze of boxes, but too many can quickly lead to an impractical Web site. A few well thought out frames can function quite well. Keep in mind that not all users will be capable of viewing frames, so you might decide to have an alternative Web site plan. Figure 15.6 shows the basic layout of this idea.

You will have two Shockwave movies always going at once. One is the navigation movie in the left frame. It will have simple rollover buttons to let the user know that they are clickable. When clicked, each button targets the other two frames to change what is displayed. The other Shockwave movie goes in the top frame and displays the title of the current Web area the user is viewing.

After sketching out a plan for the site (figure 15.7), you're ready to begin construction.

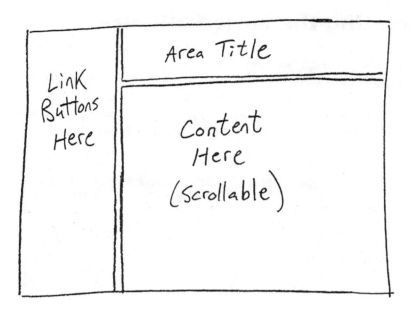

Figure 15.6
The basic layout of our sample Web site.

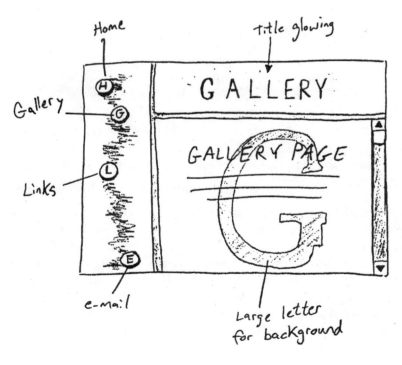

Figure 15.7
A conceptual sketch of the Web site.

Creating the Basic Structure

You need to create two starting HTML documents to set up your screen for the frames. The first HTML page divides the screen into a left and right frame. After a little experimenting, I decided to use 18 percent of the screen for the left frame and 82 percent for the right frame. I named the frames "left" and "right" and put an HTML document in each. In the left frame, I put *left.html* and in the right frame I put *rframe.html*. My starting HTML file, called *shocked.html* can be seen in figure 15.8.

Figure 15.8
The first HTML file that divides the screen into two frames.

The HTML statements important here are the three that define the frames:

```
<FRAMESET cols="18%,82%">
<FRAME SRC="site1/left.html" NAME="left" SCROLLING="NO"
➥NORESIZE="NORESIZE">
<FRAME SRC="site1/rframe.html" NAME="right" NORESIZE="NORESIZE">
```

The first statement above separates the screen into columns, which makes a vertical frame division. Using percentages instead of pixels allows the same statement to work appropriately on any monitor, independent of the video resolution. The second two statements place two other HTML documents into the two frames. They also define the frame names and set a few parameters. I decided that the left frame would not be scrollable because it will only contain the Shockwave movie with Web site links. The *NORESIZE* parameter prevents the viewer from adjusting the frame positions.

Now, to divide the right frame into two more frames (for a total of three) I created the *rframe.html* document (figure 15.9) using 20 percent and 80 percent for the positions. The top frame is named "top" and the bottom frame is named "bottom." This right frame area will be changing, but I started out using the two HTML documents that go with the home page. Notice that neither *shocked.html* nor *rframe.html* contains any actual Web page content; they are used only to set up the site into the three frames.

V

Using Lingo

Figure 15.9
The second HTML document divides the right frame into two more frames.

I planned ahead to name everything that goes in the top *something-glow.html* because the titles glow. And everything in the bottom frame is called *something-main.html* because that is the frame for the main content. So, the two HTML files for the home page are *homeglow.html* and *homemain.html*. These are empty HTML documents for now, but you have the basic structure set up and you're ready to create and assemble the pieces.

Creating the Shockwave Movies

Each area of the Web site will have a different Shockwave movie displaying the title. These will be put into the top frame. You need to create four separate movies: *Home*, *Gallery*, *Links*, and *E-mail*.

The movies are quite simple. The blurred letters were created in Photoshop by placing text on a black background then using a blur filter. Each letter was separated as an individual cast member and placed on a black background in Director. By "in-betweening" their sprite blend values, you make each letter fade in and out to give the appearance that the letters glow one by one. Figure 15.10 shows one of the glowing movies in Director.

Figure 15.10
Using sprite
blends to make
the letters glow.

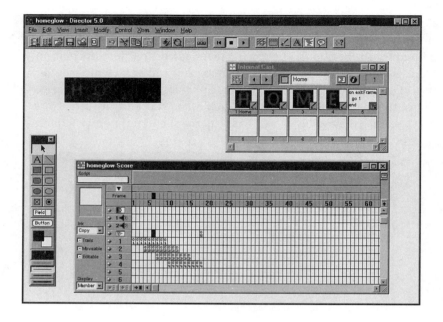

These movies are named the same as the HTML document that will contain them: *homeglow.dir, gallglow.dir, linkglow.dir,* and *mailglow.dir.* Naming the movies this way helps you to remember what movie goes on what page. With only four pages of movies it isn't too bad, but it can easily get confusing to have to remember a lot of file names.

Those four movies all are very small (under 5K) so that the user doesn't have a long download time when switching between sections. The other movie is a bit larger (27K), but only needs to load once, then stays in the left frame. It contains four buttons that navigate through the Web site. I created a background graphic, rollover, and click states for each of the buttons. The three states of the graphics are shown in figure 15.11.

The first graphic was imported into Director and placed on a black background. The rollover and click state images were also imported but were broken into individual cast members for each of the buttons. The rollover and click state cast members were placed in the score over the top of the background image in eight sprite channels (four for the rollover images, and four for the click images). The eight sprites were turned invisible using a Lingo script:

```
on exitFrame
  repeat with x=2 to 9
    set the visible of sprite x to false
  end repeat
end
```

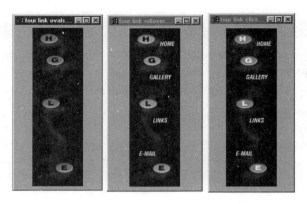

Figure 15.11
The graphics used
in the navigation
movie before being
split apart as cast
members.

You learned in other chapters how to work with rollovers and mouse clicks.
A looping frame script controls the rollovers of the four sprites by setting
them visible or invisible depending on the mouse location. For each of the
four buttons, there are two Lingo statements that need to execute to load
new HTML documents in the top and bottom frames on the right side of the
screen. The script for the "links" button, for example, looks like this:

```
on mousedown
   set the visible of sprite 8 to true
   puppetsound "robot"
   updatestage
end

on mouseup
   set the visible of sprite 8 to false
   updatestage
   gotonetpage "linkmain.html," "bottom"
   gotonetpage "linkglow.html," "top"
end
```

The statements that set the sprite visible or invisible are what control the
appearance of the button when it's clicked (it turns orange). A puppetsound
command plays a sound effect when the button is pressed. The two statements in the mouseup handler are what control the changing of the other
frames. Using the gotonetpage command, new HTML documents are targeted
to the other frames, called "bottom" and "top." See chapters 13 and 14, "Internet Lingo for Shockwave" and "Further Use of Internet Lingo," respectively, for more on using network Lingo.

The other three buttons are set up the same way—loading appropriate HTML
documents to the two frames.

V

Using Lingo

> **Note**
>
> It would have been nice to have the "e-mail" button bring up the mail window of the browser. I tried using this Lingo command:
>
> ```
> gotonetpage "mailto:pdg@ix.netcom.com"
> ```
>
> The mail window did come up, but the `gotonetpage` command inserts a slash into the address line so it reads, "/pdg@ix.netcom.com," which would not mail properly. `Getnettext` seemed to do the same thing. Perhaps future versions of Shockwave will change this. If you find a way around it let me know! Our work around here is to load a whole new HTML page in the bottom window with e-mail links. At least there is a benefit to that because more than one address can be made available.

The navigation movie, called *nav.dcr* is embedded into the *left.html* document. It is put onto a black background so the bounding rectangle isn't visible.

```
<html>
<body bgcolor=000000>
<center>
<embed src="nav.dcr" height=400 width=96>
</center>
</body>
</html>
```

The other four movies are embedded into their respective HTML documents. For an example, here is the gallery movie embedded. It looks very similar to the other embed statement.

```
<html>
<body bgcolor=000000>
<center>
<embed src="gallglow.dir" height=50 width=224>
</center>
</body>
</html>
```

Our main Shockwave movies are now complete. Others may be used in the content area (the "bottom frame") but for this example we are finished. Now we can work on the HTML documents for the bottom frame.

Backgrounds

The plan is to have large letters as the background image for the content areas. By using big areas of flat color and saving the images as 3-bit GIFs, the file size is very small even though the images are huge in physical dimensions (figure 15.12). Remember that the GIF format compresses images just like Afterburner compresses Director movies. Each of the letters ended up being only about 5K.

In the HTML document for each page, I couldn't just use a normal `<img src= "filename">` tag because my text could not flow over the top of it. Using the `<body background= "filename">` tag makes a tiled background, but I only wanted one big letter. So I created the image with a large area of blank space around the letter so the next tile wouldn't be visible. Depending on how much text and other items are placed over the background, it would have tiled eventually, but the example doesn't go very far down the page. If there were more items, you would either have to live with the tile or make the background image have even more blank space below the letter.

Figure 15.12
Using a lot of blank space spreads the tiles apart, but it compresses well because it's a flat color.

Content

The content is pretty bare bones in this example. There are just a few sentences on each page to describe the area and give you an idea of what could be put there. It wouldn't help your purposes to fill the pages with information, anyway. Figure 15.13 is called "The finished Web site" but it's really just a basic framework—you can see how more depth can be added.

Figure 15.13
The finished
Web site.

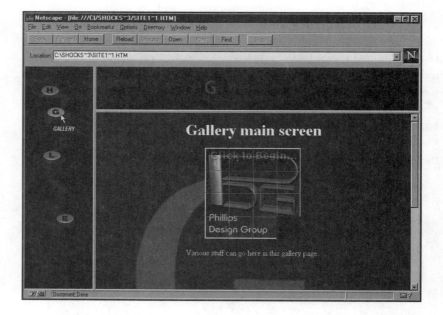

Note that the "gallery" section contains another Shockwave movie. It's a small slider game where the player has to rearrange the squares into the proper positions; you'll find this movie in the gallery at the end of this book. Having this Shockwave movie on the page means that there are three running at one time. It seems to work fine on my computer, but someone with a slower machine might have more trouble. Macromedia doesn't recommend running more than a few at a time. Feel free to push the limits, but be aware that some viewers might not appreciate it.

For Non-Shocked Visitors

This example will only be visible to viewers with a frames-capable browser and the Shockwave plug-in. Though Netscape Navigator and Microsoft's Internet Explorer are the most popular browsers and support these features, there are many browsers that do not. For people using those browsers, you may decide to have a starting Web page that gives the option of enhanced or nonenhanced. The enhanced version loads your Shockwave site, while the nonenhanced uses only basic HTML pages.

If you don't want to give the option to the user, you might choose to have a tiny movie on a basic Web page that contains a `GoToNetPage` command to load the Shockwave page. If the browser doesn't support Shockwave, nothing happens and they stay on the basic page with normal links. If the user does have Shockwave, the enhanced site will automatically load via the `GoToNetPage` command. See chapter 13, "Internet Lingo for Shockwave" for more on this idea.

From Here...

You have learned about all of the pieces of a Shockwave Web site and you have seen them put together. By this point, you should have a very good idea of how a Shocked site can be designed. But the real fun begins when you come up with your own ideas and your own creations. Hopefully, this book gives you a starting point and the fundamentals you need to Shock your Web presence:

- Chapter 16, "Using Existing Materials": Shows how to use and modify existing material for Shockwave.
- Chapter 17, "Alternatives to Shockwave": Alternatives and the techniques to use.
- Chapter 18, "Shockwave for Audio": Shows you how to use audio compression and streaming in your Shockwave movies.
- Chapter 19, "Shockwave for Authorware": Who should use Authorware, and how it's different from Director.
- Chapter 20, "Shockwave for Freehand": Learn how to use Afterburner Xtra and embed the Shocked Freehand file.

V

Using Lingo

CHAPTER 16

Using Existing Materials

A few weeks ago, my fiancée and I met with the harpist who will be playing in our wedding. We didn't have any idea what we wanted for music in the ceremony, so we asked her for some suggestions. She sat down at the harp and immediately began strumming through various songs that she already knew. Within a few minutes, we had picked out a few that we liked, and the rest of our meeting could be spent throwing a tennis ball for her big dog.

I suppose you'd like to know how this relates to Shockwave. Well, the tennis ball doesn't. But the harpist's repertoire does. Imagine if she had to learn all new songs every time she performed—every job would be a lot of work for her. But by having a group of songs that she is already familiar with, she may hardly even need to practice. Similarly, you may have a lot of existing material that can be used for Shockwave; so instead of completely building from scratch, you can use what you already have.

This chapter covers using and modifying your existing materials to be put on the Web:

- Using existing graphic images
- Modifying your CD-ROM or Kiosk projects
- Reducing frame rate and size of existing animations
- Reducing or eliminating audio
- Cutting or modifying content

Using Existing Graphics

Let's say you have a standard logo that is used on all of your printed materials: brochures, business cards, letterhead and envelopes, and so on. Before it can be used on the Web, you will need to make some modifications.

Resolution

Printed images need to be high resolution. Your average home laser printer can be 300 or 600 dots per inch (dpi). This allows for relatively smooth curves for detailed graphics. Remember dot-matrix printers? They are still around, but more for economy than graphics quality. Low resolution output results in choppy, jagged edges. See figure 16.1.

Figure 16.1
Low-resolution images show more jagged pixels than high-resolution images.

Professional output is very high resolution—often 1000-2000 dpi. This doesn't mean the images are scanned at 1000 dpi. Actually, most color photos are scanned and output at a resolution of 300 dpi; but higher resolution output means more accurate control of halftones and crisp, clean text. We won't go into details of the printing process, but the point here is that graphics must be fairly high resolution for high-quality printed work.

On-screen graphics, however, are low resolution. There's not much that can be done about it—your computer monitor displays images at a resolution of 72 dots per inch and no more. An image that is higher than 72 dpi doesn't appear more sharp or clear, it simply appears larger. This is because on-screen images are measured in pixels, not inches.

A printed image may be set at 5 inches wide. If it is 300 dpi, it will be smooth; if it's 72 dpi, it will be rough—but it will stay 5 inches wide when printed. In contrast, an on-screen graphic as displayed on a Web page is measured in pixels. A 5-inch image at 300 dpi is 1500 dots wide, which appears larger than a 5-inch image at 72 dpi—a total width of 360 pixels.

> **Note**
>
> Dots per inch on a computer screen is not necessarily an actual measurement of the number of pixels in an inch of space. A 14-inch monitor can be set to the same resolution as a 21-inch monitor, though one will appear much larger than the other. The size of the pixels changes depending on the physical size of the monitor. Similarly, a monitor in 640 by 480 mode will have larger pixels than a monitor set to 800 by 600 mode—the actual monitor size does not change, just the number of pixels used.

Enough math; your printed image is too big to be used for Shockwave. Because the computer screen is most often set for 640 pixels wide by 480 pixels high, the image needs to be reduced to that size—and actually needs to be smaller because the browser frame takes up part of the screen. You can't be sure whether people have their monitors set for 640 by 480 or 800 by 600 so it is best to be safe with the lower resolution.

Transforming the existing graphic can be as simple as opening the image in Photoshop and changing the image size to be within 640 by 480 pixels. Sometimes you may have a logo that is in another format and needs to be converted. Postscript output (.EPS) allows vector data to be used, such as curves, lines, angles, and so on, to draw the image at high resolutions. But Shockwave requires bit-map images. This may require you to use an illustration program to load the vector image, then export it as a bit-map file type.

Color Depth

As mentioned throughout the book, if anything can be displayed in a lower bit-depth, it is a great advantage for Shockwave. You might have some small images that look nice in 8-bits, but are not noticeably different as 1-bit images. If you are using 16-bit images, they definitely need to be reduced to 8-bits. Authoring using 16-bit images is fairly rare anyway.

Figures 16.2 through 16.6 compare the same image displayed in 16-, 8-, 4-, 3-, and 1- bit versions. You can see how quality is sacrificed as bit-depth is reduced. For many animation purposes, however, the motion and sound make up for lost color quality.

Figure 16.2
16-bit

Figure 16.3
8-bit

Figure 16.4
4-bit

Figure 16.5
3-bit

Figure 16.6
1-bit

Color palettes take up space, too. I recently viewed a CD-ROM project that the user moves around a 3-D world where every screen has a different color palette. It looked great having a custom palette for each view since the 256 colors were optimized for that particular image. But in Director, each custom palette is over 2K. A few is all right, but a dozen adds up quickly.

If your images already use a variety of palettes, consider creating one palette that contains most of the colors you need, then map every image to the same palette. Not only does this shrink size a bit, it makes things easier on your transitions between movie segments because you won't experience a palette flash.

Going from CD-ROM or Kiosk to the Internet

If you are used to authoring for CD-ROMs or Kiosks, you will feel like a giant boa constrictor is squeezing the very life out of your work. You no longer have 600 megabytes to fill with full screens, video clips, and sound effects. Someday, you probably will have 600 megabytes that can be downloaded quickly, but until then you'll have to do with only a few hundred kilobytes at most.

Chapter 4, "Considerations for the Internet," mentions ways of keeping file size small as you create for the Internet. Transforming your CD-ROM project follows the same rules.

Bigger is Not Better

Not only do you need to leave room on the screen for the browser controls, you probably don't even need to fill the available window. A physically small movie can be just as effective as a large one, and will most likely save on download time.

So what if your screens are already created to be 640 by 480? You have two options: Reduce the size or crop the image.

If you want everything in its same location, only smaller, you can use Photoshop to reduce the image size. Director can scale an image smaller using the `transform bit map` command, but I have found that Photoshop often does a better job—particularly if you have the original high color images to work with.

> **Tip**
>
> If you decide to shrink images, you will need to make sure that everything is scaled down equally. You may choose a new pixel size (instead of 640 pixels wide, you make it 400 pixels wide) but a better way is to use percentages. This way, you can scale all of your objects the same amount (60% for example). So if the original is 640 pixels wide or if the original is 349 pixels wide, the new size of both images will be in proportion.

If you find you have a lot of open space in your screen designs, you may want to crop or rearrange the screens. Cropping is an easy step—you just cut away the unnecessary areas around the edges. But if you have open areas within the image and want to rearrange the layout (where buttons are located, and so on), you will have more work to do. If your buttons are independent cast members in Director, this is fairly easy. But if they are created as a part of the background, you might not be able to move them as easily.

I recently had to redesign a game for Shockwave. The original size was a bit too tall, so parts of it were covered by the browser. If the user selected to hide the location and toolbar, it would all fit; or if the video display was set for 800 × 600 it would fit, but I couldn't count on either of those, so I rearranged a few things to squeeze it down. The game is seen in the Example Gallery in Appendix A (the trivia hurdles game).

Modifying Existing Animations

If you are using a 3-D graphics package or another tool to create animations, consider size and frame rate as you create the animation. Some software is easier than others to use to modify this.

You might think you need 15 frames per second to accurately represent the animation. But try it at 10, or even lower. The fewer the frames you have, the smaller the file size it is.

I recently wanted to modify an animation that we used on a CD-ROM so that it could be made into a Shockwave movie. I asked the person who created it to make a scaled down version of it. Without much difficulty, he exported only a few frames at a reduced size. After importing the frames to Director, I had a smaller version of the same animation at a slower frame rate. It still looked OK and was much smaller for download time.

Reducing Audio

Audio is a killer when it comes to file size. If you don't need the sound, go ahead and take it out completely. But some sounds are worth keeping to enhance the Shockwave movie. The easiest way to reduce their size is to modify their format. Change all the sounds to 8-bit, 11.025 kHz. If that sounds too terrible, use 8-bit, 22.050 kHz.

Be sure to check the audio in a sound utility. Sometimes there is a short amount of silence before or after the actual sound. You might not hear it, but it can make the file size of the sound larger than it has to be.

If music can be looped, definitely do so. If it can't, it might be best to leave it out completely. A few seconds of a tune might not be worth the wait for the end user.

For longer audio clips, you can use streaming audio. You will need SoundEdit 16 to create a special file format to be used over the Web. Chapter 18, "Shockwave for Audio," covers this process more thoroughly.

MIDI is not currently supported by Shockwave. It would be efficient for file size, but may be difficult to predict the user's configuration of MIDI instruments. There may be other MIDI utilities that function over the Internet that could be used in addition to Shockwave. Being able to utilize a variety of audio and video options is a definite benefit to any Web site or multimedia project.

Content

You were hoping I wouldn't mention this. There are few things worse than having to cut out some of the content of your existing material. It's like putting a hacked-up version on the Internet, leaving out large parts of your hard labor.

You are often going to have to cut out entire parts of your project that are not absolutely necessary. You will have to evaluate every animation, button click, rollover, image, sound effect, and so on, to determine if it is necessary for the "Shocked" version of the movie. You know what you intend to offer and you know what your audience expects. If it doesn't fit completely, leave it out. People will be very annoyed to download a big movie full of stuff they don't want to see.

You might consider breaking the content of your project into pieces. Give the Internet users the choice of which segment to see. Then users can just download the content that interests them without having to spend forever loading a lot of information that they have no desire to view.

Cutting content implies that your original project contained a lot of information. You might reconsider whether Shockwave is the way to go for your project. Shockwave for the Internet is still limited enough that it is not practical as a major information tool. You might just have selected elements enhanced through Shockwave, with most information in normal Web pages.

Shockwave for Intranets (using Director or Authorware) may be more useful for high-content projects. Of course, you know whether your project is designed to be viewed on an Intranet or on the Internet.

An Example Transformation

Figure 16.7 shows a screen from an existing CD-ROM project, a marketing CD for ZIPP bicycles. The project is not included on your CD-ROM, but you probably can imagine how it would work. The original work was a full-screen, interactive project with audio announcing possible choices and video clips introducing each area. This particular section used .AVI files with animations of the bicycle tires separated into pieces. The user presses one of the three buttons at the bottom of the screen to switch between the types of tires and read information while watching the videos and listening to the audio clips.

Even this one small section of the CD-ROM would be far too big to use as a Shockwave movie, so it must be modified. I decided that I would create separate HTML pages for each of the three tires. This means the user doesn't need to load the information for all three tires at once, which will help with download time.

My first step was to break the large image into pieces. The text was originally created as a bit-map image in Photoshop, but I could just use normal text in Director or as part of the HTML document. I separated the "Tires" title to be it's own image which can be displayed on the Web page as a .GIF or .JPG image. The buttons used to select each tire are cropped as .GIF images and will be set up as links to other Web pages with the other tire types. Figure 16.8 shows the images that were cut out of the original project to be used in the Web page.

Figure 16.7
An original CD-ROM project that must be modified for use in Shockwave.

I eliminated the audio voice that announces the menu options. This can be done with text just as easily. The video that introduced the tires section can also be eliminated—it's a great addition to a CD-ROM project, but simply not practical for a Shockwave application.

The only other major elements were the animations of the tires. You may remember this example from Chapter 7, "Animations to Demonstrate or Teach"—the peel-away diagram. The original CD-ROM used an .AVI file created from an animation in 3-D Studio. But to adapt it to Shockwave, we needed to make it much smaller. Instead of using linked media (such as a video clip) we exported only 12 frames from the animation. These images were then imported into Director to be animated together internally. The text labeling the diagram was created using Director's text tool.

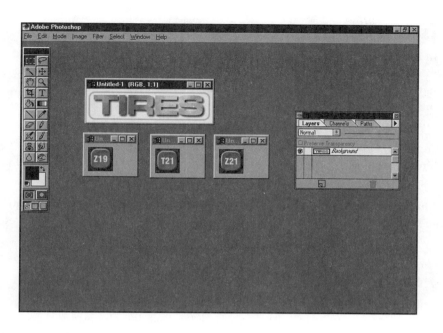

Figure 16.8
Graphics cropped from the original project.

Figure 16.9 shows the pieces compiled into a Web page. This is only one of three pages, but the other two are very similar. The only part of the page that really needed Shockwave was the animation. The text was easily typed as part of the HTML document. The title and link buttons were cropped from the original CD-ROM image.

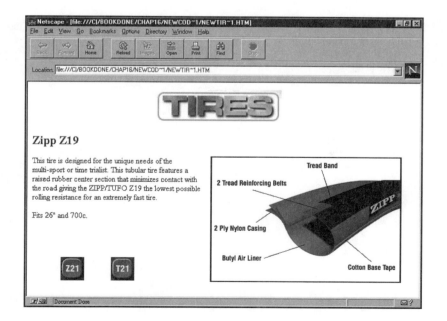

Figure 16.9
The Shocked version of part of the CD-ROM project.

Is It Worth the Effort?

In certain cases, you will need to ask yourself, "Is it really worth the effort to modify my existing material, or should I start over?" You might find that to reduce image sizes, sounds, animation frames, and whatever else, is just as much work as it is to completely start over and create a new movie from the ground up.

Sometimes you might like to take a movie and re-create it. Because I have already created it once, I know exactly what I need and I can really streamline the process to create the most efficient version of the same idea.

Much of the creation process may be conceptual, anyway. Once you have an idea and know how the pieces must fit together, it is often fairly simple to re-create a few graphics and construct a new movie.

From Here...

You may find that it is more practical to design new movies for Shockwave than it is to modify your existing material. But that doesn't mean you can't take pieces and parts from other projects and use them in your new movies.

- Chapter 17, "Alternatives to Shockwave": Offers some alternatives, such as Java, Real Audio, and others. You may find that you can achieve similar effects through other methods on the Internet.
- Chapter 18, "Shockwave for Audio": You learn to use Shockwave's audio compression and streaming functions.
- Shockwave for Authorware and Freehand are covered in Chapters 19 and 20, respectively.

CHAPTER 17

Alternatives to Shockwave

Shockwave is a great tool for creating a dynamic Web site. The biggest drawback that Shockwave, and consequently everything else on the Web, suffers from though, is bandwidth. The other thing is that the end user needs to install the Shockwave plug-in in order to see the movies. This can be seen as a drawback because not everybody who uses the Internet knows what a plug-in is. While veteran users are familiar with the requirements, new users may be confused and might not be capable of actually downloading and installing the plug-in on their systems.

So, if you are targeting a demographic that consists of "Internet Newbies," or are planning on creating HTML documents for a larger Intranet whose users will have to install the driver on every single system, you may want to consider some alternatives. If you add to this the fact that embedding more than one movie to a page is not recommended, the need for an alternative is even greater. Here are some of the options available that this chapter explores:

- Animated GIFs (Multi-Image GIFs)
- Java
- Real Audio
- Movie File Formats (.MOV, .AVI, .MPEG)

Bear in mind that these "alternatives" do not replace the easy customization, ease of use, or advanced interactivity that is responsible for making Shockwave as popular as it is (besides the fact that there was and still is a large user base of Director users before Shockwave was available). But there may be certain applications of Shockwave that can be just as easily done in other ways, and knowing when to use one or the other is the mark of a good Web page designer.

Animated GIFs

First, a look at the seemingly not-so-powerful-but-frequently-used GIF. Many people are not aware that the GIF 89a specification for the GIF file format allows for multiple images to be embedded within the file. Also, it is possible to control the placement as well as the transition times from one image to the other. This means that you can have a navigation bar, for example, that has smaller images embedded within that file that change from one to the other, while relevant information on the navigation bar's controls remain static. Add a client-side image map to this example and you have something that's dynamic and takes less time to download than a comparable Shockwave movie. An extra bonus is that browsers that support animated GIFs but not Shockwave will see your animation. Concerning GIFs, here are a few things to consider:

> Compatibility
>
> Building an Animated GIF
>
> Extra Features of GIF Construction Set

The downside is that, like Shockwave, Netscape 2.0 and above are currently some of a handful of browsers that take advantage of the extra information that the GIF89a file format can contain. Another browser that recognizes animated GIFs is Microsoft's Internet Explorer, which actually supports more features of the GIF 89a file format than any of the Netscape browsers.

As these two browsers are the two most popular browsers being used (accounting for well over 75 percent of the market), you can be sure that the time you spend creating your animated GIF won't be in vain.

> **Tip**
>
> In the event a browser doesn't recognize animated GIFs, only the first image of that GIF is displayed. If you make sure that the first image does not rely on the other elements to make sense, you will have a built-in work around for non-compatible browsers.

Building an animated GIF is an easy thing to accomplish as long as you have the right tools. The tool of choice is Alchemy Mindwork's GIF Construction Set (**http://www.mindworkshop.com/alchemy/alchemy.html**). A 32-bit version is available for Windows 95 and NT and is included on the CD-ROM.

Creating an Animated GIF

GIF Construction Set has been updated with some cool new features. One of them is an "Animation Wizard." In Windows 95, "Wizards" will take you, step-by-step, through some processes, asking you relative questions on the way. When you're done, you'll have your finished product as the "Wizard" uses the answers you supplied to do the work for you. While this makes it incredibly simple for new users to create an Animated GIF, more advanced users will prefer getting their hands dirty so that they may have more control. The "Animation Wizard" is available from the "File" menu. Below, you'll do everything by hand.

Now you're going to take an animation created in Director, export it as a series of BMP files, and create an Animated GIF. The images used in this and succeeding tutorials are located on the CD-ROM under the "tutor/anim" directory. The reasons behind using Director-created animations will become apparent later on.

After installing GIF Construction Set, click "File" then "New." At this point, all the options necessary to build your GIF are available from the tool bar. The first thing you need to do is insert a "Loop" block. First, click the "Insert" button. You will see several buttons available, but for now, select the "Loop" button.

Next, insert a "Control" block in the same manner that you added a "Loop" block (figure 17.1).

Figure 17.1
Select "Loop" from the insert dialogue.

The "Loop" block specifies how many times the GIF should run through all the "frames" that you will be adding. Although Netscape 2 does not yet support this feature, Microsoft Internet Explorer 3 and Netscape 3 do. By default, they loop indefinitely (2000 times). To change how many times the GIF loops, though, simply double-click the "Loop" block and a dialog with the relevant options appears. Double-clicking any block reveals more information.

The "Control" block (figure 17.2) sets how the image you insert is treated. Double-click it and you see that you can control whether or not there is going to be a transparent area, whether or not it should wait for user input (not yet supported by any browsers), how many milliseconds to wait before proceeding to the next frame, and how it's to be removed by the next frame.

Figure 17.2

The "Control" block dialog.

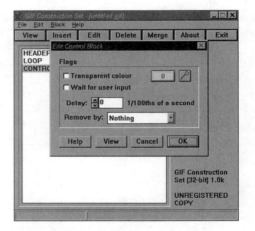

Because you're making a simple animation, insert a time of 30 milliseconds and select "OK." Now you need to insert the frames that you exported from Director.

Note

It's not necessary to convert all your frames to GIFs because the GIF Construction Set supports a wide variety of file formats. Those file formats are: *.ART (PFS: Publisher), *.BMP (Windows Bitmap), *.CUT (Dr. Halo), *.DIB (Windows), *.GIF (Compuserve), *.HRZ (SSTV), *.IFF (Amiga), *.IMG (Ventura), *.LBM (Amiga, Deluxe Paint), *.MAC (MacPaint), *.MSP (Microsoft Paint), *.PCX (PC Paintbrush), and the list goes on…
In this example, though, the frames are already GIFs.

Insert your first frame by selecting the "Insert" button and then selecting "Image." The "Open" dialog then pops up. GIF Construction set allows you to import a series of images, relieving the user of the hassle of importing each frame individually. To do so, locate your frames then select the first frame. Hold the SHIFT button on your keyboard and select the last frame of the animation (figure 17.3) to select all the frames.

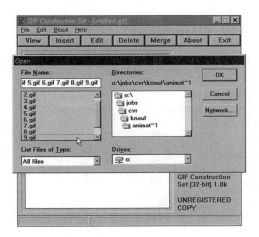

Figure 17.3
Importing a series of images into GIF Construction Set.

Curiously enough, Director is the perfect tool for creating the individual frames for an animated GIF for a couple of reasons. One is that Director excels in cell animations, making it very easy to create a 2-D animation, and the other is that Director exports a movie as a series of BMP files that use the same palette. This is very important if you want your images displayed correctly because at this point, the first frame loads when you select "OK." GIF Construction Set informs you that the image does not match the system palette and presents you with a list of choices.

Because you know that every image has the same palette, select the "Use this image as the global palette" option and select "OK." If the palettes are different, you may have to do some experimenting. Going with your system palette is an easy way to go—just be sure that all your images are remapped to the same palette (figure 17.4).

The next image that loads also triggers the palette dialog. Again, you know that all the frames have the same palette, so this time select, "Use it as it is" and "Use this selection for subsequent images" (figure 17.5).

Figure 17.4
Selecting an
option that
correctly deals
with your image's
palette is crucial
for the correct
display of your
Animated GIF.

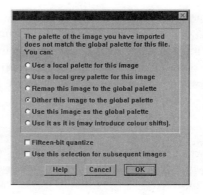

Figure 17.5
Setting the palette
dialog to import
subsequent images
"as is."

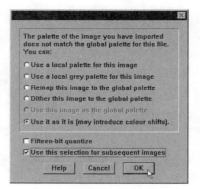

If you are using a series of images that were not created in Director, the palette issue will need to be resolved. Using your system pallete is the easiest way to go. Select "Remap this image to the global palette" as well as "Use this selection for subsequent images." This works most of the time, but if you don't get satisfactory results, experiment with the other settings.

The rest of the frames will be imported according to the settings that you have just made.

If all your frames are the same size, that is, your animation does not consist of a large image with smaller images animating over the top of the first frame, then you are almost done. If you do need to position an image, double-clicking an "Image" block lets you input, in pixels, how far away from the upper left-hand corner the smaller image needs to be.

Look at the main window. Notice that the "Header" block reflects a default image size of 640×480 and that all the frames reflect an image size of 150×136 (figure 17.6).

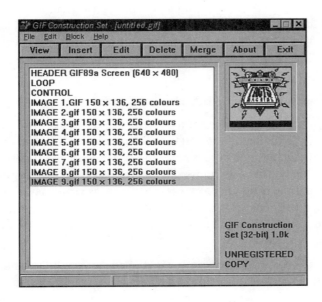

Saving your work now results in an image that is 640×480 pixels in size (the default setting). The size in the "Header" block sets the size of the GIF. Change that dimension so that it matches the dimensions of our frames by double-clicking the "Header" block and changing the sizes accordingly.

One of the last things that you need to do is to insert a "Control" block before every image. Because you already set the first control block, highlight that block, then copy it by pressing Ctrl+C from the keyboard and pasting it (Ctrl+V) before every image.

To preview the animation, click "View." The speed that your animation runs from the "View" option may not reflect how fast it runs inside of a browser, but at this point you may see each frame appear in succession. If everything looks okay, then save your file and place it as you would normally place any GIF into your Web page.

Try not to go overboard on your Animated GIF. Remember that everything on a page competes for bandwith when it comes time for someone to view it.

V

Using Lingo

Keeping the file small and efficient, which is the credo of every Web designer, should be first and foremost on your mind. What's the point of having an 80K Animated GIF, when Shockwave's compression schemes will shrink it down to 30K? Applications for Animated GIFs typically are animated bullets, banners, and small logos. These types of things make sense when implemeting them as a GIF. If your application is something larger, use your best judgement.

Embedding a Java Applet

Another way to add an animation to a Web page is through the use of Java. Of course, as mentioned in the first chapter, programming in Java is not for the faint of heart, but one does not need to be familiar with C++ to take advantage of Java. There are numerous applets (Java programs) available for free downloading off the net from sites that serve as virtual Java libraries of sorts. If you are able to find an applet that accomplishes what you want, then you're in luck. Realistically, this is probably the only way the average person will be able to use Java in his or her Web pages.

As mentioned above, Director can be used to create your 2-D animations; for example, the infamous Animator Java applet. The great thing about this is that the Animator applet merely takes a series of frames or GIFs from a Web server and displays them in sequence so that the question of whether or not each image has the same palette is no longer a concern. The Animator applet is available from one of the best Java resource sites around:

http://www.gamelan.com.

Hundreds of other useful applets are available there as well. A great Java reference published by Que is *Java by Example*.

It takes a while to decipher the documentation that comes with most applets because the creators assume that the person who ends up with his or her applets is computer literate. But, with a little effort and some trial and error, it usually isn't that hard.

Now embed the animator applet into HoTMetaL Pro 3 and animate the same series of GIFs that were used for the previous GIF Animation. After that, do the same in Backstage Designer.

Using HoTMetaL Pro 3 to Embed Java Applets

Once you have HoTMetaL Pro booted up, select the "New Page" button (remember that if you leave the cursor over a button for a couple of seconds, that a description of that button appears), then click the "Paragraph" element button, and lastly, select the icon from the bottom row of buttons (figure 17.7) that resembles a "nice hot cup" of Java.

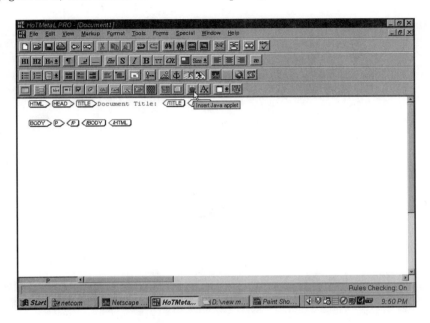

Figure 17.7
Select the Java button from the bottom toolbar.

In the window that pops up, locate the "Animator.class" file and double-click it. Delete the statement that is in the "Alt" field. You can ignore the rest of the fields in the dialog as you will change those parameters as necessary later. Select "OK."

The first thing you need to do is save your new HTML document in the same directory as the "Animator.class" file. Next you need to change the absolute URL that links the applet in your page to a relative link. The link that you now have won't work on a Web server because that link refers to files that are on your computer.

Remember that in the tutorial for embedding Shocked Director movies into HoTMetaL, a right-click anywhere between a start and end tag results in available options for those tags. As you get further into this tutorial, it may be confusing as to where a tag starts or ends as additional tags are inside them. You can try right-clicking immediately to the right of a start tag to be sure that you get the properties for that tag. For now, go ahead and right-click anywhere in between the <APPLET></APPLET> tags and select "Element Attributes" (figure 17.8).

Figure 17.8

Edit the attributes for the <APPLET> </APPLET> tags.

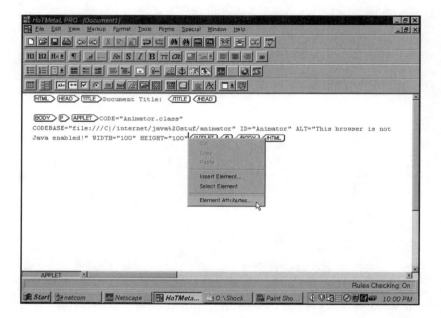

At the top of the resulting dialog, in the text field entitled "Codebase," delete everything except for the directory that holds the HTML document and the Java Applet. In this case, the directory is called "animator." Put the following characters, "…/" before the directory.

The "Codebase" of any Java applet is the directory where the applet and the other associated class files and configuration files, if any, can be found by the applet. Actually, this PARAM is not required if the applet and supporting files in question are in the same directory as the HTML file that calls it. This is a good exercise that you need to learn: The importance of specifying correct paths not only to our applet, but to anything else that is linked to your Web page, be it an image, a Java applet, or a Shocked file.

Leaving just the directory where the applet resides (without the "…/") tells the applet to look for that directory above where the applet currently is, which is incorrect. You need the applet to look in the same directory that it's in, so by putting "…/" before the name of the directory, the applet starts looking for the relevant information one directory below where it currently is. It will then look up one directory for the "Animator" directory (remember that this directory exists in this example only, unless you are using the same directory structure as this example). It sounds a little confusing, but it works.

Next, before you start adding the parameters that tell the applet what to do, set the dimensions. Again, right-click between the <APPLET></APPLET> tags and select "Element Attributes." This time you edit the width and height fields. Because you are using the same graphics as in the previous animated GIF example, you'll enter that information here, which is 150×136 pixels.

According to the documentation that came with the applet (or should have come with it) the following are available parameters and instructions that can be passed to the applet:

> Select an image to display at load time
>
> An image to paint the frames against
>
> Number of the start and end frame
>
> Time between frames
>
> Repeat
>
> Position of each frame (x,y)
>
> Order of frames
>
> Directory containing audio files
>
> An audio file to play in the background
>
> Audio files associated with specific frames

These are the options that produce external results as far as what you see and hear. In order to duplicate the Animated GIF, simply tell the applet what files to use and the amount of time to display each file, which involves items 1, 3, 4, and 5, as well as some other attributes that affect the above options.

1. First, specify the "IMAGESOURCE"—the location where each frame is located. To do this, first insert a <PARAM></PARAM> tag within the <APPLET></APPLET> tags. Place the cursor in between these tags and right-click. This time select the "Insert Element" option. From the list of valid markup that can be used, double-click the PARAM tag, as shown in figure 17.9.

Figure 17.9
Inserting a
<PARAM></PARAM>
tag within the
<APPLET></APPLET>
tags.

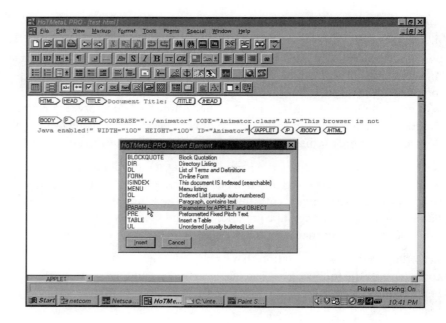

2. Now you need to edit the <PARAM> <PARAM> tags. Right-click the tags and select "Element Attributes," in the "Name" field (figure 17.10).

3. Now, enter the word "IMAGESOURCE." In the "Value" field enter the name of the directory where the images are. I'm in the habit of keeping all images separate from all other documents by placing them in a directory called "images," which is in the same location as the rest of the graphics files. Because this is the case here, enter "images" for the value. If your images are located elsewhere, substitute the location of your images here.

4. Insert another pair of <PARAM></PARAM> tags and bring up the "Param Attributes" dialog for those tags. Now insert the number of the first frame. Type in the word **STARTIMAGE** for the "Name" field and put the number **1** in the "Value" field. Repeat this process by inserting another set of <PARAM></PARAM> tags and put these words in place of the previous ones, "ENDIMAGE" and "9," respectively.

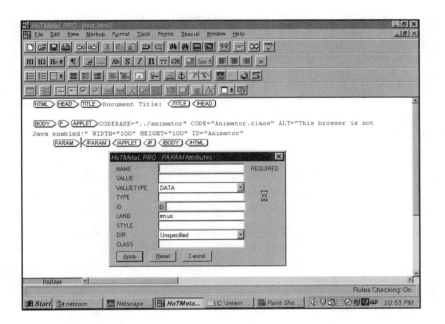

Figure 17.10
The Param
Attributes
dialogue.

The Animator Applet generates a list of file names based on
STARTIMAGE and ENDIMAGE and an additional PARAM called
NAMEPATTERN. Based on the information that you have already inserted, the applet knows that there are nine frames in total and that
those frames start at "1" and end at "9" (starting at "0" and ending at
"8" would also be 9 frames). Now that this has been established, you
use the NAMEPATTERN PARAM to tell the applet how to generate the
file names.

5. Enter an additional pair of <PARAM></PARAM> tags and insert
"NAMEPATTERN" for the name and "T%N.GIF" for the value.

What you have just done is instructed the applet to generate a series of nine
file names based on the letter "T," followed by the numbers 1 through 9
(T1.GIF, T2.GIF... T8.GIF, T9.GIF). The "%N" portion of the value entered for
NAMEPATTERN gets substituted by the number range 1 to 9. These are in fact
the names of each GIF used in the GIF Animation. If you would have put in a
value of "T%3.GIF," the file names would be T0001.GIF, T0002.GIF and so
on. The "3" after the percent symbol tells the applet that there are three zeroes in the names of the files to be used. The "N" simply tells the applet not
to put any zeroes before the predefined range of numbers (1 to 9).

One last PARAM that needs to be inserted is the PAUSE PARAM. As you did before, insert a new pair of <PARAM></PARAM> tags and bring up the "PARAM Attributes" dialogue by right-clicking on the PARAM tags and selecting "Element Attributes." Enter "PAUSE" for the name and enter a value of "100" into the "Value" field.

The PAUSE PARAM tells the applet how long in milliseconds to pause on each frame before displaying the next frame. You've instructed the applet to display each frame for 100 milliseconds.

You could have specified one last PARAM, the one that specifies how many times to repeat the animation, but if this PARAM is absent, the applet loops the animation by default.

The last thing you need to do is insert one of the frames as an image between the <APPLET></APPLET> tags. This serves as an alternative image should someone try to view your Web page and not have support for Java in his or her Web browser.

Place the cursor just to the right of the applet end tag (</APPLET>). Next, click the "Insert Image" button from the tool bar. It's the one that resembles a small outdoor scene of some mountains and the sun (remember that leaving the cursor over any button for a few seconds reveals the function of that button). You use the image T9.GIF, so in the "Image File" field from the resulting dialog box, type in **images/t9.GIF** and select "OK." All of your images are in a directory of the same name (images). This directory happens to be in the same directory as the applet and HTML document, so all that is necessary to link the alternative image is the name of the directory and the file name (this is referred to as a relative link).

You're done! Your screen, if you've duplicated this tutorial, should look like figure 17.11. Save the page and preview it in Netscape. It takes a few seconds for it to kick in, so be patient.

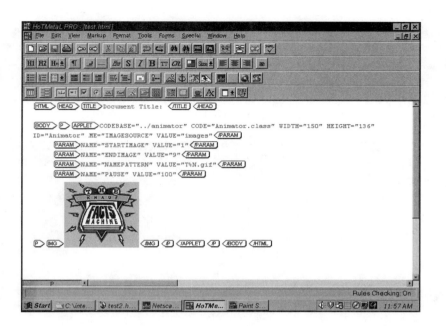

Figure 17.11
Your screen
should look like
this when you are
done embedding
the Animator Java
Applet.

Using Backstage Designer to Embed Java Applets

Backstage Designer offers an easier way to embed Java Applets than
HoTMetaL Pro by giving the user a single dialog box with all the necessary
options to completely install an applet. To begin, boot up Backstage Designer.
If it is not already installed, go to the included CD-ROM and find the
"mmbsd" directory that contains the install file. Double-click it and follow
the installation instructions.

Before you proceed, save your document in the same directory as the applet
you did in the preceding tutorial.

1. Select the Java button as illustrated in figure 17.12.

    You then get an icon that represents the Java applet you wish to insert.
    Double-click the icon and the "Java Applet Properties" dialog appears.
    All the parameters and settings related to any Java applet can be speci-
    fied and edited within this one dialog.

V

Using Lingo

2. First, you need to locate the applet you want to use. Click the "Browse" button to the right of the "Applet" field. Because you already saved this document in the same directory as the applet you want to use, the dialog box for locating files starts from the directory where the HTML document is located. For this reason, the Animator applet should be visible, so go ahead and double-click it.

Figure 17.12

Select the Java button from Backstage Designer.

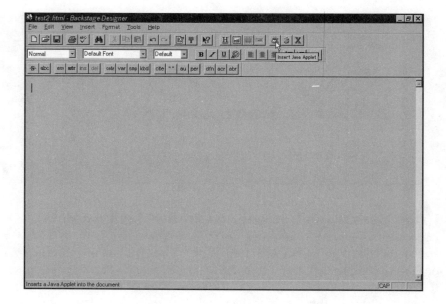

Whenever possible, Backstage Designer uses relative links instead of absolute links, so you don't have to worry about editing the path to the Applet. As you can see, in the "Applet" field, the path is indeed relative (figure 17.13).

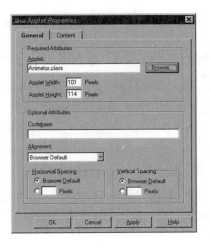

Figure 17.13
The "Applet"
field is correctly
displaying a
relative path
to the Animator
applet.

3. To insert all the parameters that you need to control the applet, click the "Content" tab. Under the "Paramaters" field, select the "Add" button. You are now looking at the "Add Parameter" dialog where you input the name of the parameter and the required value.

Basically, you duplicate the parameters used in the previous discussion. In the "Parameter Name" field enter "IMAGESOURCE" and in the "Parameter Value" field enter the directory where the images are saved. Your display should resemble figure 17.14.

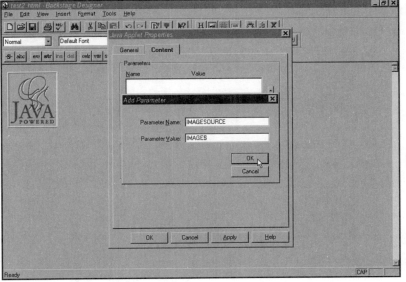

Figure 17.14
Entering the
"Name" and
"Value" informa-
tion into the
"Add Parameter"
dialog.

V

Using Lingo

4. After selecting "OK," you will notice that the information you have just entered is now in the "Name" and "Value" columns in the "Parameter" field. You enter the rest of the parameters in the same manner by clicking "Add" and then entering the required information. Enter the following "Names" and "Values":

Parameter Name: STARTIMAGE, Parameter Value: 1

Parameter Name: ENDIMAGE, Parameter Value: 9

Parameter Name: NAMEPATTERN, Parameter Value: T%N.GIF

Parameter Name: PAUSE, Parameter Value: 100

The "Parameter" field should resemble figure 17.15 when you are done.

5. Now you specify an alternative image in the event that a non-Java compatible browser is used to view your Web page. Below the "Parameters" area is an "Alternate Content" field. To activate it, click the "Image Source" box and enter "images/T9.GIF" in the field. Alternatively, you could have selected the "Browse" button and located the file that you want to use.

Figure 17.15

All "Parameter" fields after all the parameters have been entered.

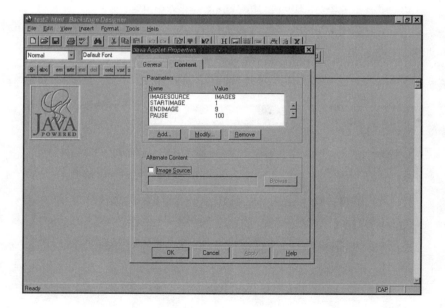

6. Click the "General" tab. The last thing you need to do before you can preview the applet in action is to set the correct Height and Width (that would be the dimensions, in pixels, of each of the frames) so that the animation isn't cropped. In the "Height" field, enter a value of "150" and in the "Width" field, enter a value of "136" (figure17.16).

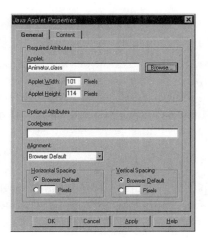

Figure 17.16
Adding the correct Height and Width for the applet.

V

Using Lingo

7. Click "OK," then save and view your HTML document in Netscape.

When using different applets, they all use the same basic structure. Read the accompanying documentation on the applet you wish to use closely, as sometimes they aren't too clear. Again, as mentioned earlier, there are many applets available for free downloading off the Internet. You can go to a search engine such as Yahoo (**www.yahoo.com**) and do a keyword search such as "Java Applets" to find some sites that have them. On the CD-ROM under the HTML directory is a file called *index.html*. View this file in your browser and you will see links that are not only related to Java, but to HTML and Shockwave as well.

On the CD

Real Audio

When Real Audio came out, it was the first technology able to deliver streamed audio. That is, as the audio arrived at your computer over the Internet, you heard it. Previously, Audio files had to be downloaded completely on a user's system before they could hear what they had. Real Audio is used on many "Radio Stations" across the Internet as well as in some Intranets.

Unlike Shockwave, where only the MIME type for the data you wish to serve up needs to be added to a Web server (besides the fact that the end user needs to have the Shockwave plug-in installed), to offer Real Audio to prospective Web surfers requires that you install the Real Audio Server on your Web server. This is subject to certain compatibility issues as there are a wide variety of Web servers being used, the majority being UNIX-based Web servers. This is a minor issue really, because the people who plan on offering this kind of service won't have piecemeal systems and cheap Web server software.

Real Audio Servers require a lot of bandwidth and a fast server. On top of these requirements, you must purchase what is referred to as "*streams*." Each "stream" is used when someone dials up your Web site and starts to receive audio. For the entire time it takes to stream the audio from the server to the user's system, that stream is unusable by anyone else.

So, if you have a popular site, you may want to have anywhere from 25 to 75 or even a hundred "streams" available. You need even more streams if the audio being served up is of long duration, meaning that the stream will be occupied for a long period of time before being released for someone else to use.

That aside, Real Audio is expensive. Expect to pay anywhere from $4,000-$14,000 to get a Real Audio Server going (the cost often includes a year or two of technical support), whereas you can put an audio file into a Web page using Shockwave for free if you already have the Director Multimedia Studio.

It doesn't take long to see that it appears as if Real Audio really isn't an alternative to Shockwave. This is especially true when one considers that, interactively speaking, Real Audio is limited to synchronizing audio with specific HTML pages. What has more impact? A Director movie with animation, rollovers, and audio tied to user-triggered events or a Web page with background audio or a narrator speaking (that Shockwave can do better)? With Macromedia's new Shockwave Audio Streaming technology, Real Audio is suddenly archaic.

Additionally, it's possible to insert WAV and MIDI files into Web pages, so that a capable browser, such as Internet Explorer (HoTMetaL Pro 3 supports Internet Explorer-specific HTML) will play those files once loaded. Although you won't benefit from streaming technology, entire songs can be downloaded quickly via a MIDI file. All it takes is a little HTML and some imagination.

Movie File Formats: MOV, AVI, MPEG

Earlier, it was mentioned that it's possible to embed audio sources into Internet Explorer. Internet Explorer also supports embedded inline AVIs. This means that you can embed a Video for Windows file into your Web page. For example, you could make an AVI file of the images used in the Animated GIF and Java examples and use it instead inside of Internet Explorer. All this requires is the software to create the AVI (such as Adobe Premier) and the associated HTML needed to embed the file.

Also, thanks to a number of plug-ins, you may also embed Quicktime movies and Mpeg movies as well. For Netscape, follow this link to get a host of third-party plug-ins:

http://www.home.netscape.com/comprod/power_pack_ summary.html

Getting plug-ins for Internet Explorer is a little different. Whenever the browser encounters something that you need a plug-in for, it will ask if you want it to get the plug-in and install it for you (this requires a connection to the Internet).

Because these require the user to have the associated plug-ins installed in their Web browser, the native support for AVIs (if you are rendering an animation using some 3-D Animation package, you can render straight to AVI), Animated GIFs, and Java that Netscape and Internet Explorer have makes them better choices if you are looking for different ways to create the examples that you have been going through.

From Here...

In summary, because more than a single Shockwave movie per page can yield undesirable results, the savvy designer can use an Animated GIF or Java applet or even an AVI for those other elements on a page. Because they load faster than the majority of Shocked movies, using these alternatives as a supplement to a movie can be a plus.

Here is a preview of what's coming up in the following chapters:

- Chapter 18, "Shockwave for Audio": Learn all about adding audio to your Web page—with Lingo and Afterburner.
- Chapter 19, "Shockwave for Authorware": Examines how it is different from Director.
- Chapter 20, "Shockwave for Freehand": Find out about the advantages of using Freehand and "Shocking" vector graphics.

V

Using Lingo

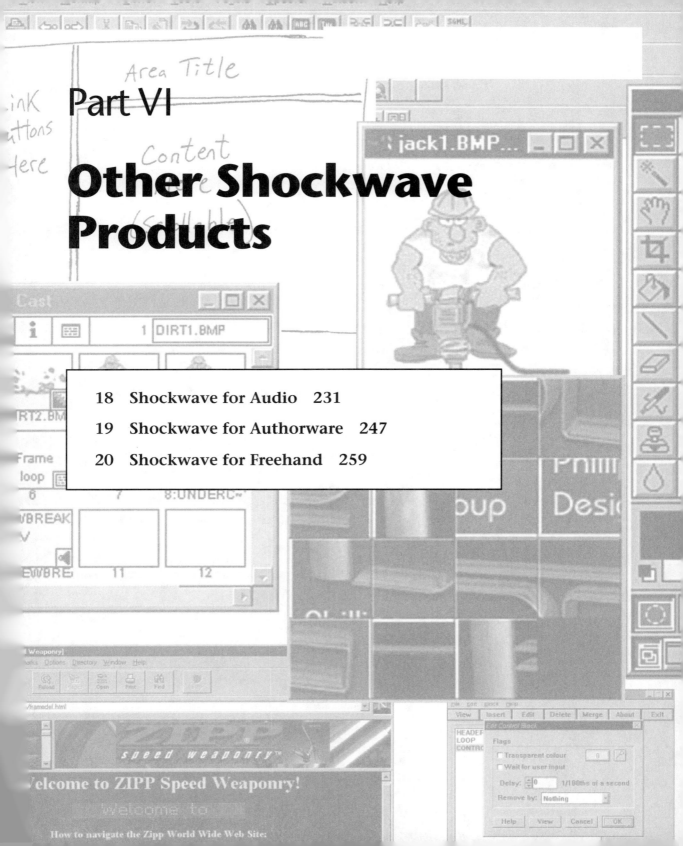

Part VI

Other Shockwave Products

CHAPTER 18

Shockwave for Audio

Two weeks *after* the first draft of this book was finished, Macromedia made public a new Shockwave development: audio compression and streaming. Very typical of the newfangled computer world, it's hard to keep up, but we have done our best to include the absolute latest possible information for you. This chapter presents the processes of including compressed audio and streaming audio in your Shockwave Web pages. This is a powerful addition to Shockwave in an area that previously was quite limited. Here's what you can expect from this chapter:

- Defines new terms and describes the process of streaming over the Internet.

- Shows you how to compress the audio files embedded within your Director movie.

- Shows how to create your own compressed audio files using Macromedia's Sound Edit 16 software.

- Describes the new Lingo used to control the streamed audio.

- Includes an example of a Shockwave "Music Stereo" to show you exactly how this process works.

What Is Streaming?

Ever tried to build a brick wall? Me neither, but it works well for an analogy. You can't build the whole thing at once; instead, you put one brick on at a time. Going bit by bit, the whole wall is eventually built. This is the principle of *streaming*.

You may remember this concept if you read the chapter about Shockwave for Authorware, because it uses the process of streaming. The way a normal Shockwave for Director movie works is to download the entire movie across the Internet, then play it within your browser. In earlier versions of Shockwave, all sound files needed to be included within the movie. So if the movie contained a 60K audio clip, the whole thing would need to be loaded before it could be played.

What streaming does is separate the sound file from the rest of the Shockwave movie. Then it breaks the sound file into little pieces that can be loaded a little bit at a time as needed. You obviously can't listen to an entire three-minute song at once, so streaming allows Shockwave to load only a few seconds at a time for seemingly real-time audio. It starts by loading a few seconds as a buffer, then immediately plays those few seconds while more data is loaded.

Previously, a three-minute song was out of the question for Shockwave because few people would be willing to wait that long to hear it. But with the process of streaming, the user is occupied listening to the music (and possibly interacting with the rest of the movie or Web page) as the audio information is slowly loading in the background. You could potentially have megabytes of audio data, but if the user is enjoying the music, he or she will hardly notice that it's downloading.

Compressing Audio for Shockwave

There are really two enhancements that Shockwave can offer to audio. We have mentioned streaming already, which is a separate compressed audio file that is loaded by the Shockwave movie. The other feature is compressed sound *within* the Director movie. Where Afterburner previously compressed only graphics and other elements, it will now compress the audio cast members embedded within the movie. For shorter sound clips, this is very beneficial because you may want immediate access to the sounds instead of a delay that results from streaming.

> **Note**
>
> Be sure you have the latest version of the Shockwave plug-in and Afterburner installed. If you don't, you will soon be lost because you won't have certain extras this chapter refers to that are installed in Director, SoundEdit 16, or your browser.

Compressing Sounds Embedded in Director

This audio compression feature only works with version 5 of Director. The SWA Compression Xtra is included with Afterburner to offer controls for the compression of audio cast members (it will automatically be added to your Xtras menu when you install Afterburner for Director 5). Figure 18.1 shows the available features when you select "Shockwave for Audio Settings" from the Xtras menu.

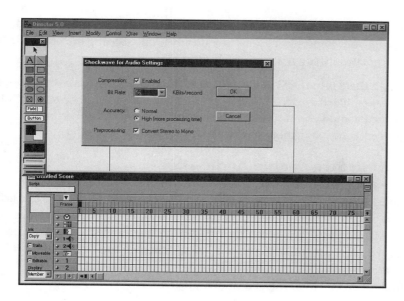

Figure 18.1
Options using the Shockwave for Audio Xtra.

Of course, if you have no audio imported as cast members, this doesn't make any difference to your movie. But with audio cast members you have several options from the Xtra menu.

First, you can choose to disable the audio compression. Why you would want to disable it I don't know, but you may have your reasons—troubleshooting, perhaps.

Another option is bit rate. This determines the quality and final size of the compressed audio. A higher setting produces larger files that are higher in quality. Lower settings compress the audio more, but may lose some quality. For most sound effects, you may find that you can't tell much difference in quality, but the choice is up to you. I did a small test on compression rates and found the following. An original Director movie of 164K contained a sound clip recorded at 22.050 kHz and 16 bits that was 156K within the cast. Choosing 160 as the bit rate resulted in a compressed .DCR file of 79.3K, and choosing a bit rate of 32 compressed the file to a final .DCR size of 18.5K. The higher rate did sound better, but the low-bit rate did not sound too bad considering the incredible reduction in file size.

The menu gives the option of normal or high accuracy in the audio compression. While the higher accuracy is claimed to take longer processing time, I have found Afterburner to be a very fast conversion anyway.

Finally, you may choose to automatically convert stereo sounds to mono. Stereo sounds are twice as large as mono sounds, so this is usually a good practice if your imported audio is not already mono. Setting the bit rate to 32 will automatically convert stereo sounds to mono.

That's all there is to the SWA Compression Xtra. Once you have the settings the way you like them, the Afterburner Xtra will automatically compress all embedded audio to your specifications. You don't need to input these settings every time; your choices will remain as defaults.

Creating Streamable Audio Files

We are about to deliver some bad news to Windows users. To create the compressed files to be streamed you must use SoundEdit 16, a software package developed by Macromedia only for the Macintosh (figure 18.2). I'm sure many Macintosh users are leaping with glee at the chance to be one up on Windows (something that isn't too common lately due to the vast number of Windows users) but I wouldn't be surprised to see the arrival of either SoundEdit 16 for Windows or a similar program developed to allow Windows users to create streamable audio files.

There are two Xtras for SoundEdit 16 that are also included with Afterburner. The SWA Export Xtra actually does the compressing and exporting, and the SWA Settings Xtra gives you control of the compression settings. Both are put into SoundEdit 16's Xtras folder. The plug-ins allow you to take a standard audio file from SoundEdit 16 and export it in a new format with the extension .SWA which is compressed to reduce download time for streaming over the Web.

In SoundEdit 16, begin by opening the audio file that you wish to export. Macromedia recommends you work with 22.050 kHz files, though you may use 44.100 kHz files also. If they are already 8-bit or 11.025 kHz files, they should be upsampled to 16-bit and 22.050 kHz for exporting. Note that an 11 kHz stereo file will automatically be converted to mono when exported.

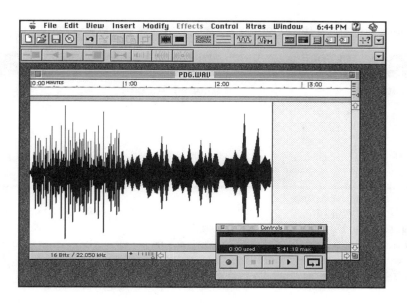

Figure 18.2
SoundEdit16 for
Macintosh.

From the Xtras menu, choose "Shockwave for Audio Settings" to control the
options for the SWA file (figure 18.3). The settings are similar to those in the
Director Xtra. You will need to select a bit rate for the streamable file. Keep
your target audience in mind when selecting a bit rate. Lower rates should be
used for modem users over the Internet, while higher bit rates can be used for
T1 lines or Intranet projects.

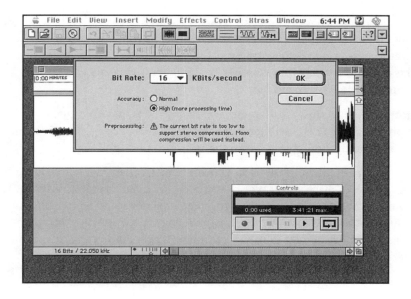

Figure 18.3
Using the
Shockwave for
Audio Xtra in
SoundEdit 16.

VI

Other Shockwave Products

Macromedia offers the following suggestions for bit rates (see table 18.1):

Table 18.1 Bit Rates for Streamable Audio Files	
Bit Rate	**Intended Audience**
64 Kbps-128 Kbps	T1 connection
32 Kbps-56 Kbps	ISDN line
16 Kbps	28.8 modem
8 Kbps	14.4 modem

You have the option of converting stereo audio files to mono when exporting. Like the Director Xtra, a bit rate of 32 or less automatically converts to mono. When the settings are chosen, press "OK" to close the settings box. Before exporting, you should close the Levels palette if it is open.

From the file menu, choose Export and select .SWA File from the "export type" menu. Enter a file name and choose Save to export the file. The settings you chose earlier will be used as the new SWA file is created. Pretty simple. The file is now ready to be uploaded to the server and streamed by the Shockwave movie.

Controlling the Streaming Files in Director

So, you have an SWA file all ready to stream across the Web. This section describes how to import and control the SWA file in your Shockwave movie. Director 5 uses yet another Xtra for this purpose. (Don't worry, all of these Xtras are automatically put where they should be.) This one is called the SWA Streaming Xtra.F file in the cast.

Before you are confused, we are not *embedding* the actual SWA file, we are simply inserting a cast member that is the SWA type. It is sort of like a linked media element, though we control the reference through Lingo.

From the Insert menu in Director, choose "Other," then "SWA Streaming Xtra." This will place a new type of cast member in an available position. This is somewhat abstract because the cast member is not really referencing the actual SWA file, it is just a generic cast member type. You will want to name this cast member to refer to it easily through Lingo. Editing the cast member properties (the "i" button) brings up an options box that really has no options except for the member name (figure 18.4). You may also enter the name directly in the cast member window in the name space.

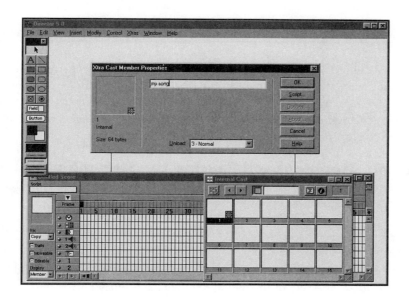

Figure 18.4
Naming the
SWA Streaming
cast member.

You will soon see how easy it is to control the SWA cast member through Lingo. We begin with the basic commands, then cover some additional available features.

Set the URL of the SWA Cast Member

When you insert an SWA Streaming cast member, it has no reference to tell it what SWA file to play. By setting the URL, you give a specific location and file name for the SWA file. You may include an entire HTTP address, or just the file name if the SWA file will be located in the same directory as the Shockwave movie. To do this, you use the Lingo term: URL of member "name." For example:

```
set the URL of member "mysong" = "http://www.pdgroup.com/shock/
➥music.swa"
```

The above Lingo statement would set the URL of the SWA cast member named "mysong" to the HTTP address of the actual SWA file, called *music.swa*.

> **Caution**
>
> It is important that you type the exact URL address correctly. Many servers may not allow file names longer than eight characters plus the extension and the names may be case-sensitive.

You only need to have one SWA cast member because you can't stream more than one sound at a time. By controlling the URL through Lingo, you may have more than one possible SWA file that can be referenced by the SWA cast member. The user may press different buttons in the Shockwave movie that set the SWA cast member's URL to play different sound files over the Web.

Playing, Stopping, and Pausing the Streaming Audio

The commands for playing, stopping, and pausing could not be simpler than they are. The syntax is as follows:

```
play (member "name")
pause (member "name")
stop (member "name")
```

Let's say I have an SWA cast member that I have named "long music" and I have already set the URL of the member. I may have a play button with the following script attached:

```
on mouseup
    play (member "long music")
end
```

Other buttons could be scripted to pause or stop the music in the same way using the other two commands. When an SWA file is paused, it freezes the song until the play command is again initiated. The stop command ends the streaming, and a subsequent play command will restart the audio file from the beginning.

Preloading

Preloading is a way of protecting the streaming file from breaking up. Preloading for five seconds, for example, loads five seconds of the sound before the Shockwave movie begins playing it. By giving it a head start, you have a buffer so that if the network connection slows down, there's still audio information to play and the sound doesn't stop. Playing a streaming SWA file automatically preloads a small amount without specifying, but you can choose to determine when and how much is preloaded using Lingo commands.

The following Lingo sets the amount of time that is preloaded in seconds:

```
set the preloadtime of member "name" = number of seconds
```

Then, I may even begin preloading before the play command is given. This way, a few seconds could be loaded when the movie starts so that the sound begins immediately when the user clicks a button to play it. To start pre-loading without playing, use the preloadbuffer command. The syntax is as follows:

```
Preloadbuffer (member "name")
```

So a specific example might look like this, where "songfile" is the name of the SWA cast member I want to preload for 8 seconds:

```
on exitframe
    set the preloadtime of member "songfile" = 8
    preloadbuffer (member "songfile")
end
```

The State of the Streaming File

At any time, you may check the state of a streaming SWA file. This will tell you if the file is playing, preloading, stopped, and so on. To check this state, use the Lingo: *state of member "name."* The result is returned as an integer that is translated in table 18.2. If the value is 3, for example, the file is playing. The following handler puts a message in a field if the sound is playing.

```
on ckeckplay
    if the state of member "mysong" = 3 then put "Now playing the
    ➥song." into field "songstatus"
end
```

Table 18.2 contains the possible results of the *state* function.

Table 18.2 Possible Code Results of the State of a Streaming File	
Value	**Returned Meaning**
0	stopped
1	preloading
2	preloading finished
3	playing
4	paused
5	done
9	error

Checking the Duration and Percentages of an SWA File

Lingo commands are provided to check the duration of a streaming file (in seconds), the percentage of the file streamed from the server, and the percentage of the file that has been played. The three Lingo terms are *duration of member "name," percentstreamed of member "name,"* and *percentplayed of member "name."* These values may only be checked after the command has been initiated to play or preload the SWA file, otherwise they return zero (0).

The following example handler could be used to check the progress of a streaming file and put the results in three text fields:

```
on checktime
    if the state of member "mysong"=2 then
        put the duration of member "mysong" into field "howlong"
        put the percentstreamed of member "mysong" into field
        ➥"pstreamed"
        put the percentplayed of member "mysong" into field "pplayed"
    end if
end
```

Checking the Bit Rate of an SWA File

Similar to checking state, duration, and other characteristics, you may check the bit rate of an SWA streaming file using *the bitrate of member "name."* If the file was created with a bit rate of 16 Kbps for example, this function would return the value 16000. This handler puts the bit rate of the current streaming file into a variable called "gbrate."

```
On checkrate
    global gbrate
    if the state of member "mysong"=2 then set gbrate=the bitrate of
    ➥member "mysong"
end
```

Checking Errors with the SWA File

If you have problems streaming a file, you may wish to check what the particular error is. Two functions are provided to check and return error messages: "geterror" *(member "name")* and geterrorstring *(member "name")*. If you only want an integer representing the error, use "geterror".

"Geterrorstring" results in a text string describing the error. For example, the following handler checks for an error and puts the results into a field named "whaterror."

```
on checkerrors
    if geterror (member "mysong") <> 0 then
        put geterrorstring (member "mysong") into field "whaterror"
    end if
end
```

If geterror returns zero (0), there is no error. Table 18.3 lists the possible results for both "geterror" and "geterrorstring".

Table 18.3 Error Code Results for *geterror* and *geterrorstring*	
geterror()	*geterrorstring()*
0	OK
1	memory
2	network
3	playback device
99	other

A Streaming Audio Example

We created an example for you to look at and take apart (or possibly use in your own Web page). This is a Shockwave "Stereo" to play streaming SWA files. It is designed to be useful in more than one situation because values for the SWA URL are passed to the movie through the embed tag in the HTML document. Open the movie *stereo.dir* on the CD-ROM to see how it's made. *Audio.html* loads the .DCR version and uses two .SWA files also located on the CD-ROM in the chapter 18 directory.

Collecting the Pieces

The graphics created include the main music control panel with buttons to play, to pause and stop the sound, as well as controls for volume and song selection. Buttons with highlighted symbols also show when the song is playing, paused, or stopped. Figure 18.5 shows the graphics used.

The SWA audio files in this example were taken from Macromedia's demonstration sites. You may run this from the CD-ROM using the *audio.html* file, but the concept works the same over the Internet.

Assembling in Director

The creation of the movie is fairly straightforward, though you should think ahead about how you want to construct the embed tag in the HTML document. It's also tricky using network Lingo scripts because they cause errors in Director; they are only understood through Shockwave. If you are careful, you will be able to create the movie without running the completed version until it is embedded for Shockwave.

Figure 18.5
Graphics used in the Shockwave Music Player.

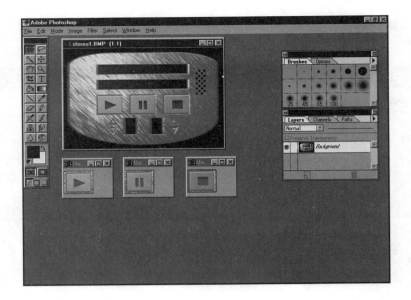

Basic Functionality

Set up the buttons first, leaving out the network Lingo until the buttons work properly with the changing graphics. The play button remains lit when pressed, the pause button only lights when the play button is on, and the stop button turns off both the play and pause buttons. You can control these using the "visible" property of the three sprites. Once these buttons work properly, you're ready to start working with the SWA cast member, though you can't test the movie until it's embedded.

Choosing the SWA Streaming Xtra from the Insert/other menu, I added the SWA member to my cast then named it "song." In a beginning frame script, I put the following:

```
on exitFrame
   set the url of member "song" = externalparamvalue("sw1")
   set the preloadtime of member "song" = 5
   put externalparamvalue("sw2") into field "title"
   set the visible of sprite 2 to false
   set the visible of sprite 3 to false
   set the visible of sprite 4 to false
   updatestage
end
```

The "set the visible…" statements simply hide the highlighted buttons that become visible when clicked. I planned ahead to use four external parameters:

"sw1"—the URL of the first song

"sw2"—the title of the first song

"sw3"—the URL of the second song

"sw4"—the title of the second song

The above script sets the URL of my SWA cast member equal to the external parameter "sw1," which will be entered later in the HTML embed tag. I could have used the external parameter named "swURL" but this may confuse me when I want to pass a second URL value in the embed tag, so I decided just to use all custom parameters. My script sets the preload time of the SWA cast member to be five seconds. It also puts the song title into a field named "title" by retrieving the external parameter "sw2."

The next frame script loops while waiting for the user to choose to play, pause, stop, and so on. While it loops it updates the status of the current song using a case statement:

```
on exitFrame
  case (the state of member "song") of
    0: set status="Stopped"
    1: set status="Preloading"
    2: set status="Preload done"
    3: set status="Playing"
    4: set status="Paused"
    5: set status="Done"
    9: set status="Error"
  end case
  put status into field "song status"
  go to the frame
end
```

I created another text field named "song status" that displays the results of the `state of member "song"` command. Because I don't want just a number displayed in the text field, I had to use a case statement to translate the numbers into text strings.

The rest of the scripts are all attached to buttons. Because I already set the buttons to appear and disappear depending on how they are clicked, I just need to add the network Lingo to start or stop the audio streaming. The play button, for example, looks like this:

```
on mousedown
  set the visible of sprite 2 to true
  set the visible of sprite 3 to false
  updatestage
  play (member "song")
end
```

VI

Other Shockwave Products

It first turns the highlighted play button visible in sprite 2 and turns the pause button invisible in sprite 3 (whether it was invisible already or not). Then it begins the SWA streaming using the *play (member "song")* Lingo. The stop and pause buttons look similar, but turn different sprites visible and use their respective Lingo commands to control the audio.

Adding Extra Features

For more features, I added two other options for the user to control. Up and down arrows control which song to play and the volume of the music.

Note

I only have two songs available to play, though you could use more. There are quite a few external parameters that can be used to pass values from the HTML tag to the movie (in this case, URLs and song titles) but if you had a very long list, you might decide to load the information from a text file using the getnettext command.

For the song control buttons, I added another text field to display the song number, then scripted the up and down buttons. The up button script, for example, looks like this:

```
on mouseUp
  global gsongnum
  if gsongnum<>2 then
    stop (member "song")
    set the visible of sprite 2 to false
    set the visible of sprite 3 to false
    updatestage
    set gsongnum=2
    set the url of member "song"=externalparamvalue("sw3")
    put externalparamvalue("sw4") into field "title"
    put gsongnum into field "songnum"
  end if
end
```

The above script first checks if the current song is already the highest number (2) by checking a global variable. If it's not, then the up arrow switches to song 2. It stops the current song if it's playing, turning off the play or pause buttons also. Then it sets the URL of the SWA cast member to the external parameter "sw3" and the song title to the external parameter "sw4." The down arrow button looks similar, but switches back to song number one.

The volume buttons use the Lingo *soundlevel* to control how loud the song plays. Another text field displays the sound level (an integer from 0 to 7). The script for the volume down button is as follows:

```
on mouseUp
  set the soundlevel=the soundlevel -1
  put the soundlevel into field "vol level"
end
```

Of course, the volume up script is identical, but increments the sound level instead of subtracting from it.

Afterburner and Embedding the Movie

After saving and compressing the movie into a .DCR format, you're ready to write the embed tag in the HTML document. It looks like this:

```
<embed src="stereo.dcr" height=300 width=400 sw1="song1.swa"
➥sw2="An unknown song" sw3="song2.swa" sw4="Some Orchestra Music">
```

After the standard height and width parameters, I put the four external parameters that will be read by Lingo for the URLs and song titles of the SWA files. Because the SWA files are in the same directory as the Shockwave movie, they need only the file name. I could have specified the entire HTTP address.

Figure 18.6 shows the final movie as seen in the browser. Run it from the CD-ROM to hear the music streaming.

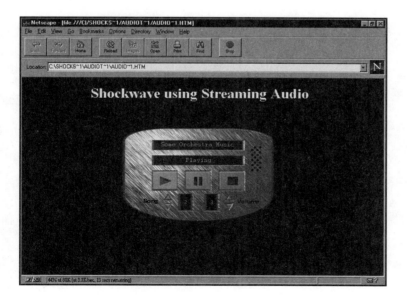

Figure 18.6
The Shockwave Audio Player.

From Here...

The addition of compressed audio is a significant accomplishment in multimedia on the Web. As with any new development, it's exciting to think of the possibilities made available through this technology. You will surprise your Web visitors and invite their return by continuing to update your Shockwave Web site with the latest enhancements.

The speed that multimedia springs up on the Web suggests that it is not ready to stabilize. It shouldn't at all surprise you if, by the time you hold this book in your hands, there is a new development called "Shockwave for Video" that allows streaming video clips. Perhaps it's not yet available or practical for the public, but it is there somewhere along with dozens of other ideas waiting for their chance to be developed.

- Chapter 19, "Shockwave for Authorware": Covers the basics of using Shockwave for Authorware for large multimedia projects over Intranets.
- Chapter 20, "Shockwave for Freehand": Describes Shockwave for Freehand, using scalable vector graphics on the Web.
- Appendixes at the back of the book give further information, including a gallery of Shockwave examples.

Shockwave for Authorware

Now that you thoroughly understand the concept and uses behind Shockwave for Director, it's important to know that Macromedia has developed a similar product for its high-end authoring package, Authorware. The name, coincidentally enough, is Shockwave for Authorware, and its uses are similar to Shockwave for Director with some key differences. Here is what you can expect from this chapter:

- Describes exactly what Shockwave for Authorware is and how it is different from Shockwave for Director.
- Learn who should use Shockwave for Authorware and a few suggested applications of it.
- Shock an Authorware presentation with a specific example given as a demonstration.
- Discuss related problems and limitations.

Learning How Shockwave for Authorware Is Unique

It is important to first describe the differences between Director and Authorware. As you may already know, Director started as a tool for creating two-dimensional cell animations. It is for this reason that the interface of Director takes on a "cell-by-cell" look that stretches out into infinity. It has only been recently that the package has evolved into an authoring platform. Because of its base in two-dimensional animation, its interface is clumsy for interactive presentations that are by nature nonlinear. Enter Macromedia's solution, Authorware for both Windows and Macintosh. Since its introduction, Authorware has been billed as a "high-end" authoring solution with emphasis on the interactive programmer. Authorware has an extremely intuitive interface that allows for flow-line style building of presentations (see figure 19.1).

Figure 19.1

The Authorware interface.

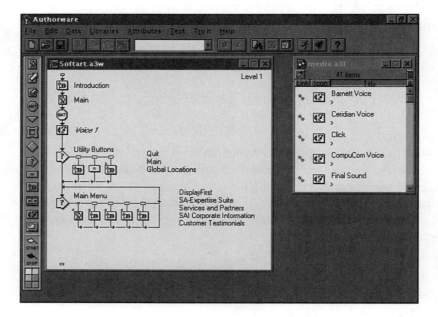

Until recently, Director was still the package of choice because of its ability to use Shockwave to get from a local machine to many machines networked together. Now, with the introduction of Shockwave for Authorware, Macromedia's high-end authoring system can also deliver applications over a network. But wait—there is a key difference between the two types of Shockwave. Shockwave for Director can deliver a presentation over the much-talked-about **Internet**. Shockwave for Authorware must use an **Intranet**.

What is the difference between these dramatically different platforms with spellings that are so similar a casual reader can mistake them as the same word? Well, the Internet is a global connection of servers that can be accessed by any old Joe with a PC, a modem, and a phone line. The Internet is typically slow to download information because of the restrictions of modern phone lines.

An Intranet, on the other hand, is typically set up within a company and is a connection between internal PCs and a network server. Intranets provide a much quicker access time of data because of larger bandwidth and improved communication devices. For instance, many computers connected to an Intranet have a network device installed, rather than a modem, and have a direct connection to the network. The network interface allows for a much faster transfer rate because it is not limited to a telephone connection.

While the Intranet limitation exists with Shockwave for Authorware, it works just like Shockwave for Director because it uses Netscape Navigator or another browser to download and view information off the network. Many companies are just now discovering the potential of this new medium, and are excited about the growth of Shockwave for Authorware in the future.

Who Should Use Shockwave for Authorware?

As with any new technology, the first question to ask is, who would benefit from using it and how? I think the answer to the first part is unquestionably large companies with an Intranet currently installed. The second part of the question is a topic exploding in the corporate world: What are some of the applications of Shockwave for Authorware?

The most important application that companies are finding useful for Shockwave is training. With companies becoming more and more concerned with the quality of training for their employees, Shockwave for Authorware allows a detailed training program to be accessible from any PC that's connected to the Intranet. Not only can trainees have access to on-line text describing their jobs in detail, but also to high-quality audio and video that will reinforce ideas and increase retention.

Previously, employers would have to designate a room as a training room for new employees. Also, they would have to fill this room with multimedia-capable PCs for each trainee to use. Then, they would have to schedule a time for the new employees to attend a training session. All of these things were taking away valuable resources from the company and costing a lot of money to maintain. With a training module written in Authorware and "Shocked," new employees can sit at their own computers at their own leisure and review training material.

Another important application of Shockwave for Authorware is internal communication. One of the most important tenets of any successful business has always been strong internal relationships. In order to develop these relationships, effective communication is essential.

In the past, things like newsletters informed employees about what events were planned for the company, how the company was doing financially, company history, new employee information, and so on. With Shockwave for Authorware, a company can develop an on-line newsletter that's accessible from any computer in the building. Not only does it save on printing costs, but the medium is enhanced with the addition of, for example, a full-motion video of the president describing company positioning or a narration of upcoming events over an animated calendar.

How to Use Shockwave for Authorware

Now that you are convinced that Shockwave for Authorware is the perfect solution for your business, you need to know how to use it. The basic procedure for creating a "Shocked" presentation is simple; just follow these steps:

1. Take an existing Authorware program file (you must have Authorware 3.5).

2. Put it through Macromedia's Afterburner for Authorware.

3. Embed the map file in an HTML document, and then view it using a Web browser that has the Shockwave plug-ins.

The following gives in-depth details about each of these steps.

The first step is to choose an existing Authorware 3.5 presentation or create a new one. Creating a new presentation may be the option you choose, because, like authoring for CD-ROM and kiosk development, there are certain limitations to keep in mind while programming, the most important of which is the size of the video you are attempting to play. With presentations coming from a CD-ROM or hard drive, the computer must only spool enough information into memory to start a video playing. Then, new frames of video are accessed in real-time from the disk.

However, with the speed of current Intranets, videos must first be downloaded to a user's local machine before it can be played back. People who use the Internet are all too familiar with waiting for items to download to their computer; but, the smaller the video files, the less time it takes. Of course, before Shockwave for Authorware, playing video files over an Intranet was impractical and presentations were limited to text only.

The next step is to put the Authorware 3.5 program file through Macromedia's Afterburner for Authorware. Afterburner breaks the presentation into smaller chunks of information that can be more readily accessed from a network. In order to accomplish this, you must first package the program without the run-time player of Authorware. This creates an .app file that Afterburner can read (if you package the file with the run-time player, the result is an executable file with an .exe extension).

When you select your file to use, Afterburner then asks you for the destination of the *map file* (.aam) it creates. A map file is a text file, created by Afterburner, that is essentially a log of transpiring events as the presentation is being "Shocked." It records things such as the names of the individual packets of information, the location of any external files such as movie files, Director files, and so on.

The next thing Afterburner asks you for are Segment Settings. These settings describe how the "chunks" of information are produced. The first thing you type in is a four-character prefix that you want each file to end up with. (Afterburner automatically adds four digits representing a hexadecimal number, starting with 0000.) This prefix can be any four characters that you want to use to keep these files organized.

Next, you can specify the file size of each chunk produced. The default setting is 16,000 bytes, which is a good choice for most presentations. You can choose to make the chunks larger or smaller depending on your own project. After that, Afterburner takes over and begins producing files.

Your last step is to embed the map file into an HTML document. Even people who are not familiar with HTML programming can easily do this step. An HTML document is just a text file that enables you to add statements. The statement for a "Shocked" Authorware piece is:

```
<EMBED SRC="mypiece.aam" WIDTH=640 HEIGHT=480 WINDOW=onTop>
```

Where "mypiece.aam" is the name of the map file you produced, WIDTH and HEIGHT are the screen size of your presentation, and WINDOW describes how the presentation appears in the browser. The options for WINDOW are as follows in table 19.1:

VI

Other Shockwave Products

Table 19.1 Possible Commands for the WINDOW Option	
Command	**Definition**
inPlace	Displays the piece embedded within the HTML page in the browser window. You can use inPlace only in Windows.
onTop	Displays the piece in a separate window on top of the browser window. This makes your piece look more like a separate application.
onTopMinimize	Displays the piece in a separate window and minimizes the browser. This setting makes your piece look the most like a separate, stand-alone application.

At this point you have completed the process, and now all you have to do is open the HTML document inside the Web browser. The two requirements for viewing a "Shocked" piece are that you must have a compatible browser, such as Netscape Navigator, and you must have the Shockwave for Authorware plug-in. Installing the plug-in is as easy as downloading an executable file from Macromedia's Web site, double-clicking it to launch an installer, and following the instructions. You will find that total functionality has been maintained and viewing a presentation over the network is as dynamic as pulling it from a CD-ROM or hard drive.

Software Artistry—A Shocked Example

Recently, Phillips Design Group was given the opportunity to create an interactive CD-ROM for Software Artistry, an Indianapolis-based company specializing in help desk software for large corporations. The CD was graphically dynamic and contained video, audio, and a full demonstration of each module in a family of software. The piece, created entirely in Authorware, was a perfect test for Intranet application using Macromedia's Shockwave. The following is a step-by-step procedure to "Shocking" Software Artistry's presentation:

Packaging the Existing Presentation

The first step in Shocking the presentation is to package the existing Authorware project. The actual files are not included on the CD-ROM, but you can follow the procedure and adapt the concepts to your own project. The steps are as follows:

1. Open Authorware Professional 3.5 and open the Software Artistry program file *softart.a3w*.

2. Under **File** in the menu bar, choose **Package**.

3. Choose **Without Runtime** from the pull-down menu and click **Save File(s)** and **Package** (see figure 19.2).

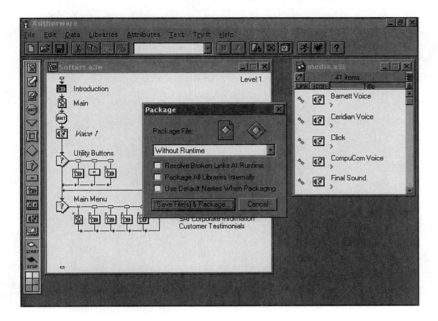

Figure 19.2
Packaging the existing presentation.

4. Give the packaged file the name *softart.app* and the associated library file the name *media.apr*.

Putting the Packaged File Through Afterburner

With the presentation packaged without the run-time player, you are now ready to use Afterburner. Note that Authorware, Director, and Freehand all have separate Afterburner programs. You must use the Afterburner for Authorware program.

1. Open Afterburner 3.5 and click "OK" to get past the introductory screen.

2. Select *softart.app* as the packaged Authorware file (see figure 19.3) and then choose **OK**.

3. Select *softart.aam* as the destination map file (see figure 19.4) and choose **OK**.

Figure 19.3

Selecting a
packaged
Authorware file
in Afterburner.

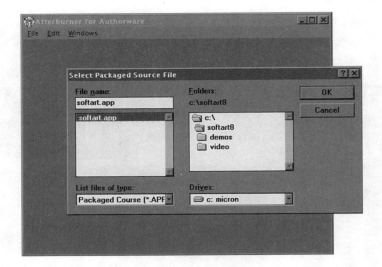

Figure 19.4

Afterburner creates
a map file.

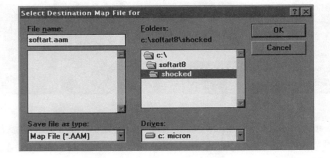

4. Accept **soft** as the four character segment prefix and **16000** as the segment size (see figure 19.5).

5. Wait. This particular packaged file was 17 MB and on a Pentium 166MHz with 16 MB of RAM it took approximately 12 minutes to produce the .aam file and associated file segments.

6. Select *media.aam* as the destination map file for the packaged media library.

7. Accept *medi* as the four character segment prefix and **16000** as the segment size, as described above.

8. Wait again. The file size of this packaged library is 8 MB and on the same machine it took four minutes to finish the job.

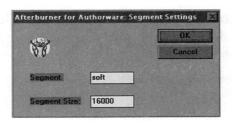

Figure 19.5
Accept the
segment prefix
and size as shown.

After finishing the preceding steps, Afterburner automatically opens the
softart.aam file for viewing and editing (see figure 19.6). Afterburner includes
editing features so that if the name of a file or its location changes, you can
easily edit the .aam file without re-Shocking the Authorware piece. Editing
within Afterburner is relatively easy and involves simply double-clicking a
line in the file. At that point, different dialog boxes appear, depending on the
operation being performed. When you are finished, simply save the file and
the changes take effect.

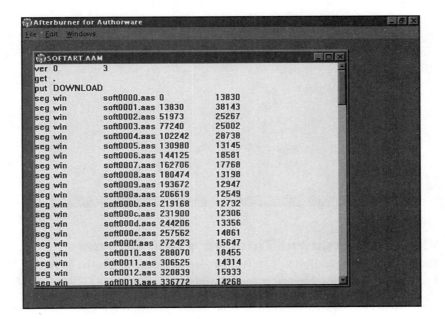

Figure 19.6
Viewing and
Editing the
.aam file.

Embedding the Map File Into an HTML Document

You are almost finished now—you need only make reference to the Shockwave file in the HTML document.

1. Open an existing HTML document using a simple text editor such as Write for Windows.

2. Add the line `<EMBED SRC="mypiece.aam" WIDTH=640 HEIGHT=480 WINDOW=onTop>` where the individual options are as described previously (see figure 19.7).

3. Save the document as ***softart.html***.

Figure 19.7
Adding the Shockwave statement to the HTML document.

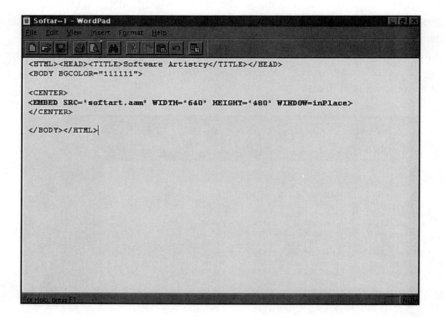

```
<HTML><HEAD><TITLE>Software Artistry</TITLE></HEAD>
<BODY BGCOLOR="111111">

<CENTER>
<EMBED SRC="softart.aam" WIDTH="640" HEIGHT="480" WINDOW=inPlace>
</CENTER>

</BODY></HTML>
```

View the Document Through a Web Browser

The Shocked presentation is now ready to be viewed through the browser. The steps in Netscape Navigator are described below.

1. Open Netscape Navigator 2.0 or later.

2. Choose **File**, then **Open File**.

3. Select *softart.html*.

4. A dialog box opens, stating that it's about to run *softart.aam* and asks "Would you like to trust this file?" This is a security option built into Shockwave for Authorware. Because there are video and Director files that need to be downloaded onto the user's local hard drive, it must ask permission first. Click "Yes" and the presentation begins (see figure 19.8.).

Figure 19.8
The presentation
as seen in Netscape
Navigator.

Problems and Limitations

Just when you think this software is perfect in every way, be advised that Macromedia's Shockwave for Authorware is still being developed on a daily basis, so there are still some problems and limitations.

> **Tip**
>
> An immediate problem you may find is that after installing Shockwave for Authorware and trying to run the Software Artistry presentation through Netscape's Navigator, you get an error dialog box stating that it's unable to locate the external movie driver for the embedded Director files. After hours of testing and such, you may find that you have to do a custom installation of the Director external movie drivers. By copying the necessary files from your Authorware subdirectory to **c:\program files\netscape\navigator\program\plugins\np32asw**, you're able to get Shockwave to find the necessary drivers.

The Afterburner interface is clearly in the testing stage. It would be good to see a much more user-friendly interface. The days of editing text documents to accomplish tasks are over. Users demand an interface that clearly describes options and presents many help features. You may also notice that depending on the background colors you have chosen for Windows, text entry boxes, and sometimes buttons, do not match.

As far as limitations go, Shockwave for Authorware deals with the boundaries of technology in several ways. First of all, there are speed limitations when using a product over a local area network. Designers must keep the size of video and audio elements small because of slow download times. Another limitation is the type of computer that's being used to view the "Shocked" piece. Not all users of the network will have computers that are capable of displaying high-color graphics or video.

From Here...

Macromedia's Shockwave for Authorware is a revolutionary product in the quest to find better ways to communicate via the computer. Whether it's training, information about current events, or other corporate happenings that depend on effective communication for their success, Shockwave proves that a currently installed Intranet can handle multimedia-style presentations. Perhaps in the next year Shockwave will evolve into an Internet tool, where Authorware pieces can be viewed on the World Wide Web. With the future holding so many uncertainties, there is one thing for sure: Macromedia is and will be there with its cutting-edge products and vision.

- Chapter 20, "Shockwave for Freehand": Describes the process of using Shockwave for Freehand and how to "Shock" vector graphics.
- Appendix A, "Example Gallery": Includes a variety of Shockwave examples for you to examine.
- Other appendixes and a glossary of terms are provided with further information.

Shockwave for Freehand

Shockwave for Freehand enables high-quality vector-based graphics to be placed in Web pages. Unlike raster images, vector graphics are very small and load much more quickly. The Shockwave package consists of two components that are in the form of "Xtras." They are the URL Manager Xtra, which allows the addition of URL hotspots to your Freehand graphics and the Afterburner Xtra, which compresses your Shockwave Freehand files.

A unique ability that is a major feature in Shockwave for Freehand is that the user may zoom in and pan the screen around to get a closer look at a Freehand graphic, without suffering from a loss in image quality due to the inherent nature of vector files.

An application for this technology that comes instantly to mind would be detailed maps and technical illustrations. But before you rush out to publish your Freehand art as Shockwave files, a few things need to be done to ensure that it appears as intended.

This chapter leads you through the following:

- Important considerations
- Using the Urls Xtra
- Using the Afterburner Xtra
- Embedding the Shocked Freehand File
- Limitations
- Setting the MIME type on your Web Server

Important Considerations

First, be sure to change the unit of measure in your Freehand document from whatever unit you are currently using to "points." This is important because any image or embedded object, such as Shockwave, that is placed or embedded into an HTML document, usually has the dimensions of that object coded into the HTML. As in the case of the `<EMBED></EMBED>` markup, the dimension attributes are mandatory, and given in pixels. By setting the unit of measure within your Freehand document to "points," you are approximating pixels per inch or screen resolution (72 points/pixels per inch).

To change the unit of measure in Freehand, you must go to "Window," then select "Inspector" (see figure 20.1).

Figure 20.1

Use Freehand's "Page Inspector" to change the unit of measurement.

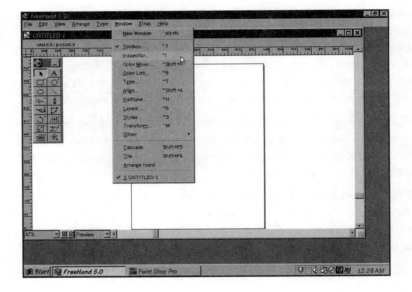

Select the unit of measure field and highlight "points" if it's not already selected (see figure 20.2).

Secondly, creating a graphic that only occupies a couple of square inches in Freehand ends up occupying an 8"×11" area (which is quite large in points/pixels) unless the page size is adjusted to fit around the graphic itself.

To change the size of the page, bring up the "Inspector" again. If you have a number of items on the page, select and group them all together. Next, move the group to the lower left-hand corner of the page. With the group still selected, click the "Object Inspector" button from the "Inspector" dialogue as shown in figure 20.3.

Toward the bottom of the Inspector dialogue, notice the Width and Height fields that are the last two fields under "Dimensions." Write down these dimensions because they represent not only the size of your Freehand illustration, but the new page size that you want your document to be. For simplicity's sake, round these numbers up. Dimensions that include decimal places may be valid in Freehand but will not be valid when it comes time to embed the Shocked Freehand document into a Web page.

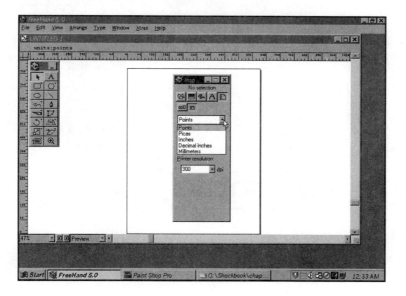

Figure 20.2
Select the unit of measure field and highlight "points."

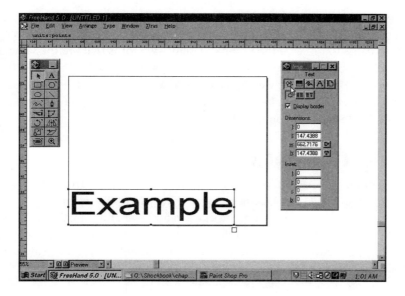

Figure 20.3
Select the Object Inspector from the Page Inspector Dialog. Note that our example text is still selected and in the lower left-hand portion of the page.

VI

Other Shockwave Products

Next, select the "Page Inspector" in the "Inspector" dialogue. Toward the bottom of the dialogue, there is a drop-down list. Select this list and scroll down to "Custom." Observe that the "X" and "Y" fields underneath the drop-down list are no longer dimmed. These two fields are where you insert the dimensions that were written down earlier. After you type a number into a field, hit "Enter" to make the change take effect (figure 20.4).

Figure 20.4
Select "custom" for the page size and enter the appropriate dimensions into the X and Y fields.

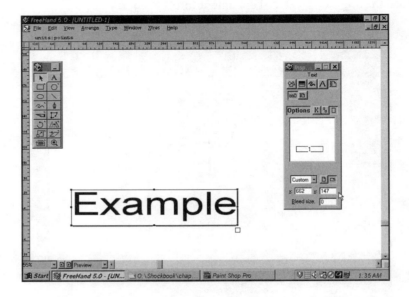

Additionally, keep the use of custom fonts to a minimum. Chances are that the end user doesn't have the same fonts on their system as you do. Try to use a system's default fonts or, if you must use other fonts, try converting them to paths to preserve the original design. Two fonts that are the same on Macs and PCs, though, are Courier and Times. Also, unused colors, layers, and imported images that were traced should all be removed from the document. Finally, objects can be simplified by having excessive points removed through the "Simplify" command.

Using the URLs Xtra

All the commands related to adding links are available from the URLs (Uniform Resource Locator) Xtra dialogue that is accessible from the "Windows," "Other" menu once Shockwave for Freehand is installed. To install the plug-in for Netscape and the Xtra for Freehand, go to the Shockwave folder on the CD-ROM and double-click the executable. If you have already installed Shockwave for Director or Authorware, the Freehand files are already installed.

To add a new URL, select "Window," "Other" and then "URLs" as illustrated in figure 20.5.

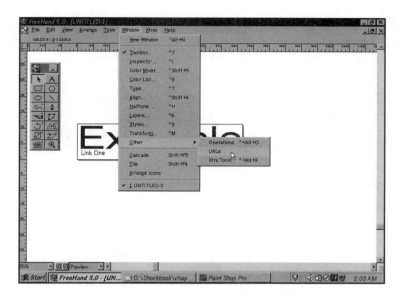

Figure 20.5
How to get to the URL manager in Freehand.

Click "Options" from the URL dialogue and then select "New." Type in the absolute or relative URL into the "New URL" field and then press enter (see figure 20.6).

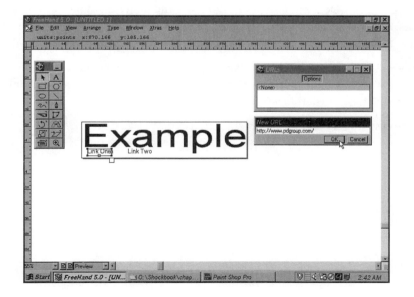

Figure 20.6
Enter the destination of the link that you wish to add.

Next, to apply that URL to a specific element, click and drag the desired URL onto the object that is to serve as the "hot area" for that URL. An alternative method of assigning URLs is to select one or a group of objects, then select the URL that you want to be associated with those objects. Remove URLs by selecting the objects, then selecting "None" from the URLs dialogue. The same can be accomplished by dragging and dropping the "None" option onto the desired objects.

When creating URLs, remember that a URL cannot be assigned to a group of objects that have been "grouped" together, as selecting any one of the objects within that group selects the entire group. Also, when using relative URLs, be sure to use a URL that is relative to the location of the Shocked file on the server and not the HTML document that it is embedded into. If you are unsure, using an absolute URL will work every time.

An absolute URL consists of the protocol, (HTTP); the address of the Web site, which usually consists of "**www.mywebsite.com**," and the directory or file that is to serve as the destination for the link. Basically, it would look something like this: **http://www.mywebsite.com/myfile.html**.

Using the Afterburner Xtra

Now that you are satisfied with the links in your Freehand document, it's time to prep it for use over the Internet. Open up the file that you want to Shock in Freehand, then under "Xtras," "Afterburner," (see figure 20.7) select the "Compress Document" option. Enter the file name that you want to use when prompted. You may also choose to enable the "Lock" option if you want to thwart any future attempts to open the file (see figure 20.8).

Non-locked compressed Shockwave Freehand files can be opened in Freehand with the Installed Xtras by choosing the "Decompress Document" option under the "Xtras," "Afterburner" menu.

Compressed Freehand files have the extension "*.FHC."

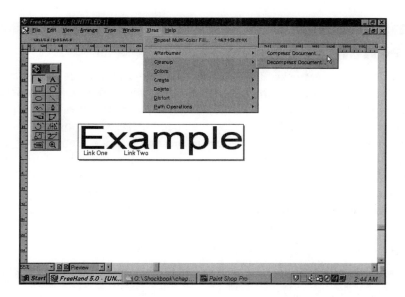

Figure 20.7
Select "Compress Document" to prepare your Freehand document for the Web.

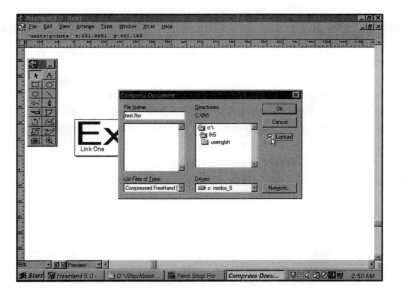

Figure 20.8
The "Save As" window when "Compress Document" is selected. You may choose to lock your file here.

Embedding the Shocked Freehand File

As with embedding Shocked Director files, additional parameters exist that allow for further control of the embedded object. These additional parameters are not available in the previously mentioned HTML editors (HotMetaL Pro 3 and Backstage Designer). However, as in embedding Director movies, these additional parameters are not necessary to succesfully embed compressed Freehand files. Basically, follow the same procedure for embedding Director movies, and, if you would like to add these extra features, you may do so by opening the HTML document in a text editor and adding them by hand. The following explains the available parameters and the associated HTML in detail.

The HTML for embedding a Shocked Freehand file would be:

```
<A><EMBED SRC="your_file.fhc" WIDTH="120" HEIGHT="80"></EMBED></A>
```

The keyboard commands for controlling the pick tool (used for selecting links), the zoom tool (for magnifying areas of interest) and panning (to view those areas of the image that are "off the screen") are available via keyboard key combinations. Because most users are unfamiliar with these commands, a tool bar can be added to the top or bottom of the Freehand document. This toolbar can be added via some extra HTML in the <EMBED> markup. If you want to include a tool bar, you may wish to increase the height of the Shocked Freehand file by 20 pixels (points) because the tool bar spans the width of the Shocked piece and occupies 20 pixels of vertical space. Neglecting to do so will result in part of your image being obscured by the tool bar. Also, for the entire tool bar to be displayed, the Freehand file must be at least 85 pixels (points) wide. The HTML for adding a tool bar to the top of the above example would be:

```
<A><EMBED SRC="your_file.fhc" WIDTH="120" HEIGHT="80"
TOOLBAR="TOP"></EMBED></A>
```

To place the toolbar on the bottom simply replace the "TOP" parameter with "BOTTOM."

The keyboard commands that are available are:

1. **Zooming In**

   Mac: Command+Click

   PC: Right Click

2. **Zooming Out**

>>**Mac:** Command+Option+Click
>>
>>**PC**: Alt+Right Click

3. **To return to 1:1**

>>**Mac:** Command+Shift+Click
>>
>>**PC:** Shift+CTRL or Shift+Right Click

4. **Panning**

>>**Mac:** Hold down the Control Key and click and drag
>>
>>**PC:** Hold down the Space Bar while clicking and dragging

Here are a few things to remember when using the tool bar:

- To return to normal "Cursor" mode, you must click the arrow tool after choosing the other tools.
- Links are only available in "Cursor" mode.
- An image can be returned to a zoom state of 1:1 by clicking the Shockwave logo.

Finally, remember to send (FTP) your files to the server in BINARY. Sending them as anything else, such as ASCII, renders them useless. This is because BINARY sends the files on a byte-by-byte basis exactly as the file is, whereas ASCII tries to send the file as if it were a text file, which it is not, and that destroys the contents of the file.

A really good FTP package for PCs can be downloaded via your Web browser from various sources, such as:

>**http://www.jtec.com/**
>
>**http://www.windows95.com/apps/ftp.html#wsftp**

You can download a shareware FTP package for the Mac called Fetch 3.0.1 from the following addresses:

>**http://wwwhost.ots.utexas.edu/mac/index-by-date.html**
>
>**http://wwwhost.ots.utexas.edu/mac/internet-ftp.html#fetch-301**

VI

Other Shockwave Products

Limitations

Shockwave for Freehand does not support the following:

EPS images.

Display of such postcript lines and fills such as "textured" and "custom" are not supported.

Externally linked TIFFs don't display.

Text effects, tabs, and kerning don't save.

The last page that was active in a multi-page Freehand document that's compressed will be the page that is displayed in Netscape. The other pages will be available by panning to either side.

Only Shocked Freehand files that are embedded into an HTML document print from Netscape on the Macintosh. Opening a compressed file into Netscape via Netscape's "Open File" command outside of an HTML document and then attempting to print results in a system crash.

The opposite is true on the Windows side, with the exception of the system crash; a blank area appears where the Freehand document should be when printing.

Setting the MIME Type for Freehand Files

Just as in Director movies, serving up Freehand files from your Web server requires that the MIME (Multi-purpose Internet Mail Extensions) types for Freehand files be properly set up. If you are unfamiliar with how to do this or do not have access to the Web server that you use, have the Server Administrator do the following for you.

How to Configure UNIX Servers

In the file that registers file types, enter the following information or give this information to the Administrator who will be doing this for you.

MIME Type: image

Sub Type: x-Freehand

Extensions: fh4, fh5, fhc

Notice that two of the extensions are the extensions for native Freehand 4 and 5 documents. It is possible to embed uncompressed Freehand files into your Web pages once the Shockwave plug-in for Freehand is installed and the proper MIME types have been set. However, because smaller often times means better on the Internet, serving up uncompressed Freehand files is often undesirable because the file takes longer to download than compressed Freehand (*.fhc) files.

Also, using native freehand files (*.fh4 and *.fh5) means that the end user could open your file and do whatever they wanted with it. Compressing the image and enabling the "lock" option when compressing your Freehand file will prevent this.

Configuring Mac HTTP Servers

The following information needs to be added to the *MacHTTP.config* file by someone knowledgeable about the server, preferably the server's Administrator.

> BINARY .FH4 TEXT * image/X-Freehand
>
> BINARY .FH5 TEXT * image/X-Freehand
>
> BINARY .FHC TEXT * image/X-Freehand

Configuring WebSTAR Servers

If you are using WebStar server software, do the following:

1. Run the application called WebSTAR Admin
2. Locate and select your server in the "Pick a Server" window
3. Choose "Suffix Mapping" from the "Configure" Menu
4. Choose the following settings from the "Suffix Mapping" dialogue box:

> Action: Binary
>
> File Suffix: .FH5
>
> File Type: TEXT
>
> Creator: *
>
> MIME TYPE: image/x-Freehand

Repeat the above process to register the .FH4 and .FHC suffix types. Again, if you are unfamiliar with your server or do not have access to it, have the server Administrator register the MIME types for you.

From Here...

Also included in this book are three Appendixes to help you apply the information, concepts, and ideas presented in previous chapters. The following references are:

- Appendix A, "Example Gallery": Walks you through a variety of examples using Shockwave.

- Appendix B, "Shockwave Toolkit Reference": Lists the various software packages used for creating Web pages, as well as where to find them.

- Appendix C, "Glossary": A technical listing of terms used in this book.

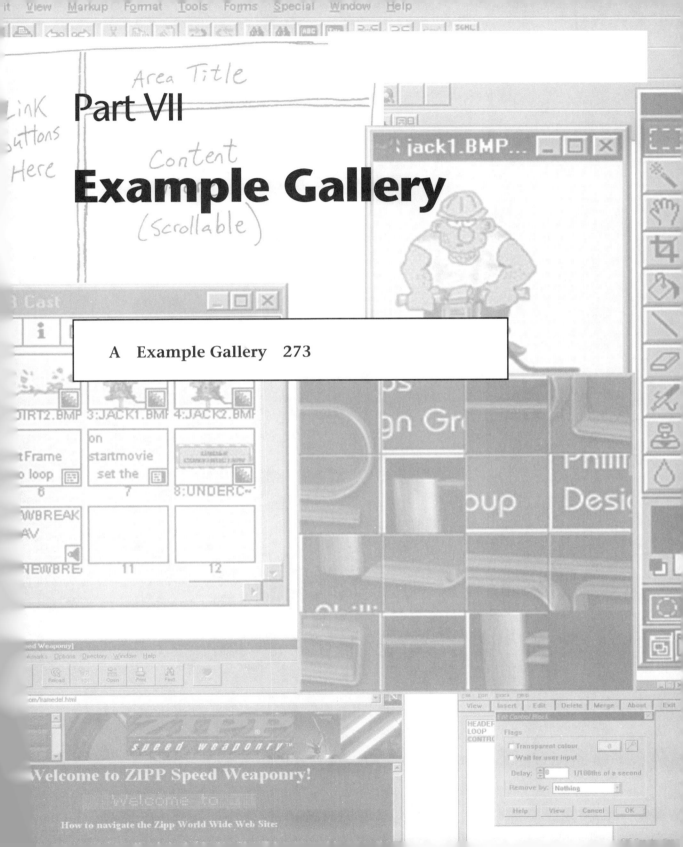

Part VII

Example Gallery

Example Gallery

Some of the examples from this book are conveniently placed in this appendix for you to browse through. There are also several examples that are not mentioned in the book that you will want to check out; they are in the second part of the appendix.

On the CD-ROM, you can load the HTML document called *append-a.html* in the Appendix A directory. This will allow you to easily see each example in the context of your Web browser. The source for each example may be a .DCR file, but .DIR files are also included so that you may open them in Director to see how they are created.

Each example gives the HTML file name, the Director file name, the compressed size, and a brief description of the movie.

Examples Used in This Book

The first section contains many of the examples contained in this book. You may decide to look here for examples and ideas rather than paging through the chapters to see sample Shockwave movies. Only select movies are displayed in this section; examples used merely to demonstrate a basic concept are not included in the appendix.

Flashing "NEW"

HTML example: new.html

File name: *new.dir*

Size compressed: 4.33 K

Description: The flashing "NEW" movie is an extremely simple movie that is small enough to place just about anywhere on the page to draw attention to an item. If you have a list that is continually changing, you may want to put it near the latest items added to the list so that the user can quickly see the current additions.

The movie is merely two frames alternating between each other. The same effect could also be achieved through an animated GIF (figure A.1).

Figure A.1
Using a small movie to draw attention to something.

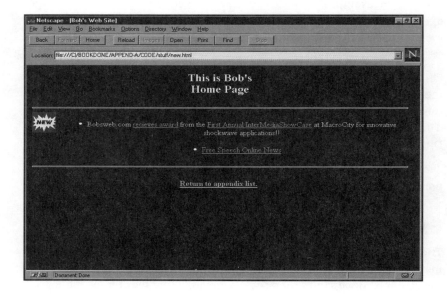

Animated "Home Page" Title

HTML example: home.html

File name: *home.dir*

Size compressed: 5.04 K

Description: This is a generic title for any home page. The letters zoom in from off the stage and remain jiggling in place. This is a fairly simple animation using very little Lingo. The graphics were intended to be placed on a black background so that the bounding rectangle of the movie would not show up once it has loaded (figure A.2).

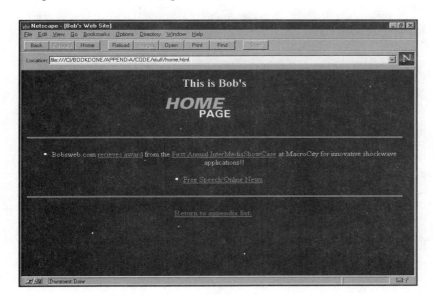

Figure A.2
An animated home page title.

Under Construction

HTML example: notdone.html

File name: *jack.dir*

Size compressed: 32.8 K

Description: A cartoon character vibrates with a jackhammer as a sign drops down to inform the viewer that the page or site is not yet completed. The sound effects were intentionally stopped after playing once so that the viewer is not annoyed while he or she stays on the page (figure A.3).

Figure A.3
An animation alerting the viewer that the page is under construction.

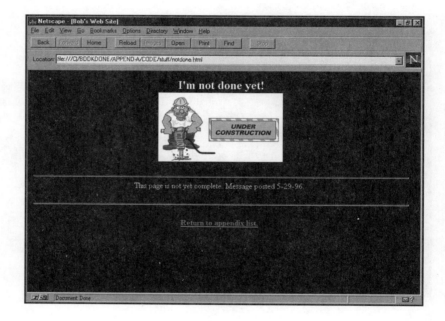

Animated Street Map

HTML example: map.html

File name: *map.dir*

Size compressed: 12.9 K

Description: This is an informative movie that describes how to reach a location. The basic concept can be adapted to any map. As an animated dot travels along a path on the map, text announces road names and turns. Though large in physical dimensions, the map is fairly lightweight in file size due to flat colors and character text (figure A.4).

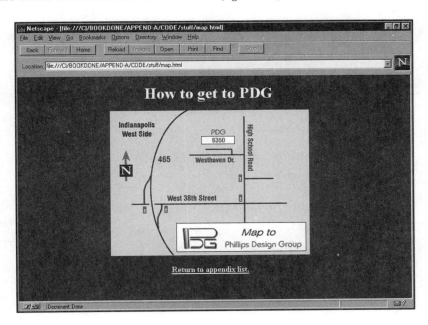

Figure A.4
An animated road map offering directions.

Bicycle Tire Animation

HTML example: tires.html

File name: *tires.dir*

Size compressed: 144 K

Description: In this example, the layers of a bicycle tire are peeled away and the various parts are labeled. This example might be easily understood with a static image, but you can imagine how some technical diagrams could be enhanced through motion. 144 K is a hefty price for this simple movie, but someone looking for detailed information may be willing to wait (figure A.5).

Figure A.5
Animating a technical diagram of a bicycle tire.

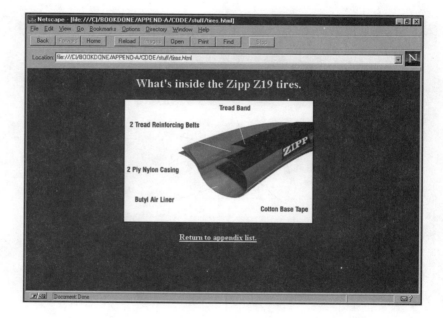

Pulsing "Gallery"

HTML example: gallery.html

File name: *gallery.dir*

Size compressed: 11.9 K

Description: The pulsing "Gallery" image is only one image that is in be-tween using sprite blends and scaled size. The background color is intended to match the background of the Web page for a seamless movie. Palette issues can often be confusing. My testing found this to be an exact match when running in 24-bit color mode (millions of colors), but slightly off in 16-bit mode (thousands of colors) (figure A.6).

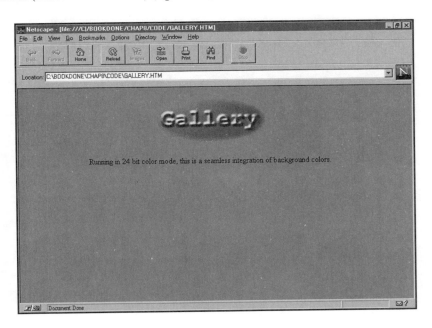

Figure A.6
The pulsing image matches the background color of the Web page.

Animated Shockwave Logo

HTML example: texture.html

File name: *texlogo.dir*

Size compressed: 16.3 K

Description: Matching a textured background is another way of seamlessly integrating a Shockwave movie to a Web page. This example animates the Macromedia Shockwave logo over a textured background. The same image was used in the HTML document and in the Director movie to create tiled backgrounds. The animation itself is a few sprite blends, stretches, and colored 1-bit images (figure A.7).

Figure A.7
Matching a patterned background with this animated Shockwave logo.

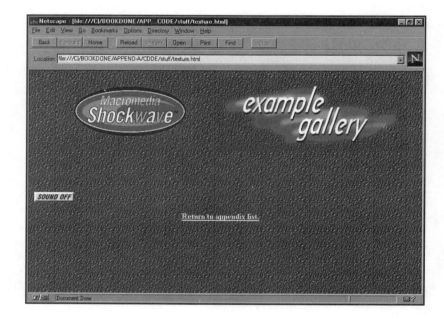

Rippling PDG Logo

HTML example: pdgwave.html

File name: *pdgwave.dir*

Size compressed: 32 K

Description: The rippling logo movie is static until the user passes his or her mouse over the movie location. Then the animated logo ripples while a sound effect plays. Definitely one of the bells and whistles of a Shockwave page—a bit useless perhaps, but still fun (figure A.8).

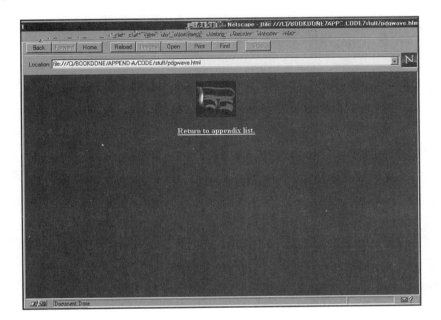

Figure A.8
The logo quivers as the mouse rolls over it.

Using a Go-To Loader

HTML example: prepare.html

File name: *prepare.dir*

Size compressed: 4.74 K

Description: This movie goes along with the next movie *pdgmain.dir*. It's a very small movie that downloads quickly to eliminate the ugly white box that Shockwave usually begins with. Then it calls another movie and animates an image while the larger movie loads (figure A.9).

Figure A.9
The quick-loading go-to file.

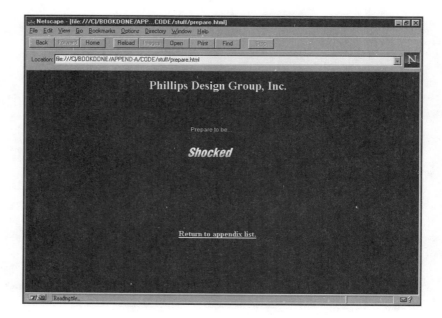

Because you are running this from a CD-ROM, there will be very little delay in loading the larger movie, but the download time over the Internet would be much longer.

PDG Navigation Movie

HTML example: prepare.html - loaded by the preceding movie

File name: *pdgmain.dir*

Size compressed: 148 K

Description: This movie offers an interface for the user to select the area of the Web site to visit. A slider moves left or right and a laser beam zaps the words that are possible choices for the user. The accompanying Web pages are not included on the CD-ROM—this is just to show the navigation movie as an example (figure A.10).

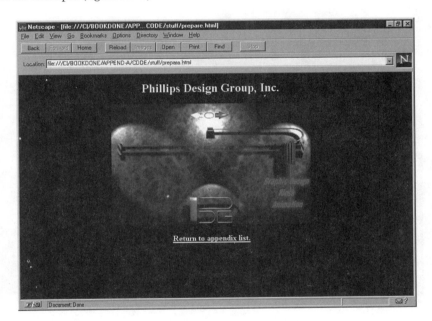

Figure A.10
PDG's navigation movie.

Retrieving Text from the Internet

HTML example: getnet.html

File name: *getnet.dir*

Size compressed: 4.42 K

Description: This is a simple utility that lets you experiment with some network Lingo. It will only work in your browser while you are connected to the Internet. You may enter the http location of any text file (or HTML document), and the movie loads the item and displays it in a scrollable window. Other network information is also displayed—error, done state, ID number, and last modified date (figure A.11).

Figure A.11
A utility to test the Internet Lingo functions.

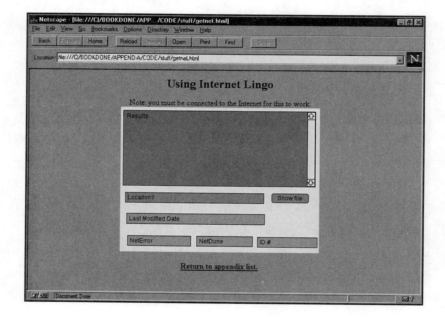

Line Graphing Movie

HTML example: graph.html

File name: *graph.dir*

Size compressed: 8.55 K

Description: This compact but powerful movie takes a series of numbers that the user enters and creates a line graph. The Lingo programming uses lists to store and retrieve the information. The scale of the graph is adjusted to fit the data. By itself, this may not be the most useful movie, but used to load data via a `getnettext` statement, this could be a very valuable tool for Web sites that report data (figure A.12).

VII

Example Gallery

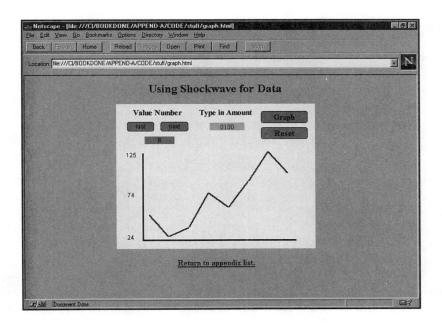

Figure A.12
A movie that graphs data entered by the user.

A Completely Shocked Site
HTML example: shocked.html

File names: *nav.dir*, *homeglow.dir*, *gallglow.dir*, *linkglow.dir*, and *mailglow.dir*

Sizes compressed: (in order of above list) 17.6 K, 2.61 K, 4.48 K, 2.56 K, 2.87 K

Description: This entire site was described in detail in chapter 15, "Putting It All Together: A Shocked Site." The page is divided into three frames. In the left frame, a Shockwave movie allows the user to navigate the site. In the top frame, another Shockwave movie displays the title of the area the user is currently viewing. The bottom frame contains the content of the site itself. By targeting frames, the navigation movie and the title movies can stay visible while the user scrolls through the content of the Web site (figure A.13).

Figure A.13
A Shockwave site using multiple movies and frames.

Streaming Audio

HTML example: audio.html

File name: *stereo.dcr*

Size compressed: 39.8 K

Description: This example demonstrates audio streaming using several
.SWA files. The HTML document passes file names and descriptions to the
movie using external parameters. The movie loads and plays the streaming
files. Running from the CD-ROM will be fast, of course, but streaming over
the Web is relatively fast as well. The movie loads fairly quickly also because
the streaming files are externally loaded (figure A.14).

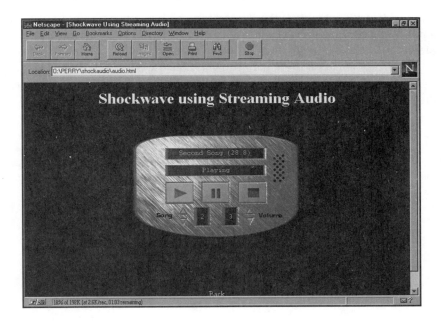

Figure A.14
A Shockwave
site that uses audio
streaming.

Other Shockwave Examples

This section contains a few movies that were not used as examples in this book, but you may find them helpful in understanding more about Shockwave and Director, and helpful in giving you ideas for your own Web site.

The Slider Puzzle

HTML example: puzzle.html

File name: *puzzle.dir*

Size compressed: 39.7 K

Description: Remember this old puzzle game? It may have had numbers or letters or a picture, with one position left open. Then you slide the other pieces around to try to get them in order. The logic is fairly straightforward. A Lingo script checks if the square you click has the open square next to it. If it does, the squares are switched. When the squares are in proper order, it jumps to a different frame to alert you that you have won (figure A.15).

Figure A.15
A small puzzle game that everyone used to play.

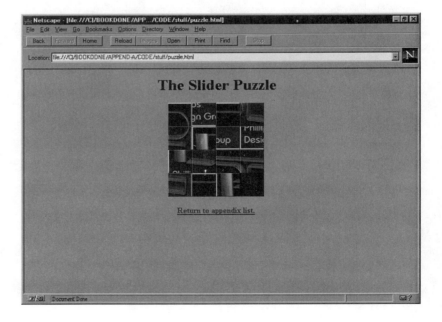

Animated Web Counter

HTML example: counter.html

File name: *counter.dir*

Size compressed: 29.5 K

Description: All over the Web you will find counters proudly displaying the number of visitors a Web page has received. (Of course, this is usually inaccurate because it doesn't really count how many people have seen the page. One person could hit the same page ten times and it would count all of them.) This Shockwave movie is an animated Web counter that gives the appearance that thousands of people are hitting the Web page, until the counter finally breaks from the strain. The numbers of the counter are the same cast members animated in different ways for each digit. The only interaction involved is the option of turning the counter on or off by clicking it (figure A.16).

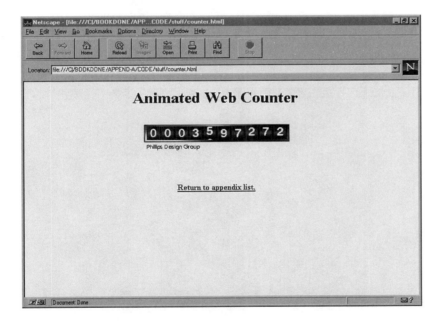

Figure A.16
An animated Web counter.

Finish Line Challenge

HTML example: finline.html

File names: *finstart.dir* and *finishnt.dir*

Sizes compressed: 5.81 K, 80.5 K

Description: Used on the Finish Line athletic shoe store Web site, this game loads trivia questions using the `getnettext` command. The trivia questions can periodically change while the game remains the same. Using lists, the questions are randomly chosen while a timer keeps track of the player's speed. After passing ten hurdles by correctly answering questions, the user is taken to another Web page with a winning certificate (figure A.17).

> **Note**
>
> The game will not work properly from the CD-ROM because it calls a text file that must be retrieved from the Internet. The game may or may not be at the Finish Line Web site at the time you are reading this (www.thefinishline.com). To play the game from the CD-ROM, run the file called *finline.exe* which will load the text file using a `fileio` command.

Figure A.17

The Finish Line trivia game loads questions from a text file.

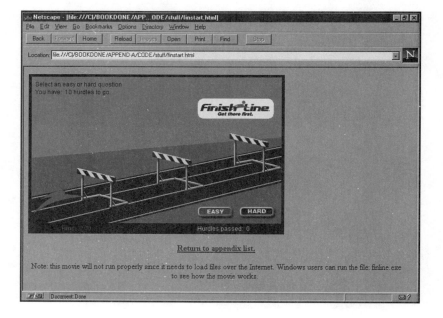

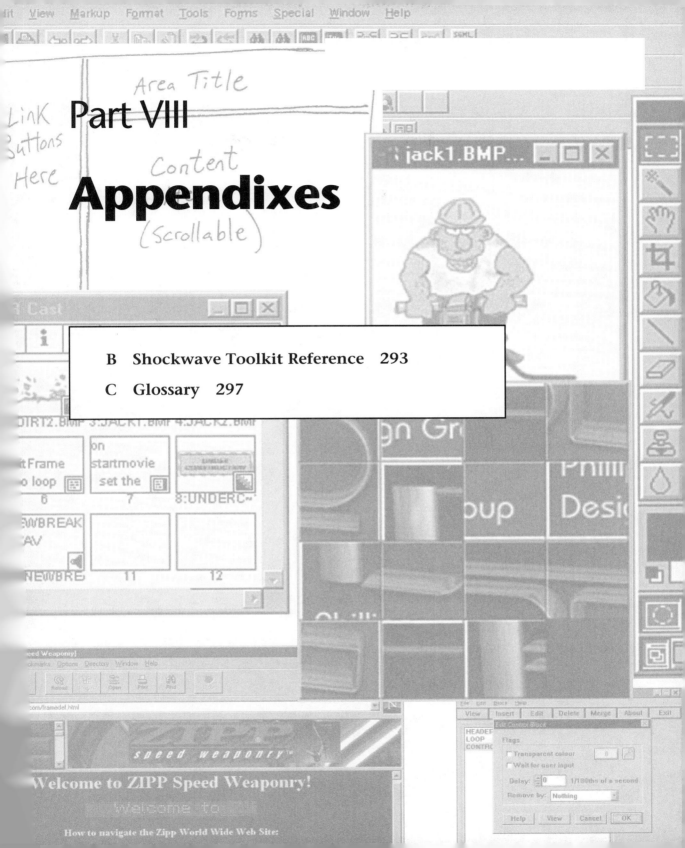

Part VIII

Appendixes

Shockwave Toolkit Reference

This reference is meant to give the budding Web designer an idea of the various tools that are used for creating Web pages and graphics for the Internet. They are available from various sources, and some you can even download off the Internet for free.

Professional Software Packages

Below you will find the tools that serious Web developers use to create graphics and build Web pages. The cost of these packages will most likely prevent the average user from obtaining some of them (well, legally anyway) as they are not cheap. But, if you want the ability to create professional-looking graphics, this is the stuff to get.

Adobe Photoshop

For years Photoshop has been regarded as the industry standard among graphics professionals for color correcting and image manipulation. With added support for third-party plug-ins, the creative capabilities of this program have been greatly expanded.

GIF 89a Plug-In for Adobe Photoshop

One of the many things that's not only very useful but free off the Internet is the GIF 89a plug-in for Photoshop. This excellent little utility lets you create transparent GIFs within Photoshop. What sets this apart from any other program is that unlike the rest, you can select more than one color to be made transparent. It's available from the Adobe site at **http://www.adobe.com**.

GIF Construction Set from Alchemy Mindworks

Animated GIFs are quickly becoming the standard way to add basic animation due to the native support for the file format by many browsers. GIF Construction Set gives the user the ability to build basic and complicated animated GIFs from many different file formats.

Macromedia xRes

Excelling in graphics for print media, xRes can also export your images as GIF89a files as well as progressive JPEGs and PNGs.

Alien Skin Software's Black Box

A suite of plug-in filters for Photoshop, The Black Box contains 10 filters that allow you to create bevels, drop shadows, and 3-D effects quickly and easily. Each filter can be user customized.

Adobe Acrobat

Files created using the Acrobat PDF Writer retain the original look of the document over multiple platforms, ensuring that your message is delivered as intended. Acrobat Readers are available for Mac, DOS, Windows, and UNIX.

Macromedia Director Multimedia Studio 2

If you don't already own Director and are planning on purchasing it, this is the package to get. Bundled with Director is xRes, an image manipulation program; SoundEdit 16, a sound manipulation program; and Extreme 3D, an application that allows you to create 3-D scenes and animations.

Caere's OmniPage Pro

If you are confronted with the task of getting information from a stack of printed material typed into a Web page, OmniPage can help. This powerful OCR accurately and easily converts scanned documents into editable text that can be imported or opened in your favorite HTML editor.

SoftQuad's HoTMetaL Pro 3

This powerful, professional Web page builder supports not only the new HTML 3.2 spec, but has added support for Netscape Extension as well as Internet Explorer Extensions.

Included in its feature list is a built-in image map editor for client-side, server-side image maps, and a built-in frames editor, along with a built-in color selector that relieves the user of converting RGB to HEX.

Incontext Web Analyzer

Once your Web site is complete, you may want to run Web Analyzer on it to be sure that all your links, from hyperlinks to embedded multimedia files, are linked up correctly. This program searches through a site and shows you a graphical representation of the structure, including all in-and-out links as well as all file types, sizes, titles, and dates as they were last modified. Once a problem is found, you can launch your favorite HTML editor to take care of the problem from within Web Analyzer. ❖

VIII

Appendixes

Glossary

Afterburner   A utility that is freely available at Macromedia's Web site that compresses a Director movie for use over the Internet.

animation   Any process where multiple images are presented rapidly, giving the illusion of motion.

Applet   A program created using Java that can be inserted into HTML documents via the <APPLET></APPLET> tags.

Authorware   A multimedia authoring tool made by Macromedia that excels in delivering highly interactive applications, which can include video, audio, animation, and even Director Movies. Authorware-made applications can be used for Intranets.

Backstage Designer   An HTML editor that features WYSIWYG Web page creation. Made by Macromedia, it offers a very easy way to add Shockwave movies to any Web page.

bitmap image   A graphic format that records color information about each individual pixel of an image.

Browser   A program that functions as an "interface" for viewing HTML documents. Typically, browsers (e.g., Netscape, Mosaic, and so on) are used for retrieving data off the Internet, hence the phrase "browsing the net."

cast member   In Director, an element to be used in the movie. Cast members can be bit-map images, vector graphics, sounds, scripts, and so on.

clickable image maps   An image within an HTML document that has multiple "hot spots" defined within the image, so that when a user clicks in a predefined area, the associated document is loaded. There are two kinds of image maps: client-side image maps and server-side image maps.

client-side image map   A clickable image map that differs from traditional image mapping in that when a user clicks an image, the browser does all the processing required to interpret the action and return the desired result. Browsers that support this type of image map are Netscape 2.0, Microsoft Internet Explorer 2.0, Enhanced Mosaic, and later versions.

DCR   The file format that results when a Director movie (DIR or DXR) is compressed through Afterburner.

DIR   The native Director file format.

Director   A multimedia-authoring tool from Macromedia. Director is the tool used to assemble Shockwave movies.

DXR   A protected Director movie that cannot be edited—typically used as the final stage of a Director movie before distribution.

embed   The embed HTML tags <EMBED></EMBED> allow for a wide variety of objects to be placed or "embedded" within HTML documents. Shockwave movies are placed in Web pages using the embed tags.

frames   A way to divide the window in a browser into any number of subwindows. Each subwindow may contain a unique HTML document and each document may have links "targeting" different subwindows for displaying relative information.

Freehand   A vector-graphics-based design program from Macromedia.

FTP   File Transfer Protocol. This is the protocol used to transport files over the Internet from one computer to another.

GIF   The most widely used graphics format on the Internet. GIF stands for Graphics Interchange Format and provides lossless compression for images with 256 colors or less.

handler   In Director, a complete group of Lingo statements set to perform when the handler is called. Handlers are stored in scripts.

home page   The first or top level document in a Web site.

HoTMetaL Pro   A professional HTML editor that supports HTML 2.0 and all the Netscape Extensions. The current version, Version 3.0, supports embedded objects, Active X Objects, JAVA applets, and scripts.

HTML   Hyper Text Markup Language. This is the language used to build Web pages. Browsers rely on HTML to tell them how to display information.

HTTP   Hyper Text Transfer Protocol is used to transfer HTML documents from a Web server to a user's Browser.

Internet   Local area networks (LANs) that are all connected by a common communications protocol.

Intranet   An Intranet is an internal network of computers based on the standards of the Internet. Intranets are not accessible through the Internet, as they are meant to provide information only to the employees of some organizations and typically have a much higher bandwidth than what the vast majority of users experience with 28.8 or 14.4 dial-up connections.

Java   Java is a programming language developed by Sun Microsystems that is similar to C++. It is platform independent, which makes it perfect for use over the Internet. Java programs, called "Applets," can be placed in HTML documents to perform a wide variety of functions.

JPEG   Like the GIF file format, JPEG is another image format in wide use across the Internet in Web pages. The JPEG format differs from the GIF format in that you can generally achieve higher compression ratios than what can be achieved with GIFs, but with a loss in quality. JPEG also supports 24-bit color images.

Lingo   The programming language of Director. The commands are very similar to the English language, allowing Lingo to be relatively easy to learn.

list   The Lingo equivalent of an array. Lists are variables with multiple slots to store information. They may be linear lists (single items) or property lists (labels with a value).

Macromedia   The guys who made this book possible. More information can be found about this fine company at **http://www.macromedia.com**.

markup   Another term for referring to HTML tags, which define the layout of HTML documents.

MIME   Multipurpose Internet Mail Extensions. The format used to transfer files, the MIME Type of a file tells browsers and servers how to process files. This is important because without setting the MIME Type for Director movies, a server will not know what to serve up the file when it is called.

movie   The term Macromedia has chosen for a Director file. The analogy runs throughout the software—cast members, score, stage, and so on.

palette   A collection of available colors used by an image. An 8-bit palette, for example, is a group of 256 different colors, each in a particular position.

PhotoShop   A professional image-editing program that is the program of choice among artists and designers. It is made by Adobe.

playback head   In Director, the position holder in a movie. Without any modification, the playback head will move from the beginning of the score to the end, executing any commands it encounters. The playback head can be controlled through Lingo to move to various locations in the movie. The playback rate (in frames per second) controls the speed of the playback head.

puppet   In Director, any element (sprite, tempo, palette, and so on) that is controlled by Lingo commands where usually it is controlled through the score.

VIII

Appendixes

resolution   The value of detail in a bit-map graphic image. Measured in dots per inch, onscreen graphics are usually 72 dpi, while printed graphics are often 300 dpi or higher.

rollover   The term used to describe an event that occurs when the mouse moves over a certain area of the screen; for example, highlighting a button to alert the user that he or she may click there.

score   In Director, the tool that organizes and controls all of the elements in the movie. The playback head travels from point to point in the score and executes the commands recorded there. Sprites, scripts, palettes, and other elements can be positioned in the score to perform a certain way.

script   In Director, a group of Lingo statements organized to execute certain commands. There are different types of scripts: frame, sprite, cast member, and movie scripts. The Lingo statements must be organized into handlers within the scripts.

server-side image map   The most widespread type of clickable image mapping. This type of mapping requires the server that the Web page resides on to do all the processing. The sequence of events that returns the desired result is more involved in this type than in client-side image mapping, and therefore not as fast.

Shockwave for Authorware   The technology that allows the embedding of Macromedia Authorware files into HTML documents for multimedia presentations over Intranets.

Shockwave for Director   The technology that allows the embedding of Macromedia Director movies into HTML documents for multimedia display over the Internet.

Shockwave for Freehand   The technology that allows the embedding of Macromedia Freehand files into HTML documents for scalable vector images over the Internet.

sprite   In Director, a cast member that is placed on the stage using one of the 48 possible channels in the score.

stage   In Director, the visible area of the movie where all of the action takes place. Cast members that are placed on the stage become sprites and are controlled by the score.

streaming   The process where a large file is broken into small pieces that are loaded only as they are needed. Shockwave for Authorware and Shockwave for Audio both use the streaming process.

URL   Uniform Resource Locator. A URL contains the address where a file resides and usually also contains the scheme that describes how the file is to be retrieved. The scheme used for much of the Internet is HTTP.

variable   An item that may change depending on certain events. In a programming language, variables are used to store information that can potentially be modified.

vector image   A graphic format that records geometric information to define the properties of an image. Angles, curves, lines, boxes, fills, and other properties are included in the vector format.

Web Server   Any one of the wide variety of computers that is configured to deliver data over the Internet.

WYSIWYG   An acronym that stands for What You See Is What You Get. It's commonly used to describe an application's interface. It refers to the ability to see onscreen any graphics, text, or other elements as they appear in the final creation.

Index

Check out Que® Books on the World Wide Web
http://www.mcp.com/que

As the biggest software release in computer history, Windows 95 continues to redefine the computer industry. Click here for the latest info on our Windows 95 books

Make computing quick and easy with these products designed exclusively for new and casual users

Examine the latest releases in word processing, spreadsheets, operating systems, and suites

The Internet, The World Wide Web, CompuServe®, America Online®, Prodigy® —it's a world of ever-changing information. Don't get left behind!

Find out about new additions to our site, new bestsellers and hot topics

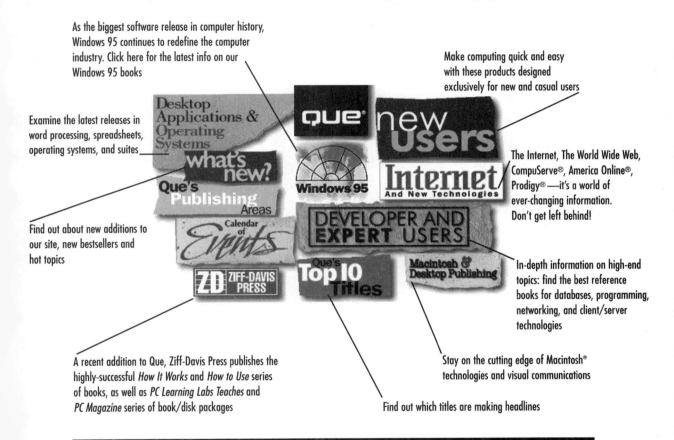

In-depth information on high-end topics: find the best reference books for databases, programming, networking, and client/server technologies

A recent addition to Que, Ziff-Davis Press publishes the highly-successful *How It Works* and *How to Use* series of books, as well as *PC Learning Labs Teaches* and *PC Magazine* series of book/disk packages

Stay on the cutting edge of Macintosh® technologies and visual communications

Find out which titles are making headlines

With 6 separate publishing groups, Que develops products for many specific market segments and areas of computer technology. Explore our Web Site and you'll find information on best-selling titles, newly published titles, upcoming products, authors, and much more.

- Stay informed on the latest industry trends and products available

- Visit our online bookstore for the latest information and editions

- Download software from Que's library of the best shareware and freeware

Use Shockwave on Your Web page and Win $1000!

Turn the page for details...

Shock Your Site and Win $1000!

Be the most creative with Shockwave on your Web Site and win $1000 from Que Corporation.

Que Corporation, Macromedia, and Phillips Design Group are sponsoring a Shockwave contest where the grand prize is a check for $1000. Any owner of a publicly accessible Web page (United States only) is eligible, providing they meet the criteria outlined in the Official Rules.

Entry into the contest is simple, just follow these steps:

1. Incorporate Shockwave for Director, Authorware, Freehand, or Audio on your Web page(s).

2. Read and comply with the official rules.

3. Use the entry form (provided) and mail or email your entry information to Phillips Design Group (PDG) before June 30, 1997.

> **Note**
>
> Please note that only one page (URL) per site, per person, is eligible for entry.

Entries will be judged by Phillips Design Group. Each entry will be assigned a score between 0 and 1000 points, based in equal parts upon creativity, suitability to task, attractive design, and ease of use. All entries will be accessible from links on the official contest page (www.mcp.com/que/cyoshockwave).

From all entries received by June 30, 1997, the one entry with the highest score will be awarded the $1000 Grand Prize. (In the event of a tie the prize will be divided equally among the entrants with the tie winning score.)

To enter the contest, fill out the following form or email the information directly to PDG at shockwave@pdgroup.com.

Name: _____

Address: _____

_____

City, State: _____ Zip: _____

Contact
Phone (day):_____ Email Address: _____

URL of page/site to enter: _____

Send to: Shockwave Contest
                  c/o Phillips Design Group, Inc.
                  6350 Westhaven Drive
                  Suite C
                  Indianapolis, IN 46254

or Email: shockwave@pdgroup.com

All entries must be received by June 30, 1997.

Official Rules

The contest begins October 4, 1996 and ends June 30, 1997. The contest is sponsored by Que (imprint of Macmillan Computer Publishing, 201 W. 103rd St. Indianapolis, IN 46290) and endorsed by Macromedia (600 Townsend, San Francisco, CA 94103).

ELIGIBILITY

The contest is open to residents of the United States excluding Vermont. Employees, officers, directors, of the sponsors and judges and their immediate family members, and their parent companies, affiliates, subsidiaries, and advertising, and promotion and legal advisors, are not eligible to participate. Void where prohibited by law.

Entrants must own a Web page that incorporates Shockwave for Director, Authorware, Freehand, or Audio as of the date of entry and through June 30, 1997. All entries must be original and not infringe on any rights of any party.

HOW TO ENTER

No proof of purchase is required. To enter, create a Web page that uses Shockwave, or incorporate Shockwave into an existing Web page and follow one of the procedures outlined below:

A) Email the following information to Phillips Design Group shockwave@pdgroup.com by June 30, 1997.

Name

Address

City, State Zip

Contact phone number (daytime)

Email address

URL of page to be entered

All entrants by email will receive a confirmation email message, notifying them that their entry was received.

or

B) Fill out and mail the form on the reverse side of this page to Phillips Design Group by June 30, 1997.

All entrants by mail will receive a confirmation letter, notifying them that their entry was received.

CONDITIONS

By entering, participants agree to be bound by these complete Official Rules and the decisions of Que and Phillips Design Group, which shall be final. Sponsors, Judges and the employees, officers, directors, shareholders, agents and representatives of Sponsors and Judges, including their parent companies, affiliates, subsidiaries, and advertising, promotion and legal advisors are not responsible for and shall not be liable for: (i) late, lost, delayed, damaged, misdirected, incomplete, illegible or unintelligible entries; (ii) telephone, electronic, hardware or software program, network, Internet or computer malfunctions, failures or difficulties; (iii) errors in transmission; (iv) any condition caused by events beyond the control of the Sponsors or Judges which may cause the Contest to be disrupted or corrupted; (v) any injuries, losses or damages of any kind caused by or resulting from participation in the Contest; or (vi) any printing or typographical errors in any materials associated with the Contest.

By participating in the Contest, you agree to release and hold Sponsors and Judges, their employees, officers, directors, shareholders, agents, representatives of Sponsors and Judges, including their parent companies, affiliates, subsidiaries, and advertising, promotion and legal advisors harmless from any and all losses, damages, rights, claims and actions of any kind in connection with the Contest.

Failure to comply with the Official Rules may result in a disqualification of your entry and prohibition of any further participation in the Contest. Fraudulent entries will be prosecuted to the fullest extent of the law. Void where prohibited by law.

JUDGING

Entries will be judged by the staff of Phillips Design Group and scored on the basis of creativity, suitability to task, attractive design, and ease of use. All decisions of the judges are final. All entries will be available for public viewing from links on the "Creating Shockwave Web Pages" web site (www.mcp.com/que/cyoshockwave). From all entries received, the one entry with the highest score will be awarded a certified check from Que for $1000. In the event of a tie, the prize will be equally divided among the entrants with the tie winning score. The grand prize will be awarded by September 1, 1997.

By accepting the prize, the winner grants the sponsors the right to use his or her name and likeness for any advertising, promotional, trade, or any other purpose without further compensation or permission, except where prohibited by law.

If the prize is won by a minor, it will be awarded to the minor's parents or legal guardian.

CONTEST RESULTS

After June 30, 1997 the results and winner of the Contest will be available on the Que Contest Web page (www.mcp.com/que/cyoshockwave).

Complete and Return this Card
for a *FREE* Computer Book Catalog

Thank you for purchasing this book! You have purchased a superior computer book written expressly for your needs. To continue to provide the kind of up-to-date, pertinent coverage you've come to expect from us, we need to hear from you. Please take a minute to complete and return this self-addressed, postage-paid form. In return, we'll send you a free catalog of all our computer books on topics ranging from word processing to programming and the internet.

Mr. ☐   Mrs. ☐   Ms. ☐   Dr. ☐

Name (first) ☐☐☐☐☐☐☐☐☐☐☐ (M.I.) ☐   (last) ☐☐☐☐☐☐☐☐☐☐☐☐☐☐

Address ☐☐☐☐☐☐☐☐☐☐☐☐☐☐☐☐☐☐☐☐☐☐☐☐☐☐☐☐☐☐☐☐☐

☐☐☐☐☐☐☐☐☐☐☐☐☐☐☐☐☐☐☐☐☐☐☐☐☐☐☐☐☐☐☐☐☐

City ☐☐☐☐☐☐☐☐☐☐☐☐☐☐☐☐☐☐   State ☐☐   Zip ☐☐☐☐☐ ☐☐☐☐

Phone ☐☐☐ ☐☐☐ ☐☐☐☐   Fax ☐☐☐ ☐☐☐ ☐☐☐☐

Company Name ☐☐☐☐☐☐☐☐☐☐☐☐☐☐☐☐☐☐☐☐☐☐☐☐☐☐☐☐☐☐☐☐

E-mail address ☐☐☐☐☐☐☐☐☐☐☐☐☐☐☐☐☐☐☐☐☐☐☐☐☐☐☐☐☐☐☐☐

1. Please check at least (3) influencing factors for purchasing this book.

Front or back cover information on book .... ☐
Special approach to the content .... ☐
Completeness of content .... ☐
Author's reputation .... ☐
Publisher's reputation .... ☐
Book cover design or layout .... ☐
Index or table of contents of book .... ☐
Price of book .... ☐
Special effects, graphics, illustrations .... ☐
Other (Please specify): _____ ☐

2. How did you first learn about this book?

Saw in Macmillan Computer Publishing catalog .... ☐
Recommended by store personnel .... ☐
Saw the book on bookshelf at store .... ☐
Recommended by a friend .... ☐
Received advertisement in the mail .... ☐
Saw an advertisement in: _____ ☐
Read book review in: _____ ☐
Other (Please specify): _____ ☐

3. How many computer books have you purchased in the last six months?

This book only .... ☐   3 to 5 books .... ☐
2 books .... ☐   More than 5 .... ☐

4. Where did you purchase this book?

Bookstore .... ☐
Computer Store .... ☐
Consumer Electronics Store .... ☐
Department Store .... ☐
Office Club .... ☐
Warehouse Club .... ☐
Mail Order .... ☐
Direct from Publisher .... ☐
Internet site .... ☐
Other (Please specify): _____ ☐

5. How long have you been using a computer?

☐ Less than 6 months   ☐ 6 months to a year
☐ 1 to 3 years   ☐ More than 3 years

6. What is your level of experience with personal computers and with the subject of this book?

	With PCs	With subject of book
New	☐	☐
Casual	☐	☐
Accomplished	☐	☐
Expert	☐	☐

Source Code ISBN: 0-7897-0903-1

7. Which of the following best describes your job title?

Administrative Assistant .... ☐
Coordinator .... ☐
Manager/Supervisor .... ☐
Director .... ☐
Vice President .... ☐
President/CEO/COO .... ☐
Lawyer/Doctor/Medical Professional .... ☐
Teacher/Educator/Trainer .... ☐
Engineer/Technician .... ☐
Consultant .... ☐
Not employed/Student/Retired .... ☐
Other (Please specify): _____ ☐

8. Which of the following best describes the area of the company your job title falls under?

Accounting .... ☐
Engineering .... ☐
Manufacturing .... ☐
Operations .... ☐
Marketing .... ☐
Sales .... ☐
Other (Please specify): _____ ☐

Comments: _____
_____
_____

Fold here and scotch-tape to ma

9. What is your age?

Under 20 .... ☐
21-29 .... ☐
30-39 .... ☐
40-49 .... ☐
50-59 .... ☐
60-over .... ☐

10. Are you:

Male .... ☐
Female .... ☐

11. Which computer publications do you read regularly? (Please list)

_____
_____
_____
_____
_____
_____
_____
_____
_____
_____

Licensing Agreement

By opening this package, you are agreeing to be bound by the following:

This software product is copyrighted, and all rights are reserved by the publisher and author. You are licensed to use this software on a single computer. You may copy and/or modify the software as needed to facilitate your use of it on a single computer. Making copies of the software for any other purpose is a violation of the United States copyright laws.

This software is sold *as is* without warranty of any kind, either expressed or implied, including but not limited to the implied warranties of merchantability and fitness for a particular purpose. Neither the publisher nor its dealers or distributors assumes any liability for any alleged or actual damages arising from the use of this program. (Some states do not allow for the exclusion of implied warranties, so the exclusion may not apply to you.)